Ancient Footprints of the Colorado River
Revised Edition

Ancient Footprints of the Colorado River
Revised Edition

Alfredo Acosta Figueroa

Front Cover Design: By Cesar Guevara
Front Cover Art: Blythe Giant Intaglios-Geoglyph image of Ometeotl, the creator.

Map of the Mexica Migration on the Colorado River from Aztlán led by Tezcacoatl of the Four Teomamas, depicted carrying Huitzilopochtli on her back going to Mexico/Tenochtitlan.
(Boturini-Siguenza Codex)
Map by Alfredo A. Figueroa

Ancient Footprints of the Colorado River

Thunderbird eagle in the Big Maria Mountains overlooking Blythe California.

Thunderbird Eagle, Cuautlehuanitl, in Nahuatl, means ascending sun/eagle. This is the eagle that is on the Mexican Flag. The eagle is the naguali of the sun. The creator's profile image of Huehueteotl is the shadowed peek in the background.

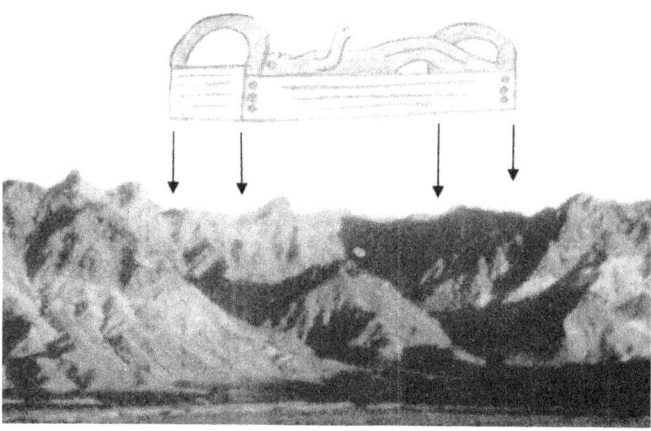

The image of the cradle below the Thunder Bird Eagle during the winter solstice.

Shown is the cradle rising out of the base of the Thunderbird Eagle that forms a small valley between the small black peak, Tepatl. This drawing shows where the cradle of Aztlán is located. The shadow of the human image in a cradle represents the birthing of Huitzilopochtli during the winter solstice.

Azcatitlan Codex Fold 12, Lamina XII, which depicts a glyph of Malinalxochitl, mother, watching over her baby, the first human in the cradle.

The Azcatitlan Codex Fold 12, Lamina XII, depicts a glyph of Malinalxochitl, mother, watching over her baby, the first human, which is in a cradle on top of a metate, (rug), representing earth. Geographically, this is the original image of Chac-Mol, and it is located at the base of the "thunderbird eagle" on the Big Maria Mountains facing south, over looking the Palo Verde Valley. It is referred to as Chac-Mol by the Maya, and Xiutecutli by the Nahua. Based on this evidence, after 54 years of research, thus, Palo Verde/Parker Valleys, "La Cuna de Aztlán. "

In memory of my daughter, Xochitl, my youngest daughter now deceased. Her name means flower in Nahuatl, the last day of the 20-day Aztec Sunstone Calendar month when we as humans are in full blossom.

Xochitl continues to live in us and like a flower,
reminding us to appreciate the beauty of life.

Copyright 2002, 2011 © by Alfredo Acosta Figueroa
Cuna de Aztlán, Blythe, California

First Printing 2002

Second Printing 2012

All Rights Reserved

Published by La Cuna de Aztlán Publishing Company

No part of this work may be reproduced or transmitted in any form or by any means, electronic or mechanical, including photocopying, recordings, or by any information storage and retrieval system without written permission from the author, except for inclusion of brief quotations in a review.

TABLE OF CONTENTS
Forward Dr. Abel Amaya
Preface Boma Johnson, Gilbert Lopez Leivas
Dedication Page
Acknowledgement
Introduction
Chapter 1: The Lower Colorado River Basin Valleys
1.2: The Indigenous Nations
Chapter 2: La Cuna de Aztlán: Origin and Ethnology
2.2: The Heron: Symbol of Aztlán
2.3: Azteca/Mexica: The Migration from Aztlán
2.4: Mexico/Aztlán: The Relationship to Mexico/Tenochtitlan
2.5: The Search for Aztlán
2.6: The Destruction of the Island of Aztlán
2.7: Aztlán: Consciousness in the Southwest
Chapter 3: The Blythe Giant Intaglios
3.2: The Bouse Fisherman Intaglio
3.3: Omeyocan: The Diamond of Infinity
3.4: The Mule Mountains and Kokopilli/Quetzalcoatl
3.5 The Return of Quetzalcoatl
Chapter 4: The Pleiades and New Fire Ceremony: Measurement of Time
Chapter 5: Mathematical Symbolism of the Nahua People
5.2: Comparing Symbolic Illustrations
Chapter 6: Cuauhtémoc: Symbol of Liberation
6.2: Revelation of Cuauhtémoc's Tomb
6.3: Homage to Florencio Yesca
6.4: Cuauhtémoc Spiritual Pilgrimage
6.5: From the Cradle of Aztlán to the Tomb of Cuauhtémoc
Chapter 7: Peace and Dignity Journey of 1992
7.2: The Second Peace and Dignity Journey of 1996
7.3: Blythe, California and Ixcateopan, Guerrero: Sister Cities
Chapter 8: Why we do not know our Indigenous roots?
Chapter 9: Xicano
9.2: Xicano Poem
9.3: The Renaissance of Aztlán and the Xicano Student Movement
9.4: Philosophy and Our Reencounter with our Indigenous culture
Chapter 10: La Cuna de Aztlán Sacred Sites Protection Circle
10.2: In Memorandum of Humberto "Bert" Corona
10.3: In Memorandum of Professor William Hensey
Primary Resources: Personal Interviews
Nahuatl/Mexica Glossary
Bibliography
Biography of Alfredo Acosta Figueroa

ILLUSTRATIONS

La Cuna de Aztlán: Azcatitlan Codex-Inside Cover Page

Xochitl Glyph

Map of Lower Colorado River Valleys of Indigenous Reservations

Alexander Von Humboldt's 1804 map of Antigua Residencia de los Aztecas (½ page up right)

Heron, Symbol of Aztlan

Aubin Codex, Island of Aztlan, Siguenza Codex, Boturini Codex Migration from Aztlan

Thomas Banyaca and Phil Smith and Hopi Prophecy Petroglyph

Four directions map from Mexico/Aztlán to Mexico/Tenochtitlan

Sonora State Symbol with four directions symbol and two peaks

Geoglyph of the four directions

Borgia Codex Plate 72 of the four directions

Vindobonensis Codex Fold 23, of Equinox Sunrise

Diego Duran's History of the Indies of New Spain Codex, Plate 4, The Azteca in Coatepec

Thunderbird eagle image in the Big Maria Mountains

Fundacion de Tenochtitlan Mexico with the eagle on a cactus on a rock

Blythe Giant Intaglios

Vatican Codex A of the Giants and Ometeotl

Figure sculptures of dog and jaguar in Palenque, Chiapas and other sacred sites

Florentine Codex, Book Five, Fold 11v. "Los Gigantes,"

Bouse Fisherman

Tlaloc-Ixtlilxochilt Codex

Aztec Sun Stone Calendar, Tonalmachiotl

Map of Omeyocan Diamond

Cicimitl Geoglyph

Cicimitl Magliabecchi Codex

Cuitlahuac Flag

Mule Mountains with image of Cicimitl

Kokopilli/Quetzalcoatl Geoglyph Image

Codex Magliabecchi-The Creator's image as the bearded Quetzalcoatl

Geoglyph of the Pleiades Star Cluster

Petroglyph of the Pleiades Star Cluster

The Pleiades star cluster (M45) is a group of stars
Codex Telleriano-Remensis of New Fire Ceremony
The Fejervary-Meyer Codex of Xiuhtecutli
Geoglyph of Quetzalcoatl's Cross
Picture of the sun setting on the "V" of Eagle Mountain
Picture of Cuauhtemoc, descending eagle
Statue of Cuauhtemoc at Ixcateopan Plaza
The tomb of Cuauhtemoc
Homage to Florencio Yesca (picture)
Picture of Dr. Salvador Rodriguez
1985 Cuauhtemoc Spiritual Pilgrimage participants
Picture of Chief Victor 'Sky Eagle' Lopez, of the Chumas
Alfredo Figueroa with Dr. Salvador Rodriguez, December 9, 1990
1992 Peace and Dignity Journey, Colorado River Organizing Committee in Desert Center
1992 Peace and Dignity Journey organizer Gustavo Gutierrez and runners
1996 Peace and Dignity Journey Ixcateopan, Guerrero
The 16 Level Spanish Caste Society System
Blythe students picketing, 1972
Students singing on the picket line, 1972
ERU students on the front cover of the 'Militant Magazine.'
Bert Corona, University of California, Riverside
Cesar Chavez in Blythe
Joaquin Murrieta
La Mexicanidad-El Chicanismo
Thomas Banyaca and Phil Smith at Hotevilla, on the Hopi Reservation, 1996
Ron Van Fleet standing at Palo Verde Peak Point petroglyphs
Mateo Leivas, Steve Lopez, Alfredo A. Figueroa and Angel Alvarez at the Tlatelolco Ruins
Tloque-Nahuaque Symbol
Picture of Mr. William Bill Hensey
Picture of Carlos LLegar, Patrick Connolly, and Mr. William Bill Hensey
Picture of Alfredo A. Figueroa, Biography
Back page cover- Kokopilli/Quetzalcoatl

FOREWARD

El Ser Chicano y No Ser Revolucionario Es Una Contradicion
(To be Chicano and not to be Revolutionary is a Contradiction)

Ever since the conquest of Mexico by Hernan Cortez on August 13, 1521, there ensured an historical debate about the origin of the Mexica/Azteca. Who were they and more importantly, where did they come from? In the second edition of "Ancient Footprints of the Lower Colorado River, La Cuna de Aztlan," El Maestro, Alfredo A. Figueroa, has provided us with an incredible account of the founding of the Mexican Nation. The information he defines is presented with passion and thought that argues for the origins of the Mexicas in the Lower Colorado River Basin Valleys. ?Y porque no? Esta es la tierra que lo vio nacer y crecer y formarlecer el gran pensador que es hoy.

So strong is El Maestro Figueroa's conviction and account of the ancestry of the Mexicans that it tends to persuade you that something really happened in the area close to the Blythe, California. In the best tradition of the Latin American writers and thinkers; El Maestro Figueroa raises significant methodological and epistemological questions that are not only intellectually important to defining Mexica history but defines a paradigm that extends to the Chicano experience.

As Bert Corona would remark, "We are a race of thinkers; Let the academic mechanics struggle over the facts." The Chicano Studies Curriculum has included, by historical demand and logic, the role of the Mexica in Chicano history. And for this contribution to the debate of the Nahua Civilization we owe a debt of gratitude to El Pensador de la Cuna de Aztlan, El Maestro Alfredo Acosta Figueroa. Gracias amigo y colega.

Yo soy Aztlan
Yo soy la Revolucion
Yo soy Chicano,

Dr. Abel C. Amaya
CSU Dominguez Hills

PREFACE

The monograph, "Ancient Footprints of the Colorado River, La Cuna de Aztlan, " by Alfredo Figueroa of Blythe, California is nearly as much a statement about his beliefs and political involvement with the Chicano Movement as it is a statement about the long lost location of Aztlan.

And perhaps rightly so, for his life experience along the Lower Colorado River and his research about his cultural origins can hardly be separated. However, to this researcher who has not yet personally experienced the Chicano Movement, the two issues, though related to him, are yet separate for those who have a different heritage age.

My comments concerning Alfredo's research will therefore address only his thesis concerning the possibility that Aztlan was located in the Palo Verde/Parker region of the Lower Colorado River and the associated migration to the Valley of Mexico. This choice is in no way intended to question or slight the interaction between these two. It is a matter that this researcher knows little about the more modern Chicano Movement, which has a direct connection to the location of ancient Aztlan, other than the notion that both events are related to the same Lower Colorado River Region.

Working for the Bureau of Land Management as an archaeologist along the Lower Colorado River for 25 years did not exactly prepare me for the concept of Aztlan perhaps being in this region. I have been very aware of the problem of determining the original location for Aztlan since my years in high school, when my grandfather, James H. Johnson, told me of his belief that Moctezuma had at one time lived in the northern reaches of his empire and had himself returned to the American Southwest where he had buried much of his gold and treasure, which he realized would otherwise be lost to the coming of the Spaniards.

Since my early days, before becoming an archaeologist, not much has come to my attention to even be concerned about the Aztec homeland of Aztlan. Than came Alfredo's research and main thesis. Could his work be considered a vital breakthrough on this old problem? I have read and reread what Alfredo has gathered as his primary line of evidence to support his thesis. I see many difficulties in his reasoning and lines of evidence yet I see enough good evidence to intrigue me. I have gained enough personal insight into his thesis which convinces me that as a whole, the idea of the Lower Colorado River being the so-called, "Lost Aztlan," is not that wild of an idea. I believe the whole concept does merit our attention and more in depth research, especially by those who can check Alfredo's various lines of evidence and add to his work without any strong bias for or against the thesis. I believe that he has opened to all of us a legitimate body of future research which I tend to think will eventually support his primary conclusion.

Is it possible that the whole idea of the southwest abandonment is the beginning of the eventual arrival of the Nahua into the Valley Mexico, beginning around AD 1325? Is it possible that Aztlan was a greater geographic area including much of the southwest, but in particular, the red rock country of the Ancestral Puebloans (Anasazi) with several core areas, including the Lower Colorado River cultural area? With Alfredo's work as a jumping off point, perhaps further work will surprise us all and tell a more complete story of the mysterious land called Aztlan.

Boma Johnson,

Retired Archaeologist,
Bureau of Land Management,
Yuma, Arizona

PROLOGUE

Those who read this book will be enlightened in the ancient cultures of our Native American forefathers in the North American continent. It was our forefathers who made impressions on the desert floor in the form of giant intaglios.
It is through these geoglyphs and numerous other sacred sites that are found along the lower Colorado River Valleys, that we can now compare them and inter-relate them with the Aztec Codices. They are completely similar, thus establishing a connection with our past which is drawn out in the desert.

People will now have a better understanding of our ancient civilization that still exists here in the desert and that of the Uto-Aztecan Confederation of Anahuac which was nearly all destroyed by the conquistadors. The invaders had no understanding of the knowledge that was left both in the Aztec Codices and the ancient structures that remain to this day in Mexico.

The Europeans failed to recognize our rich cosmic traditional culture which has caused the loss of this priceless connection. It is this slow methodical strangulation of our Native American heritage that we need to understand and acknowledge.

Modern civilizations has lent itself to the total destruction of its past by the modernization of the southwest in the form of roads, natural gas energy plants, solar energy plants and off-road race courses and so on. Not to mention the religious trends that totally failed to understand and recognize a cosmic traditional culture that had existed for thousands of years.

The desire to develop energy plants on these ancient sacred sites is in fact a ploy to completely obliterate our cultural heritage under the guise of renewable energy.

The information that you will obtain from this book is virtually non-existent and disregarded in the non-Native American world because it has always been portrayed as theory or myth.

Preservation of these sacred sites should be as important as our United States constitutional rights. There are over 10 laws that protect the rights of indigenous sacred sites, therefore the preservation of our Native American culture should be emphasized and enforced to its fullest extent.

Gilbert Lopez Leivas

Member, Colorado River Indian Tribes Reservation
Fisrt Chair of La Cuna de Aztlan Sacred Sites Protection Circle

DEDICATION

I dedicate this revised edition of the historical Ancient Footprints on the Colorado River, The Cradle of Aztlán, to my parents, Carmen Mollinedo Acosta and Danuario Gomez Figueroa, who formulated the foundation of who I am as a person, and what I stand for today.

My mother, being the fourth generation of the Colorado River, was born and raised in southern Arizona. She nourished and disciplined me to become a good human being. She taught me the great values and principles in life, including that of honesty. Through a humble Catholic upbringing, she instilled in me a sense of compassion for all humanity. Her name, Carmen, will live forever in the "Little Maria Mountain Range" on the mountain peak that bears her name. In Blythe, California in the neighborhood of "El Barrio del Cuchillo," a street is also named in her honor.

My father, Danuario, of Pima/Yaqui descent, fiercely protected his independence and went to all extremes to be self-sufficient. He demonstrated to us not to depend on anyone to survive and he instilled in my brothers and my sister, the philosophy that one should never forget that "your boss is your biggest enemy," and one should always work for oneself.

I dedicate this work to my brothers and my sister, Norah, with whom I shared my childhood experiences. My brothers, Danuario, Miguel and Gilbert, were with me in the early days of the Xicano and Civil Rights Movements. Together, we learned to fight against political and racial injustices. We also helped organize other communities to unite and create changes in racist educational and political systems, without fear of repercussions from those in power.

This work is also dedicated to my wife, Demesia Macias, who has stood by me throughout these 57 years and to my (sacred number) nine children: Alfredo, Carmela, Patricia, Maria, Jesus Roman, Guadalupe, Angelica, Humberto Cesar, and Xochitl Edwina (now deceased). This book will serve as the example that will enlighten them to follow path that will lead them to the truth of their roots and origin, "Neltiliztli," to seek the roots and fundamental truth of our purpose, as humans, here on Mother Earth.

I also dedicate this book to the spirit of Cuauhtémoc and Joaquin Murrieta, the forerunners of the Xicano Movement. This dedication is also to the struggles and causes of my two deceased mentors: Humberto 'Bert' Corona, Father of the Modern Xicano Movement and Cesar Estrada Chavez, co-founder and president of the United Farm Workers Union. These two great men served as my mentors in my pursuit and fulfill-

ment of serving humanity; the most rewarding endeavor in my life. I served under these two men diligently for decades without ever deviating from my own family responsibilities and never yielding from my principles, traditions, and most importantly, my indigenous culture.

Overall, and primordial, I wish to acknowledge the founders of La Escuela de la Raza Unida, the only independent Xicano K-12 alternative school in the United States. La Escuela has been fundamental in the development of the research in search of Aztlán. Under the leadership of Carmela Figueroa Garnica and Rigoberto Garnica, La Escuela continues to be successful and efficient after 39 years in existence.

We are also grateful to the numerous teachers who volunteered and who believed in "La Causa de la Escuela," (the school's cause). These teachers helped us with the expansion of La Escuela over the past 39 years. La Escuela would never have succeeded without their commitment and loyalty.

This dedication is also in appreciation to all of our dear friends who dedicated their unselfish time in the pursuit of the goals and principles of the Xicano Movement of the 1960s and 1970s. At the height of the movement, one of the goals was to become self-sufficient and establish Xicano alternative schools similar to La Escuela through out the nation.

This work is also dedicated to Hopi traditionalist Elder, Thomas Banancya (deceased) who was entrusted with the ancient Hopi prophecies and whom was an ardent pursuer of the truth of the Mexica. He was instrumental in reconnecting our indigenous culture with Mexico and the Lower Colorado River Basin, which begins at Spirit Mountain, located northwest of
Needles, California.

Finally, and foremost, I would like to wholeheartedly thank the Creator, "Ometéotl," the supreme divinity that has no name and has all the names, who vested in me this knowledge and wisdom that for centuries has been denied to us, the indigenous people. "Por mi raza habla mi espiritu." My spirit speaks for my people. The truth speaks through Ometéotl on behalf of all humanity. The compelling evidence presented in this book will shed new light upon our native culture, tradition and our origin in the Colorado River.

This newly revised second edition of "Ancient Footprints of the Colorado River," The Cradle of Aztlán, is the first book of a series of 13.

Blythe, CA   Alfredo A. Figueroa

ACKNOWLEDGMENT

This book was made possible thanks to the hard work of the following people. I am in debt to them for their generous dedication and contribution in this monumental task of editing and typing the manuscript that has spanned for more than three decades.

I will forever be grateful to my daughter, Demesia Patricia Figueroa Pinon, whom for the past two decades has been in the forefront of editing and composing my research.

I am thankful for my high school teacher and longtime friend, confidant and political advisor, Professor William H. Hensey, Jr., (now deceased) who was responsible for organizing the first draft of this manuscript. He was one of the few Anglos who understood the Mexica culture and traditions and who encouraged me to pursue my research in Mexico City. This trip to Mexico City finally came to fruition in 1990.

To my very good friend, Noreen Sullivan, who was my colleague in the United Farm Workers Union and in the struggle for immigrant rights. Noreen spent numerous days diligently editing my English grammar and written thoughts of the first edition and drove from San Diego to Blythe during the hot summer months.

Special words of appreciation go to Elva Garza who edited the Spanish translation of some of my text for the first edition of this book, and to Patricia Felix for correcting the style and revising and translating the text of this second edition in Spanish and formulating the chapters. I am thankful for Maria Lopez, for her long hours of dedication and for typing and reorganizing the text in English for this second edition.

My appreciation also is for Mr. Boma Johnson, retired Bureau of Land Management archeologist, for his invaluable assistance, contribution and foresight in identifying the location of many geoglyphs and sacred sites located along the Colorado River, an area that extends from Needles, California in the north, and south to Yuma, Arizona. These geoglyphs were the missing links to an obscured puzzle which lead to the location of the long-sought 'mystical' Aztlán. I thank him for his excellent recommendation in formulating a more simplified understanding of the text. His unselfish contribution will always be cherished by all indigenous people and future generations.

I am very thankful to the following people for providing me with their knowledge of the Mexica/Mayan culture. They were instrumental in assisting me with the documen-

tation as well as with the interpretation of the Mexica/Mayan codexes, and other information concerning our traditional cosmic culture. I would like to acknowledge Professor Jose Manuel Garcia "Acamapixtli," Nahuatlaca/Lecture of the Mexica Tradition and writer, Maestra Estrella Newman, of the Mexicanidad Movement, (confidant of Dr. Salvador Rodriguez's) and to Hunbatz-Men Mayan Shaman and traditionalist.

A very special recognition goes to my late cousin, Professor Francisco Figueroa of Trincheras, Sonora. In 1958, he gave me the historical book, entitled, "Nociones de Historia de Sonora," by Laureano Calvo Berber. This book provided me with the fundamental clues for my research and it contained a map with a depiction of Aztlan located above the confluence of the Colorado and Gila Rivers. This information intrigued me so much that it initiated the journey in the pursuit of the origin of Aztlán here in the Colorado River that eventually led to the publication of my first book. My cousin also encouraged me to continue my research regarding Joaquin Murrieta's genealogy in Trincheras, Sonora, which lead to the founding of the International Association of Descendants of Joaquin Murrieta.

A special recognition goes to all the people involved in the environmental movement in the United States, Mexico and the entire world. They have carried the banner of leadership in the protection of Mother Earth. Also special thanks to Cynthia Babich, director of DEL AMO Action Committee of San Pedro, California, for her generosity in contributing to the publication of this second edition.

Above all, we are forever indebt to the Creator for the blessing of being born in the Palo Verde and Parker Valleys and for bestowing on us the knowledge of our cosmic cultural tradition.

We are thankful to our native traditionalists who have survived the 500 years of the European onslaught. The knowledge of our native traditionalists has been preserved for thousands of years and passed down for generations. We have been empowered by their nihilistic attitude toward European dominance. Without their persistence in protecting this knowledge it would have been extremely difficult to have cross-referenced the Mexica Codexes with the mountain images, geoglyphs, petroglyphs and pictographs which lie in the surrounding Lower Colorado River Valleys. The time has come to know the truth of Aztlan.

INTRODUCTION

This book is the result of more than fifty-three years of research which includes the many field studies and observations that we have done throughout the years that were conducted in the Lower Colorado River Basin Valleys and in Mexico.

This book is centered in the area of Blythe, California in the Palo Verde/Parker Valleys. The unique research that is presented in this book opens a Pandora's Box of unknown history that remained lost for centuries. Most of the work is based on the sacred images that are in the surrounding mountains which provide a majestic view seen from our home located in the ancient Barrio de Acacitli, today's El Barrio de El Cuchillo.

The Xicano Movement has motivated the foundation of this book and provided the vision for the social activists that gave birth to the ideals that fueled the Xicano movement to its height. This in-depth research brings forth the truth of the Azteca/Mexica place of origin of Aztlán, and of our forefathers, Moctezuma and Cuauhtémoc. Our participation in the Xicano Movement and the search for the truth of the origin of our indigenous roots has been more than just a hobby or fad; it has been our way of life.

For over five decades, we have felt the presence of a power that has given us the inexplicable mystical energy and the impetus to continue the research and reveal the information that we have collected in this book.

One day, future generations will also be motivated to seek the true knowledge of their own heritage which in Nahuatl means, Neltiliztli, "To seek the roots of the truth, leaving no stone unturned and no shadow of doubt."

We are at the end of the Era of Pisces which correlates with the end of the Fifth Sun as shown in the Azteca Sun Stone Calendar. We are in transition of the beginning of the Era of Aquarius in 2012. We must be prepared for changes on the earth and be cognizant of our existence as humans on earth.

Time is measured and time is based on the rising of the Pleiades to its zenith. The Seven Sisters constellation rises to its zenith every fifty-two years, and the last time this event occurred was on November 14, 2003. This cosmic mathematical event is recorded on the Azteca Sun Stone Calendar and is referred to as the Binding of the Years.

Fortunately, we are entering a new era whereby historical information written by the European conquerors is repudiated for its blatant distortions. These erroneous writings are no longer accepted blindly by people without critical appraisal. Worldwide, indigenous people are relying less on faith and more on historical facts left by ancient people whose evidence is now revealing the truth of our traditional cosmic relationship on earth.

One of the main objectives in the teachings of the history of the Xicanos/Mexica has been to identify the true location of Aztlán some where in the southwest area of the United States.

Until now, most writers dismissed the existence of Aztlán (together with Xicomoztoc - birthplace and origin of the Nahua Nations) as a mythical place. In the past, such deceptions prevailed because of the lack of research and specific investigations that failed to follow through with intensive studies conducted within the southwest, especially in the Lower Colorado River Valley Basin. In addition, most investigators neglected to study the connections between the Lower Colorado River Native nations, and the Mexica Codex and cultural traditions of the indigenous people of Mexico. They allowed the current border between the United States and Mexico to separate indigenous people, their traditions and their culture.

Our research was conducted within the lower Colorado River basin valleys and is based on the sacred mountain images, sacred ancient trails, landmarks, pictographs, petroglyphs, intaglios/geoglyphs, solstices and equinoxes. These overwhemingly geographical and cosmological connections cannot be denied. Our research is also based on the native oral language, traditional songs, and history of the lower Colorado River basin Valleys.

The map of the Treaty of Guadalupe Hidalgo is one of the official United States documents that substantiate our compelling evidence of the location of Aztlán. This map was drawn by Alexander Von Humboldt in 1804 and was later used as the official map of the signing of the Treaty that ended the Mexican/American War on February 2, 1848. This will be explained in detail in the following chapters.

We have called the area of the Palo Verde/Parker Valley "La Cuna de Aztlán," because the old Island of Aztlán was located in the Colorado River Indian Tribes Reservations (CRIT) as shown in the Boturini Codex.

The Azcatitlan Codex shows La Cuna de Aztlán portrayed

by a child in a cradle. The child that is shown in a cradle represents the birth of humanity. Below the cradle is a "petate" (mat), which represents earth, and to the right of the cradle there is a woman, who represents Malinalxochitl/Chimalma which is the child's mother. The cradle is well manifested in the Big Maria Mountains, thus the origin of La Cuna De Aztlan.

In this research we factually challenge the accepted version of The Bering Strait theory that states civilization migrated from Asia to the Western Hemisphere. The Bering Strait theory is just that, a theory. This ill-conceived theory was used as a tool to justify the massacres committed by the invaders against the natives of Anahuac who refused to accept their beliefs of their religion. This theory denied future generations the truth about their roots and their true history and continues to generate mass confusion among native nations. This theory erroneously states that the native inhabitants of the Turtle continent came from the so called "Old World," the Eurasian continent. The natives of Anahuac were not of the "New World," and Christopher Columbus did not discover America. We know this is false. Currently, this theory is being challenged by archeological, biological and linguistic evidence. We know that there is just "one world," and that civilization left from the continent of Anahuac and migrated throughout the world. It will take time to rewrite history about the truth of our origins as humans. Still, we are confident this research will provoke more historians to investigate for themselves and challenge the history written by European conquerors.

The abundance of geographical and cosmological evidence found in the Lower Colorado River Basin Valleys serves as a guide for further in-depth studies. Our quest for knowledge is now coming to light. The dual prophecy of the last Mexica Tlatoani Cuauhtémoc will be fulfilled: "Our Sun will shine again and the greatness of Mexico/Tenochtitlan will never perish."

One of the main organizations that inspired our pursuit in seeking the truth of Aztlan has been the Escuela De La Raza Unida.

The ERU's successes are fulfilling part of that Mexica prophecy of cultural rebirth. ERU was born out of conflict and throughout its thirty-nine years of existence, it has been able to expand and overcome numerous barriers brought upon by that same conflict and struggle, as a means of growth.

The birth of the Escuela de la Raza Unida and the Xicano Alternative School Movement served as the catalyst that opened the door to a new horizon, escalating our quest and persistence in the revelation of the truth of Aztlan and of our indigenous origins on the Colorado River.

The historian Altamirano said: "If you want to know who the Tolteca and Azteca were and what they did, don't rely on the history books, but rather, go to the state of Guerrero, Mexico and visit the indigenous villages located in the heart of the mountains where the natives have still maintained their culture and traditions."

On the same note, in Blythe, California, we say, "If you want to know where Aztlán is, come to the Lower Colorado River Basin Valleys of Palo Verde/Parker and see for yourself where our ancient ancestors dwelled and see the stories they left behind depicted throughout the valleys and its surrounding mountains."

Finally, this study and investigation by Colorado River natives has resulted in the ethnology, the true meaning, of the word Mexico/Aztlán and the location of the mystical ancient Aztlán.

Again, we emphasize that history will be rewritten by descendents of the Mexica. We are learning how to interpret the codexes and correlate them with our natural geographical surroundings as they pertain to the lower Colorado River Basin Valleys. This is the first step in challenging the deliberate lies that we find in the text books that our younger generations are being subjected to in the public schools.

Today, like the ancient Phoenix Bird, Aztlán is rising from the ashes of obscurity. Therefore, we ask that as you read this book, you remember what the famous Cuban writer, Enrique Jose Varona said to his history students: "Don't seek the truth in what a man says, but in what he does."

The evidence brought forth to you in this book provides intense thought provoking concepts that will leave you with a new found perception of who we are as a people here on earth and of our relationship with the cosmos. The wisdom of our ancestors goes back thousands of years on this earth and their "footprints" here on the Colorado River tell us their story of origin; our story of origin which has been obscured from the world for hundreds of years by the lies written by historians whose fictitious accounts served only to defend the European conquest and completely obliterate all reminiscence of our indigenous cosmic cultural traditions.

Chapter 1

The Lower Colorado River Basin Valleys

There are seven valleys that form the Lower Colorado River Basin, beginning with the Mojave Valley in the north (Needles, California) and continuing south to the Chemehuevi, Parker, Palo Verde, Cibola, Yuma and Mexicali Valleys, down to the Colorado River Delta at the Gulf of California. This magnificent oasis of the Colorado River and the surrounding mountains is the foundation of the Hokan/Mojave and Uto/Aztecan Creation Story.

The Palo Verde/Parker Valleys have been populated, since time immemorial, with different indigenous nations migrating, fulfilling their traditional obligations and traveling to the four directions. For thousands of years, the members of the Mojave, Quechan, Yavapai, Halchidom, Cocopah, Chemehuevi and other Pai and Uto-Aztecan families migrated up and down the Colorado River Basin Valleys. (Kroeber, 1976)

The early history of the Lower Colorado River indicates that there was abundant trade up and down the river, in particular, between the Palo Verde Valley and the delta where the river flows into the Gulf of California, and west to the Pacific Ocean.

The Quechan Trail, called "Xam Kwatcan" in Quechan, is the main north/south trail leading from Spirit Mountain/Avi Kwame, north of Needles, California, to Pilot Knob/Avi Kwalal, west of Yuma near Algodones, Baja California. The main east/west trail was called "La Vedera de la Liebre" (Jackrabbit Trail) and also called the Coco-Maricopa Trail and intersects where the Blythe Energy Plant was built 7 miles west of Blythe. It is situated on one of the most sacred sites parallel to Interstate-10. These are some of the most sacred historical sites in the valley. (Johnson, 1985)

While traveling west from Phoenix, Arizona, on Interstate-10, one must admire a breathtaking panoramic view of several of the Lower Colorado River Valleys (Palo Verde, Parker and Cibola). This is visible after passing through Ferra Gulch Pass in the Dome Rock Mountains which is ten miles north of Weaver's Pass, first traversed in 1540 by Melchor Diaz as he came through looking for Hernando de Alarcon. (Dellenbaugh, 1998)
Upon descending the Dome Rock Mountains one can see the majestic meandering Colorado River and the lush agricultural valleys.

Across the California state line lie the Mule Mountains, Hamock Avi in Mojave, and "Molcajete." Located northwest are the Twin Peaks (chichis or tetones, meaning breasts in Spanish) of the Big Maria Mountains and looking south one can see the Twin Peaks of the Picachos, north of Yuma, Arizona. (Hensey, 1990)

Hernando de Alarcon was the first European recorded as having visited the natives living in the area of what we now call the Lower Colorado River Valleys. In August of 1540, he sailed up the river, an estimated eighty-five leagues from the Gulf of California, up to the area of the present-day Palo Verde/Parker Valleys.

In 1604 another European, Juan de Oñate, the first governor of New Mexico, journeyed west from the town of San Gabriel de Los Españoles, on the Rio Grande. On his way he crossed a muddy, red-tinged river which he named the Colorado. This is the first recorded use of the

name. Even though the governor actually crossed a tributary (which is the Little Colorado River) instead of the main river, the name Colorado was adopted for the entire waterway. (Waters, 1984)

Oñate then traveled southward along the Colorado River. He was the first European to travel extensively, the length of the river. He passed through Aztlán from the Bill William's River fork in the north to the Gulf of California in the south.

One hundred and sixty-four years later, in 1768, Fray Francisco Garces and his biographer, Fray Font, also traveled the Colorado River upstream and down. According to Frank Waters, author of The Colorado River, Garces was among the Spaniards who regularly referred to the river as the Colorado, "because as the river passed through the red earth of the Grand Canyon during the spring months, it was tinged red." (Waters, 1984)

The author's mother, Carmen Acosta, lived in Ehrenberg, Arizona, during the early years of 20th century before any dam, weirs or levees were built on the Colorado River and she would talk about how the residents of the towns along the river had to purify their cooking and drinking water: "We had to let it stand in tubs overnight, allowing the fine, and light, dirty reddish silt to settle to the bottom before it could be used." (C. Acosta)

In regards to the era when the Mexica lived along the river, they left remnants of at least four adobe pueblo-type ruins along the Lower Colorado River Valleys. These ruins are located between the Palo Verde Valley in the north and the Mexicali Valley delta in the south. (Johnson, 1985)

According to Boma Johnson of the BLM, numerous sites along the Colorado and Gila Rivers have been reported to contain mounds of adobe ruins, but were leveled for farmland. Obviously, the meandering rivers destroyed most of these mounds as well.

In 1775, Captain Juan Bautista de Anza recorded that he came upon some ancient indigenous adobe ruins 25-miles southwest of Pilot Knob in the Mexicali Valley. He noted that these ruins were similar to the adobe ruins located at Casa Grande on the Gila River in central Arizona. Captain Anza then concluded that they represented part of the Azteca Empire that once flourished in the region. (Galving, 1965)

Lieutenant R.W. Hardy of the U.S. Army reported that on July 23, 1826 when he traveled up his namesake waterway (Hardy River) in the Lower Colorado River delta, he was told of the adobe ruins similar to the ones at Casa Grande and was invited by the natives to visit the site.

Major Samuel P. Keintzelman, commander of Fort Yuma, claimed that in 1853, while sailing up the Colorado River, he saw a large adobe ruin at the south end of the Palo Verde Valley. It was located on a detached sandy plateau and the structures bordered a settlement of the Quechan inhabitants called Hut-Ta-Me-Mi. (Forbes, 1994)

Half a century later, in 1903, a cowboy familiar with the Colorado River delta region, found some adobe ruins a few miles southwest of the junction of the Colorado and Hardy Rivers. Unfortunately, floods and farm cultivation destroyed these pueblo-type ruins before historians and archaeologists could study them for greater historical significance. (Forbes, 1994)

In 1953, Tony Cota a Blythe-area cat-skinner (tractor driver), was knocking down heavy brush and mesquite trees to clear the land for agricultural use, when he came upon some small adobe ruins containing remains of "metates" (mortars), "manos" (pestles) and broken "ollas" (jars). This was found near the Palo Verde Lagoon, located about two miles north of the town of Palo Verde, California, in an open area on a small sand dune, in an area called "La Isla," The Island. (Cota, 1974)

During the La Paz gold rush of 1862, the Chemehuevi were living in the area of present-day Blythe on the old riverbed in half submerged huts along the riverbanks called "jukis,"(hookies). (Daniel, 1970)

From 1862 to 1870 during the La Paz, Colorado River gold rush, La Paz was a thriving river port town and was located on the south end of the Colorado River Indian Tribe Reservation (CRIT). At its height, La Paz was proposed to be the capitol of the Arizona Territory. Now all that remains of La Paz are small dirt mounds that were once adobe buildings. (Setzler, 1972)

In the Palo Verde Valley the old river channel ran southwesterly, almost parallel to present day Riverside Drive, known as "La Vereda de la Liebre" (Jackrabbit Trail) by the elders. It traverses through what is known as "El Barrio Del Cuchillo." (Daniel, 1970) According to Henry Ortiz, Sr. and Ignacio "Nacho" Macias and other Chemehuevi elders, El Barrio del Cuchillo was known as Barrio La Liebre, "Acacitli," the Jackrabbit neighborhood and east Riverside Drive/Chanslorway, the area where today, the Catholic Church is located, was known as El Barrio del Conejo, Rabbit neighborhood). (Ortiz/Macias 1975)

The Duran Codex depicts an area called Acacitli, "Acatl"- meaning (tulles or canes) and –"citli" meaning (jackrabbit); Acacitli means "Jackrabbit in the tulles." The first fold of the Duran Codex depicts the rabbit and jackrabbit in front of a cave, Xicomozstoc, with two people inside of it. This historical and sacred site of Acacitli establishes another link that connects the area of Blythe with the Mexica.

In 1875, Thomas Blythe, a San Francisco-based Englishman with a reputation of an international speculator and swindler, applied to the State of California for ownership of land in the Palo Verde Valley. He applied for the land under the State Swamp and Overflow Act, as if the land was only swampland. Under this act, only swampland available could be purchased.

Blythe lied on the application stating the land was all swampland even though the northern half of the valley was part of the Colorado River Indian Tribes (CRIT) Reservation. The Chemehuevi and other nations were living and farming the area, however, Blythe blatantly lied on his application stating: "that there was no one living in the valley." (Dekens)

According to Camiel Dekens' narrative Riverman, Desertman, Thomas Blythe fulfilled this condition by claiming on his application, "to have rowed a boat all over the Palo Verde Valley area." What he neglected to mention was that his rowboat was being carried in a wagon pulled by mules throughout the valley.

Unfortunately, this tragic deception was successful and Mr. Blythe took title to 40,000 acres of prime California land. Blythe brought in the United States Army and the homes of the natives were burned, their crops were destroyed, and the natives were forced to cross the river to the Colorado River Indian Tribe (CRIT) reservation. These heinous acts reduced the reservation boundaries on the California/Arizona side, appropriating the rich gold mines on the Arizona side. (Daniels)

Gilbert Lopez Leivas stated that according to Bureau of Indian Affairs records, the original boundary of the CRIT reservation extended west roughly to the high-water-flood-stage levels. Today, the high water levels are still visible on the mesa west of Blythe, which includes most of the present-day town of the same name. (Leivas, 1982)

Chapter 1.2
The Indigenous Nations

The Lower Colorado River Basin Valleys have been home to the nucleus of many different indigenous linguistic families whom, at one time or another, came to the area and stayed for a

while and then went on their journey in four directions, called "Nahui-Ollin." Finally, some of the nations settled permanently in this area.

According to Chief Gary Harrison, the Athabaskans left the Colorado River and went north to Alaska before the last Ice Age. Many nations left the area, beginning with the Olmecas, who went south, thousands of years ago. The Chichimeca followed then the Tolteca/Yaqui in the 5thcentury, followed by the Azteca/Mexica in the 12thcentury. The Lower Colorado River Valleys have been a major crossroad within the Anahuac Continent, with some of the nations going full circle. These nations traveled in the four directions and later returned to the Colorado River Valleys. (Krober, 1976)

The major interests in this study are the three main linguistic families that claim to have originated on the Colorado River. They are the Uto-Aztecan (Nahua): Pima, Tohono O'odam, Yaqui, Hopi, Chemehuevi, Paiute, Cahuilla, Azteca/Mexica, Tarahumaras, Cora, Huichol, Tlaxcalteca, Tarascos and Chichimeca. In addition, the Hokan (Yuman) Mojave, Quechan, Kamias, Yavapai, Hualapai, Cocopah, Halchidomas, Havasupai, Pai Pai, Chumash, Pomo, Shasta, Seris (in Sonora) and the Maya Chontal (in Yucatan and Guerrero), as well as the Apache, Navajo, Janos, Athabaskan (in Alaska and Canada).

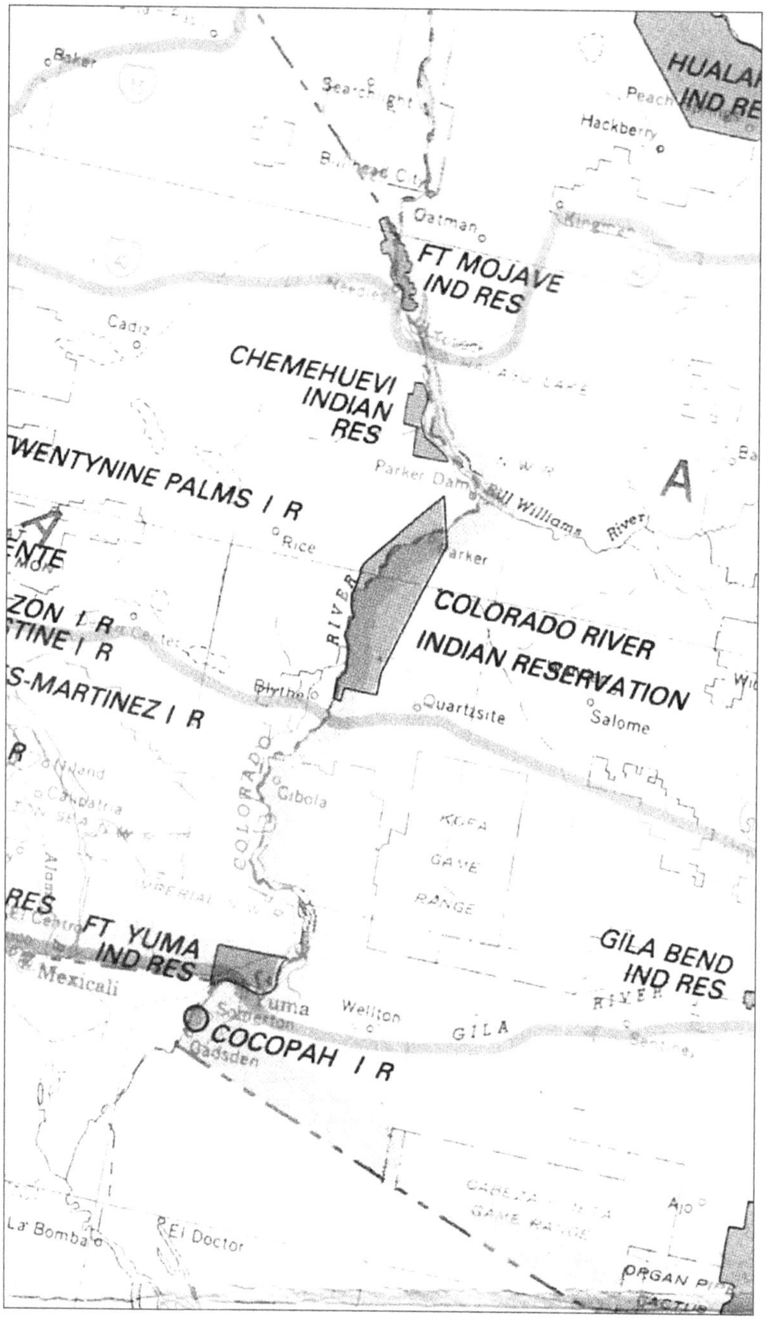

Map of indigenous reservations on the Lower Colorado River Valleys. (Taken from Department of Interior Indian Land Areas Map, 1989.)

4 Ancient Footprints of the Colorado River

There are five native reservations in the Lower Colorado River Valleys from North to South, beginning with Fort Mojave, near Needles, California, Chemehuevi, Colorado River Indian Tribes, Quechan and Cocopah, south of Yuma, Arizona. Of those five, the Mojave and Chemehuevi are the most prominent nations in the Palo Verde/Parker Valleys.

The Mojave nation boundaries to the north traditionally have been Spirit Mountain and Black Canyon, and east to the Black Mountains above Oatman, Arizona and south to the Needles Peaks, and west to the Tehachapi Mountains.

The Chemehuevi live in the valley of the same name which is located south of the Needles Peaks. Their ancestral territory extended down to the Bill Williams River fork and East, to the Santa Maria River junction, West all the way to Twenty-nine Palms, California and South, beyond the Palo Verde Valley.

The Maricopa, Halchidoma, Kaveltcadom and Kohuana were the other Hokan linguistic nations that existed in the Palo Verde/Parker Valleys. However, they were killed and driven out of the area by the victorious Mojave from the North and the Quechan from the South. The Kaveltcadom and Kohuana were conquered and assimilated. The Maricopa's went to the Gila River to live among the Pima in that area. The Halchidoma were the last of the original nations to leave the Palo Verde/Parker Valleys, circa 1830. Some of them went down into Sonora, Mexico around Caborca and Magdalena, and the rest went to the Gila River, following the Maricopa before them. (Forbes, 1994)

According to Gilbert Lopez Leivas, the Parker Valley is called "enemy house," "Ahwe-Nyava" in Mojave and "Thuhug Wantitivipi" in Chemehuevi, because of the constant enmity among the nations in the area. (Laird, 1976)

In order to ensure greater bureaucratic control over all the Lower Colorado River nations, on March 3, 1865, Congress established the Colorado River Indian Tribes (CRIT) Reservation. (History of CRIT, 1947)

The federal government tried to remove all the Mojave from their ancestral land in the Mojave Valley to the newly designated reservation in the south. The government knew of the proposed east/west railroad line that was going to be built parallel to the road going to California and it was scheduled to pass through the heart of Mojave territory.

However, the Mojave, who had been named Pipa Aha-Macave (Guardians of the River) by their Spirit-Mentor Matavilya, did not wish to break their centuries-old connection with the river and the place of their earthly origin, Spirit Mountain. Eventually, after unremitting pressure from the United States Army, Chief Irataba, and about half of the Mojave from the valley, along with a portion of the Chemehuevi and Yavapai, relocated to the CRIT reservation. (Devereux, 1951)

The original 1865 CRIT boundaries were later modified in 1867, continuing in 1874, then again in 1876 and the last one was in 1915. Due to the modifications acreage on the reservation was reduced.

In 1945 and 1957 the Federal Bureau of Indian Affairs (BIA) invited the Navajo and Hopi to settle and farm on the CRIT Reservation. (CRIT History, 1947)

In the last several decades, The Reservations Tribal Council, have successfully used the courts to regain a portion of the tribal lands located on the California side of the Colorado River which includes parts of North-East Palo Verde Valley and on the Arizona side extending south to Interstate-10. Currently, the combined CRIT reservation territory in California and Arizona approximately covers 285,000 acres.

Chapter 2

La Cuna de Aztlán: Origin and Ethnology

Aztlan is the place most commonly referred to as the place of origin of the Azteca/Mexica. Aztlan is the place where the ancestors of millions of today's indigenous people came from, including the Xicanos and Mexica. Although it has been sought for centuries, its whereabouts, until now, was a mystery.

Aztlan has many meanings, but the most recognized and accepted meaning is place of the herons due to the abundance of herons in the Palo Verde/Parker Valleys. It also means land of the whiteness because of the large white limestone deposits that are seen on the slopes of the surrounding mountains. Aztlan also means land of the rising sun because the sun rises during the equinoxes in between two peaks that form a "u" shape in the Moon Mountains, located in Colorado River Indian Tribe Reservation.

Most historians who have written about Aztlán also speculate that the Nahua nation came from northwest Mexico or southwest United States. However, scientists, researchers, and archeologists have not been able to link the Nahua/Azteca/Mexica with their ancient homeland of Aztlán, giving rise to the misconception that Aztlán existed only in myth. Yet, in the hearts and minds of Xicanos, the location of their ancestral homeland, Aztlán was just a mystery. One of the best theories regarding this issue was presented by historian Alfredo Chavero, in his book, "Mexico Atraves de los Siglos." (Teja, 1934)

Historians base their concepts on the old theory of the Hohokam (people who have gone) or the Anazasi (ancient people) and have overlooked the truth of the oral traditional history of the elders of this area. They have not pursued the connection with indigenous nations from Mexico that left the Colorado River at different intervals with some nations going south and some going east through Hopi and Navaho land. This brief research reveals the puzzle of the Hohokam and Anazasi.

After examining the geographical and linguistic evidence, our research concludes that Aztlán is located along the Lower Colorado River Basin Valleys, centered in the Palo Verde/Parker Valleys. Here on the Colorado River there was an abundance of lakes, swamps and islands which formed the old river channels.

In the Parker Valley, there is a dried river channel adjacent to the Moon Mountains where the Azteca/Mexica built dikes that separated the water from the river that flowed near by. The water was channeled into a lake called Mexico, which surrounded an island were they settled and built Aztlán.

There, the Azteca planted willow, cypress and poplar trees. The lake began to swell with numerous fish-farms, ducks, herons, wild geese, and many other types of birds. They were content with their surrounding environment and when they left on their migration south they sought similar surroundings in which to build their new homes.

The geoglyphs, pictographs, petroglyphs, intaglios, mountain peaks, rivers and swamps of the Lower Colorado River Basin Valleys bear witness to the indigenous nation creation story and their subsequent migrations. These artifacts, along with native oral traditions and the Nahuatl language, codices as well as the names of

mountain ranges and sites are all essential if one is to understand the history of Aztlán.

For centuries, the location of Aztlán had been unknown because researchers failed to study the Lower Colorado River Basin Valleys. Aztlán is clearly depicted in the Mexica Codexes like the Boturini, Aubin, and Siguenza and is in the chants of the "Bird Songs," and the bird, "Thunderbird Eagle" leads them to and from Aztlán as stated by Tibon Gutierre. (Gutierre, 1993)

According to Chuck Lamb, Retired Colorado River Indian Tribe Reservation Museum Curator, the oral histories of the Lower Colorado River Chemehuevi, Mojave, Sonoran, Opata, and Papago nations recounted that Moctezuma passed through their area.

It is important to note that there were three Moctezumas in the Azteca/Mexica history. The first Moctezuma lived in Aztlán. He was the first Tlatoani before the 1068 migration to Mexico. The first one was given the name Moctezuma. He was followed by Moctezuma Ilhuilcamina, the Cosmic Bowman, who lived four-hundred years later, reigning over the Confederation of Anahuac in Mexico/Tenochtitlan during the 15th century from 1440-1469. The reign of the third Moctezuma began in 1503 and ended when the Spanish invaded Mexico. He was killed by Hernan Cortez in 1520. They called him Moctezuma Xocoyotzin meaning "The Youngest."

Major William Emory, a surveyor with the United States/Mexico Boundary Commission, made strong references to these oral histories. He stated in his notes that during his second and final survey of the Gadsden Purchase in 1853 - 1854, these were the routes that were taken during Moctezuma's travels. (United States, 1854)

In the Geology of Wisconsin: 1873-1879 Surveys, regarding the location of Aztlan, the author, I. A. Lapham states that Aztlán was located on the shores of Lake Michigan in what is today the state of Wisconsin. However, Betancourt, Clavijero and Bourbourg believe it was located north of the Gulf of California. The Boturini and Aubin Codex as well as the historian Bancroft put Aztlán in Baja California, while Veytia, Acosta and the Ramirez Codex' place Aztlán north of Sonora. The Zumarraga and Tezozomoc Codex indicated it was in northwest Mexico, while Mendieta says it is north of Jalisco. (OSIM, 1966)

The Aubin Codex shows Aztlán as an island, and a hill (Tepetl) with a human image standing at the top. At the base on each side of the hill, is a glyph representing a house (calli). A Spanish interpreter of the codex added the word "Azteca" on top of the house image; and at the bottom of the hill he wrote "Aztlán."

According to historian Manuel Orozco y Berra, there are several great Nahua migration paths. Berra stated that: "Aztlán should be in Jalisco and has selected the island of Mexcalla, in the middle of Lake Chapala."

Modern-day Mexican historian Raul Lopez Navarro, in his 1994 book 'El Numero 13 En La Vida de Los Azteca,' states that: "Aztlán is the island state of the city of Tenochtitlan ... the Azteca just migrated around Lake Texcoco in the Valley of Anahuac."

Cecilio Robledo's, 1990 'Diccionario de Mitologia Nahuatl' claims that Aztlán is a place originally occupied by "Los Mexicanos," a name that derived from the name Azteca. He writes that Aztlán is generally believed to have been north of the Gulf of California, and adds that there is a linguistic theory correlating the Nahuatl language (spoken by the Azteca) with that spoken by natives in Arizona. Most social scientists place Aztlán in the north of Mexico, in what is now the southwest of the United States. Robledo concludes that the Azteca left southward from there on their migration.

Chilmalpahin Cuaugtlehuanitin, native of Chalco-Amaquemecan (near present-day Mexico City) and descendant of the tlatoanis of

Tenochtitlan, places Aztlán in California, in the vast region surrounding the confluence of both the Colorado and Gila Rivers. He says it is from this region that the Nahua/Azteca migrated south, during several different eras, and there is newer archeological, linguistic and ethnological research to support his conclusions.

In Dr. Alfonso Caso's journal, "El Ombligo de la Luna," he says that Mexico means "in the center of the moon," or "in the center of the lake of the moon," or "Metztliapan", in Nahuatl. Dr. Caso goes on to say that it was named Metztliapan to "remind the Nahua nations of their ancient place of origin in Aztlán, the place they left as an order from the gods. There, in the middle of the water, Anepantla was the island that was called Mexico.

Researchers like Dr. Cecilio A. Robledo in his "Dictionary of Aztequismos," say that the term Mexico is derived from: "Mexictli, name of the god Huitzilopochtli. This is where homage is rendered, in the capital city of Anahuac. Dr. Robledo also states that: "Mexictli is comprised from the syllables -metl, (maguey), -xictli, (umbilical). Mexictli signifies "umbilical of the maguey plant."(Robledo, 1990) These two interpretations by Caso and Robledo are the two most often quoted in historical research and chronicles.

Cristobal del Castillo in his 1991 book, "History of the Coming of the Mexicans and Other Nations," writes: "that the Mexica were river fishermen who lived in Aztlán and were subject to the rulers of Aztlán. Alluding to Castillo's book, writer Fernando Tezozomoc stated that "the Mexica lived in Aztlán in the middle of the water and that the leader of this place was the son of the tlatoani, Moctezuma."

Eulalia Guzman, respected archaeologist for the INAH, Instituto Nacional de Archeologia y Historia, writes in her book, "Donde Estuvo El Aztlán de los Mexica," "We know that the island of Aztlán could not have been by the ocean because the herons do not live by salt water, only fresh water." (Organo, 1966)

A lack of written indigenous documentation has made it difficult to uncover source material regarding the exact location of Aztlán and the origins of various nations. Most of the pertinent codices were deliberately destroyed by European zealots living among the colonizers in Mexico, 'silencing voices from the past.'

In their research of indigenous people, historians, archaeologists and anthropologists, have all made the same unfortunate error of classifying and categorizing indigenous people based on their given boundaries; boundaries imposed on the natives by the governments throughout the entire continent. Prior to the United States/Mexican War, indigenous people were free to roam and migrate throughout the continent as they had always done for thousands of years. Their identification has been classified and restricted to certain regions on the continent, as if they belonged to and or originated in these regions. These are not regions of their origin, but regions imposed on them by their conquerors.

Well-known historian, Paul Kirchhoff, has divided the Anahuac continent into three regions and he coined the phrases, "Mesoamerica, Aridamerica, and Oasisamerica." Aztlán has been searched for in Mesoamerica and of the three major regions, this region encompasses the area from the southern part of the state of Chihuahua down to Nicaragua. No wonder the location of Aztlán has remained unknown; no one ever looked for it in the right place.

These major regions and their boundaries should not be viewed as independent regions. They must be considered as a continent if we are to comprehend the diversity and reality of the Azteca/Mexica migrations, traditions and their origin.

The ancient tracks of the past can still be found in the hills, mountains, rocks, and mesas that surround the Lower Colorado River Valleys. Fortunately, these tracks have escaped major destruction and now bear witness to the Mexica Creation story on the banks of the Colorado River.

The geographical location of Mexico/Aztlán is now identified as the area of the Palo Verde/Parker Valley. During one of their migration intervals, the ancient Azteca/Mexica left from the ancient island of Mexico/Aztlán on the Colorado River (Lake Mexico) to settle in Mexico/Tenochtitlan, modern day Mexico City.

We have crossed-referenced the research of the origin of Aztlán with the Mexica Codexes and with the Blythe Giant Intaglios, as well as thousands of petroglyphs and pictographs that are found throughout the area. However, the most crucial evidence is the incredibly profound sacred mountain images that reveal the location of the ancient island of Aztlan, located in what is today a dried up lake bed.

The place of origin of the Mexica on the Colorado River was where the vanished island of Aztlan was located in a lake called Lake Mexico. The lake bordered the Moon Mountains on the east. This sequence is shown in the Vindobonesis Codex. There in the Moon Mountains are the petroglyphs that are the indicators left by our forefathers.

The Boturini Codex is the most accepted codex concerning the origin of the Azteca/Mexica nations. This Codex' depictions are painted all around the walls of the courtyard of the renowned National Institute of Anthropology and History Museum in Mexico City. This codex clearly shows the Nahua nations leaving an island in the first fold. On this island there is a small Teocalli (pyramid) and on top of it is the glyph (symbol) of A-tla-chinolli meaning "water, earth and fire".

In addition, there is the glyph of calli (house), and two human figures. One of these figures is Chimalma/Malinalxochitl (mother earth) and the other is Quetzalcoatl, Ce-Acatl. There is a person rowing a canoe with human footprints leading on the other side of the water, which depicts the beginning of the Nahua migration from Mexico/Aztlán.

The Nahua Nations migrated to the four-directions, "Nahui-Ollin" throughout the thousands of years from the Lower Colorado River Valleys during different eras. According to certain beliefs, the migrations began with the Azteca, Olmeca, Zapoteca, Mixteca, Tolteca, Chichimeca and finally the Mexica that migrated south to the Valley of Anahuac in the 12th century.

As the Nahua traveled they were always seeking similar places to duplicate their beloved Mexico/Aztlán and its similar surroundings. One of those locations was Mexcaltitlan, Nayarit, whose ethnology is similar to the ancient Aztlan and its surroundings. Some historians mistake Mexcaltitlan for the original ancient Aztlán. Mexcaltitlan was just one of the many stops the Azteca/Mexica made on their long journey in search of the prophesied promise land Mexico/Tenochtitlan. There is also an island called San Pedro de Aztlán.

In 1804, the eminent German cartographer and historian Alexander Von Humbolt drew a map of what was at that time called New Spain, which included present day, Mexico and Southwest/United States. Humbolt, however, never visited the Lower Colorado River Valleys, so his informants must have given him the information and copied some earlier maps. The information of some of the sites mentioned is relatively close to the actual localities here in the Lower Colorado River Valleys.

The Von Humbolt Map was the official map that was used in the signing of the Treaty of Guadalupe Hidalgo by the United States and Mexico on February 2, 1848. Mexico lost more than half of their original territory, which included Aztlan.

The map shows the "Antigua Residencia de los Aztecas," (the Ancient Residence of the Aztec), located at a junction on the Colorado River called "Concepcion" or conception, (meaning beginning). This is the first indication alluding to the location of Aztlán shown in a map which was drawn by Europeans confirming that Aztlán

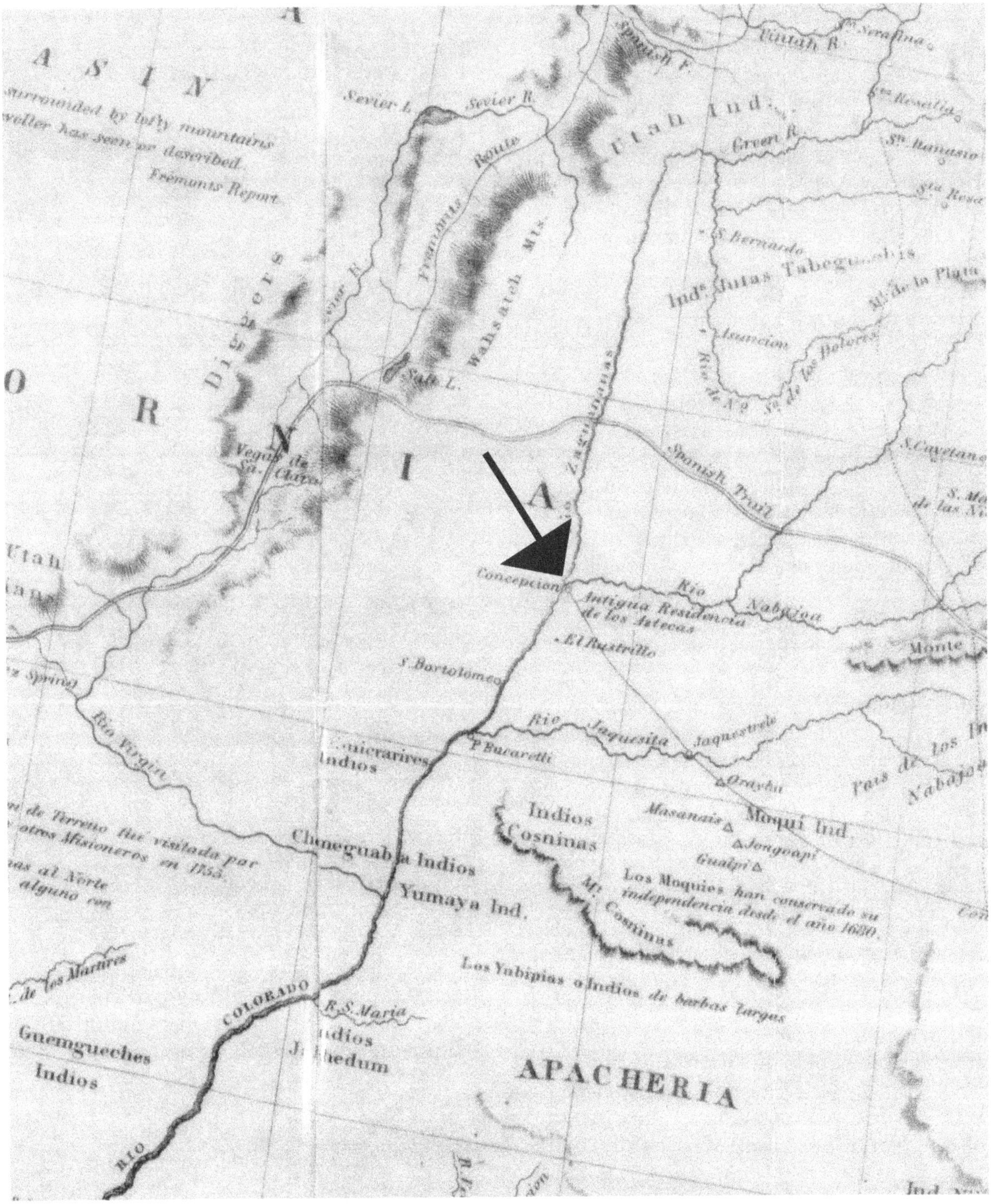

1804 Map of Alexander Von Humbolt. This same map was used for Treaty of Guadalupe, February 2, 1848. The arrow points to a place called Concepcion on the Lower Colorado River Basin that identifies La Antigua Residencia de los Aztecas, (Ancient homeland of the Azteca). This indicates that the Aztecas came from the Colorado River, with the Ancient Homeland of the Aztecas actually being from the area named Chemeguaba Indios (Chemehuevi).

Ancient Footprints of the Colorado River

was truly on the Colorado River. It also includes the Chemeguaba (Chemehuevi) nation on the Colorado River in between Rio Santa Maria and Concepcion. Further down on the Gila River the map shows the "Ruinas de las Casa Segundas de los Aztecas, meaning (Ruins of the Second House of the Aztecas). The geographic location of the ruins is approximately in the same spot where Casa Grande National monument is located in Arizona today.

Continuing southeast on the map, in the state of Chihuahua, Mexico is "Casas Tercera de los Aztecas," meaning the (Third House of the Aztecs,) which today are the ruins of Paquime in Casas Grandes, Chihuahua, Mexico.

The identity of the indigenous culture has maintained its existence due to the native cultural traditions which have persisted in the southwest despite the international border. This cultural exchange thrives also due to the continued migration of Mexicas and the Xicano activists who continue to pursue the roots of their heritage.

Our research, which includes the Azteca/Mexica migrations and their lineage from the Colorado River nations, utilizes both written documentation and physical evidence that, when combined, leaves little doubt of the existence of Aztlán in the Colorado River Indian Reservation.
The mystical island of Aztlán was located in what today is called "The Moon Ranch" at the foot of the mountain range that has the same name.

Today, the island of Aztlán has been totally destroyed by the Colorado River floods, and is now being used as farmland. The only evidence left is the dried saline river bed channel, which formed part of the old lake Mexico.

Chapter 2.2
The Heron Symbol of Aztlán

Symbol of Aztlan

Every autumn many heron, cranes, ducks, egret and many other species migrate from Canada, south to Mexico. On their way to Mexico they follow the Lower Colorado River to it's delta in the Gulf of California. Although some heron live year-round in the Palo Verde/Parker Valleys, many of them and other fowl from the north stay all winter along the river in the wildlife refuges by Havasu, Cibola and Imperial. Others, however, stay in the Lower Colorado River delta in the Mexicali Valley, or in the Salton Sea area. (Cibola National Wildlife Bulletin)

Along the southern migration trails we find heron petroglyphs in the Gila Bend area by the Gila River in Arizona and in the desert of Caborca in Sonora, Mexico. The heron petroglyphs in Caborca indicate the journey from Aztlán, land of the herons, to a place called La Provedora in Caborca. According to Boma Johnson, there are also petroglyphs and pictographs in of herons in Utah.

During the migrations, Huitzilopochtli, in the form of "the hummingbird," as shown in the Boturini Codex led the Mexica from Aztlán south to the Valley of Anahuac. The hummingbird would cry out to them, "Mexica Tihui, Tamoanchan," meaning "Mexica, seek your House."

In the mountains of the Lower Colorado River Valleys, a large white thunderbird image eagle image can be seen among these sacred mountains images and it is also depicted in the Siguenza Codex. This eagle is on top of a tree that has five branches and is talking to a group of people at the beginning of their migration from Aztlán.

The Siguenza Codex also shows the heron, (which symbolizes Aztlán and the "olla" symbolizes Xicomozstoc which represents the womb of Mother Earth.) Here in the Lower Colorado River Valleys, in Aztlán, the heron's presence ensures its connection with the Azteca/Mexica nations, which migrated thousands of years ago. The heron/crane migrations from Canada, reinforces its symbolism with Aztlán. (Cibola National Wildlife Bulletin)

The Tlaxcalteca, one of the Nahua families originally from Aztlán, carried an image of their mascot, the heron, to war, high on a banner, as it represented their native heritage from Aztlán.

Aubin Codex

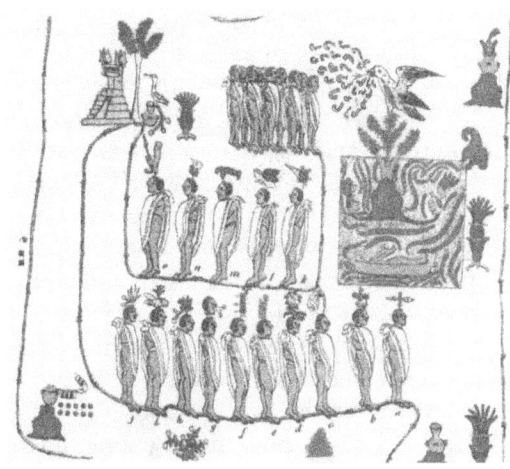

Siguenza Codex

Picture of first fold/page of Siguenza Codex which shows the Island of Aztlan with an eagle on top of tree calling to the people, "Mexica tihui Tamoanchan," meaning, "Mexica, go and seek you house." "(Vamos, adelante, busca tu casa.)" The humans on the boat represent Quetzalcoatl as he leaves to the east. The humans represent the different nations leaving Aztlan. The 'ollas' (pots) represent Chicomoztoc. The heron symbolizes Aztlan. The tree with the three branches is symbolic of Omecihualt, Ometecutli, and Ometeotl, meaning Creator. The teocalli pyramid represents Huitzilopochtli and Tlaloc..

This is Lake Mexico on the Colorado River. There is a teocalli in the middle of the island and surrounding the teocalli are the four calli/house symbols of the different nations.

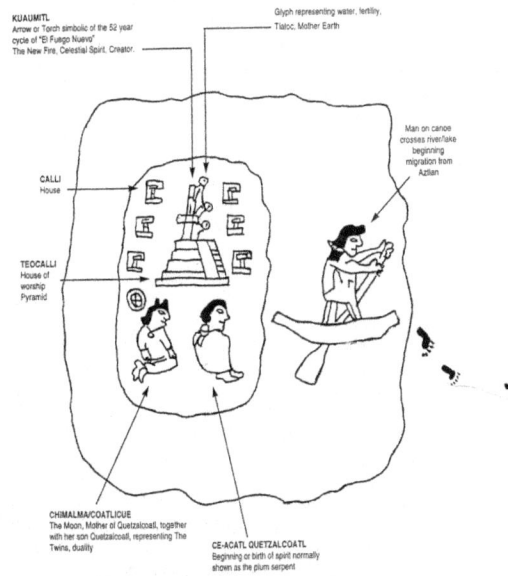

Ancient Footprints of the Colorado River

Boturini Codex

Azteca Migration from Aztlan-Man on canoe crosses river/lake beginning migration from Aztlan. The glyph on the right side of the teocalli represents Tlaloc, water, fertility, mother earth and the left side is Kuaumitl, the arrow or torch symbolize the 52 years cycle of "El Fuego Nuevo," The New Fire, Celestial Spirit, Creator. The six small houses around the teocalli represent calli. The teocalli is the house of worship. Chimalma/Coatlicue, the figure on the left with the circle with a cross, represents the mother of Quetzalcoatl, together with her son, Quetzalcoatl, representing The Twins, duality. Ce-Acatl Quetzalcoatl is on the right, representing the beginning or birth of spirit normally shown as the plumed serpent.

Chapter 2.3
Azteca/Mexica Migrations from Aztlán

Even though most Mexican historians, who have written about Aztlan, say that the Nahua nations migrated from Northwest Mexico and the Colorado River, a thorough investigation confirming this fact has never been conducted on the Colorado River.

Chimalpahin Cuauhtlehuanitzin, a descendant of the tlatoanis of Tenochtitlan whose codex is among the most respected, wrote: "Aztlán has to be in California, in the vast region along the Colorado and Gila Rivers. There, they founded the great city of Aztlán."

Dr. Alfonso Caso, former head of the National Museum of Anthropology in Mexico City and best-known scholar on this subject, said: "that through archaeological, linguistic and ethnological study, the claims of Chimalpahin could be proven." Through four decades of research and numerous investigations, we have therefore followed Caso's mythology and our conclusions verify his assertions.

According to Caso's research, nearly all of the different nations who lived west of the Mississippi River, including the Uto/Aztecan, Hokan/Yuman and Athabaskan/Apache linguistic families, extending as far as Alaska, migrated at one time or another from the Lower Colorado River Basin Valleys.

Javier Clavijero's writing's about the Nahua migrations, quotes Torquemada, who is said to: "have seen old paintings in which the migration wave was represented by a branch of the sea or a big river." Clavijero stated, "This was the Colorado River and that after passing to the north of the 35th latitude, the Nahua traveled southeast to Casa Grande, Arizona, on the Gila River, where they stayed for some time before continuing southeast to Casas Grandes, Chihuahua, Mexico." (Clavijero 1982)

Anthropologist Eulalia Guzman states that there was an Italian document in which a missionary priest affirmed to Clavijero his conviction that the Azteca came from Nuevo Mexico, which included Arizona and New Mexico. (Organo, 1966)

Other migrations that came from the Lower Colorado River Basin went northeast towards the four corners where the states of Arizona, Utah, Colorado and New Mexico meet.

In southern Utah, one can follow petroglyph footprints on trails such as the ones at the famous Newspaper Rock (north of Moab, Utah). The human footprints are the telltale signs that the Nahua nations left behind during their many migrations throughout the ages. (United States Department of Interior)

Petroglyph migration footprints can also be found at the Wenima Wild Life area near the Apache reservation in Eastern Arizona. At this site, bird claw prints are depicted alongside human footprints. (Wenima, 1995) Petroglyph footprints are also prominent around the St. George area and in the southwest part of Utah, but they can be found almost anywhere in the United States, and Mexico.

Cristobal del Castillo, a Mexica historian wrote that during the Mexica migration they were guided by Tetzauhteotl-Tezcatlipoca who transformed into an eagle and the eagle flew ahead and lead them. The Eagle was Huitzilopochtli and he communicated to them that: "I will go leading you where you are going. I will be in the form of an eagle. I will be calling you where to go. You must watch me." (Castillo, 1991)

The bird claw prints represent Huitzilopochtli in his nagualli or his animal representation. For this reason, the Eagle claw prints and the human footprints are seen side by side along the migrations trails as seen in many petroglyphs.

Major archaeological sites contain evidence that the migrations traveled through many sacred places which include Mesa Verde, Colorado and Chalco Canyon, New Mexico. The nations traveled south to Casas Grandes, Chihuahua, and on to Chalchihuites, Zacatecas, also known as the "The Turquoise City."

According to two missionaries who had visited Casas Grandes, Chihuahua, the Pima oral tradition relates that the Azteca migration south from Casa Grande, Arizona were the people who built Casas Grandes, Chihuahua. (Clavijero, 1982) Many archeological sites in the southwest, including ruins of earlier great civilizations, seem to validate this oral history as well.

Modern day Danza Azteca founder Florencio Yesca and Hopi Elder, Tomas Banyaca respected prominent Hopi elder, keeper of the Hopi prophecies, believed that the Nahua left Aztlán for political and traditional beliefs, timing their departures in accordance with the astronomical signs. They then traveled to the four directions, covering the continent. (Florencio Yesca, 1974)

According to the late Hopi shaman, Thomas Banyaca, an ancient Azteca ruin site sits on the third mesa within the Hopi Reservation, located ten miles northwest of the old pueblo of Oraibi in northeast Arizona. Banyaca stated that according to their traditions, the Hopi migrated to and from, up and down the Colorado River. He stated they traveled from the areas of Spirit Mountain and the Grape Vine Canyon northwest of Laughlin, Nevada. Banyaca personally visited the site and was looking for the ancient petrified grape vines as told to him by the ancient oral traditions of the Hopi Creation Story. (Banyaca, 1996) There, at Grape Vine Canyon, accompanied by the author and Phil Smith,

Banyaca performed a ceremonial prayer that made a moss-filled pond flow with water right before their very eyes. (Smith, 1996)

Thomas Banyaca with Phil Smith and Alfredo Figueroa, surrounded by other Ward Valley environmentalists, holding up the drawing of the petroglyph of the Hopi Prophecy. (circa 1996)

Archaeologist Stephen Lekson, who has researched the Azteca Ruins and Chalco Canyon in New Mexico, and Casas Grandes in Chihuahua, says that the members of the same families going south at different intervals constructed the sites mentioned above in a straight line.

The different Nahua nations that migrated from

the Colorado River at one time or another were not given that name until they settled at the different locations that bear their name along the migration route. The Nahua migrations from the Colorado River took place during different epochs and each epoch was given a name. The Olmeca were the first to be recorded by historians around 3,000 years ago, followed by the Tolteca, Chichimeca, Culhua and finally the Azteca/Mexica. (Capillo, 1965)

The general concept of the migrations is that most major archaeological ruins in the southwest were abandoned by the 14th century. The Azteca/Mexica left Aztlán around 1160 A.D., not because of warfare, drought or epidemics, as suggested by the historians and other researchers.

Our research reveals that they left based on the computation of the traditional cosmic 52-year New Fire Celebration which took place when the star constellation of the Seven Sisters "The Pleiades" rose to its zenith. The New Fire glyph is shown on top of the Teocalli of Aztlán in the Boturini Codex. The Seven Sisters geoglyph image is also among the Blythe Giant Intaglio geoglyph cluster.

Guided by a prophecy attributed to Huitzilopochtli, the Nahua followed the same migration path used by the herons and other migrating birds on their annual flight from the lakes of Central Canada down the Colorado River and south to Mexico. Most historians agree that all the Nahua families left from the same area at one time or another, each taking a different route. (Carpanta, Boturini Codices)

One of the first codexes about the migration of the Tolteca was written by Hueman, a Tolteca traditional leader who reigned during the journey south from Aztlán. Hueman wrote the Tolteca, "Divine Book," in which he described the migration from the red region of Huehuetlapallan, above the confluence of the Gila and Colorado Rivers. (Perez, 1972)

Most of the Pre-Cuauhtémoc codexes were destroyed by the European conquerors and over zealous priests that viewed traditional indigenous images and beliefs as evil and viewed indigenous nations as worshipers of the devil. The European distortion and misinterpretation of the codexes cast confusion upon the world and mystified the identification of the place from where the Nahua left on their journey south to Mexico/Tenochtitlan. European writers were eager to destroy all indigenous thought and traditions to justify the genocide of the indigenous nations.

During their migration from the Colorado River, the Azteca/Mexica named many of the sites along there migration route and traditionally, they named these sites after the places of their origin on the Colorado River. This tradition has caused major confusion for researchers because consequently, numerous places along the migration route were named Aztlán.

To this day, researchers have concluded incorrectly, for example, that Aztlán, Sinaloa is the true Aztlán while others say it is San Pedro de Aztlán in Nayarit, near Lake of Mexcaltitlan. There is even a place called Aztlán in the northern part of Lake Michigan. The name 'Michigan' means the same as the name 'Michoacán,' a state in Mexico. Both Michigan and Michoacán is a Nahuatl word meaning "place of the fish," alluding to the fact that the Mexica went in all four directions from Aztlán.

During their journeys south, the nations were assisted in some unexpected ways. In his book "Los Aztecas o Mexica, Fundacion de Mexico/Tenochtitlan," Alfredo Chavero, quotes Fray Torquemada saying that the Azteca/Mexica were led on their migrations by a bird that often appeared in a tree and repeatedly uttered a shrill cry (chillido) that sounded like "Mexica Tihui-tihui Tamoanchan," meaning "Adelante Mexica, encuentra tu Casa," Mexica go forward, seek your house.

Hearing the cry, the Mexica wise men, Hitziton and Tecpatzan, were compelled to follow the

bird's command. Clavero adds that in Mexico there is a bird known as Tihuitochan, whose chillido translates clearly as, "Vamos a nuestra casa," or "Let's go to our house." (Clavero 1984)

Professor Carmen G. Basurto's book, "Mexico y sus Simbolos," contains a play depicting the Mexica being led all the way from Aztlán to Tenochtitlan by a bird that shrilled "Tihui-tihui" meaning 'forward, forward.' (Basurto 1983)

Mojave oral history includes songs about a bird leading the nations, thousands of years ago, coming from a place called Yucatan. (Van Fleet) From a nearby tree, the bird would call out "Thee-yem, Thee-yem Aha-Makhav" (Mojave, go and find your destiny), shrilling the same song daily until they settled on the Colorado River at the base of Avi Kwame as known as Spirit Mountain. (Steve Lopez, 1994)

The same bird that guided and led the Hokan families up to Spirit Mountain led the Uto-Aztecan families down from the Colorado River to the Valley of Anahuac. This bird is depicted in the Siguenza and the Mexicanus Codex' and is calling the Mexica to follow him across the Colorado River. The bird is called 'tildillo' in Nahua and in English; it is called the black necked stilt. The scientific name is Himantopus Mexicanus. The bird is very common in the Lower Colorado River Valleys and breeds locally. Most of the time, it is seen out in the agricultural fields during irrigation. When they are in groups in a certain area all you can hear is their loud shrilling that resembles "tihui, tihui," which means go forward or follow me, in Nahuatl. (Bert Anderson, 2002)

According to former Bower Museum curator, Paul Apodaca, traditional bird songs are part of the Lower Colorado River Basin oral history. Recounting the migrations to the four directions, they are possibly the oldest cultural songs in the hemisphere, hailing back thousands of years.

According to Apodaca, other native songs, such as those celebrating deer, fox, mountain sheep, and salt songs, also have migration themes. These traditional songs are still sung in most of the traditional ceremonies throughout the Colorado River Basin and Mexico. Thus, the bird songs are connected with the migrations to the four directions.

Petroglyph evidence indicates that many of the Lower Colorado River nations that went south followed the Gila River from its junction with the Colorado River in Yuma, Arizona. Along the southward migration trail, the heron petroglyph is first found near the town of Gila Bend, Arizona. The migrating nations reached this area either by following the Gila River from Yuma or by using the old Halchidoma trail, which begins in the Palo Verde/Parker Valley and ends in Gila Bend, Arizona. The nations then continued to Casa Grande, where, according to Pima oral history, they constructed the large adobe structures, which today are known as the Casa Grande National Monument. (Shaw, 1993)

On their migration journey, the families continued south to the area of the Tohono Oodhan (Papagos), near Caborca and Trincheras, Sonora, Mexico, twenty-five miles west of Caborca, at La Sierra Del Alamo. There is compelling evidence found confirming the migrations from the north. On a bank of a wash called El Mural del Arroyo, there is a series of petroglyphs. One of the petroglyphs shows seven arrows depicting seven families. They are accompanied by the characteristic migration image of human footprints. In a separate petroglyph there is the explanation of the centuries-old mystery of the world-wide flood, and how the tilt of the earth's axis brought about magnetic north.

According to the late Benjamin Celeya Crespo, a Sonoran indigenous historian and amateur archaeologist, this petroglyph, El Mural del Arroyo, is thousands of years old and clearly shows the earth's axis tilted at an angle as it is skewed by the force of a passing comet, thus tilting the planet and bringing about the world-wide flood. The comet petroglyph at the Mural del Arroyo, substantiates indigenous oral his-

tory that recounts how the migrating families traveled full circle in the northern and southern hemispheres after the flood. It also indicates that the nations here in the southwest had this knowledge before they went south to central Mexico.

Mayan Shaman traditionalist Hunbatz Men, states that the Mayan Dresden Codex depicts the comet affecting the earth in the same way as shown in the Mural del Arroyo. The Dresden Codex is one of only three pre-Cuauhtémoc Mayan codexes that were not destroyed by Spanish zealots and are more accurate than the post-Cuauhtémoc documents. Their descriptions of the scientific and traditional belief of the continent's indigenous people were written before the codexes of the Hispanicize writers (tlacuilos). (Hunbatz Men, 1985)

Supporting the Dresden Codex and Benjamin Celaya's investigation is the research by H.S. Bellamy and P. Allan in their book "The Calendar of Tiahuanaca." The Tiahuanaca ruins are located at Lake Titicaca in the Andes Mountains of Peru and built before the flood. They refer to Hans Hoerbiger's cosmological theory regarding the satellite flight that passed earth, causing the earth to pull the oceans and tilted the earth off of its axis. This cosmic event created the magnetic north latitude and true north latitude on Earth. At first, Hoerbiger's cosmological theory was not recognized as plausible, but through further studies and with information cited here, his cosmological interpretations are validated and his observations will gain considerable credence. (Bellamy, 1956)

Other evidence left behind on the migration routes are the heron and tortoise petroglyphs found along the Southward migration route in the Provedora Mountains, five miles southwest of Caborca, Mexico. In the old Papago language, "Caborca" actually means "tortoise shell," and it is represented by a small hill that resembles a turtle in the out skirts of Caborca.

In combination with the heron symbol for Aztlán, the petroglyph depicts "where the people of Aztlán meet the people of Caborca." Another important petroglyph symbol representing the connection between mother earth and the cosmic bodies is also found among the petroglyphs. It is the same hourglass petroglyph found in the area of Spirit Mountain along the Colorado River. The hourglass "X" symbol petroglyph represents Tamoanchan.

In the Codex, Mexico is deciphered as the umbilical of the world and is represented as the center that connects both the top and bottom triangles of the hourglass. The top part of the hourglass represents the cosmos and connects in the center with the bottom triangle representing earth. The Mojave meaning of the hourglass is similar to that of the Mexica. According to Boma Johnson in the Hopi culture the top triangle is called Mountain of Sky and the bottom triangle is called Mountain of Earth.

The Trincheras Mountains, southwest of Caborca, are one of six Sonoran archaeological zones. The others are Rio Bavispe, Bacadehuachi, Nacori Chico, Moctezuma and Sahuaripa, and they all show evidence of Nahua migrations. (Berkowitz, 1990)

At Trincheras Mountain, there are seventeen eight-foot, terrace-like layers that begin at the base of the mountain and continue nearly all the way to the top forming a rudimentary pyramid (teocalli). Contrary to what is known about the Nahua customs and practices, some archaeologists have erroneously classified the terraces as being built for military defense or agricultural purposes. It is, in fact, a ceremonial place where the nations would perform their rituals. Located at the top of the mountain is a stone construction with a "G" or spiral design representing the Milky Way "Mixcoatl," the Cloud of Serpents.

Close to the Trincheras Mountain is a smaller hill called "La Nana," (grandmother) and the large hill is called "El Tata," (the grandfather) representing the cosmological duality. There at La Nana, among the hundreds of petroglyphs, was

a large round stone with a primitive rendering of the Azteca Sun Stone Calendar. As the Tlamantinimi (knowledge keepers) traveled south, they brought with them the knowledge of the Azteca Sun Stone Calendar from the Palo Verde/Parker Valleys.

In Trincheras and at the nearby La Playa Ruins, a large number of historically irreplaceable indigenous structures and petroglyphs have been destroyed or stolen. Treasure seekers, collectors, are responsible for the vandalism. Furthermore, some of the terrace stones of the Trincheras Mountain were hauled away by the Baja California and Sonora Railroad Lines to build bridges and other structures.

Finally, in 1947, the Mayor of Trincheras, Edmundo Sierra, put an end to this practice. Likewise in 1990, the International Association of Descendants of Joaquin Murrieta was instrumental in urging the Mexican Government to protect and fence off these sacred sites, thus protecting them from further vandalizing.

The Trincheras Mountain Culture site, as identified by archeologists, can be classified as one of the major stops on the great Nahua Migration on its southward journey. Remains of the Nahua presence can be also seen in Cucurpe, southeast of Trincheras, home of the Opatas-Eudeves. There we can see more of the petroglyph footprints called "Las Huellas del Viejo," the footprints of the ancient one. The region of Cucurpe shares a similar duality with the Colorado River Omeyocan Diamond of Infinity and is shaped by similar geographical surrounding mountain ranges, 3-peaks and a cave.

The Nahua migration continued to the center of Sonora, in an area occupied by the Sonoran nations belonging to the Opata/Pima/Cahita group which is part of the larger Uto-Aztecan linguistic families. Many nations, like the Opatas, opted to remain in what is now called "Ojo de Agua", close to the Pueblo of Huepec on the Rio de Sonora, which they named "Sonota," (Land of the Corn Cob), hence the name Sonora originated. In this area, the Opata emerged, settling along the rivers and valleys of central Sonora. (Calvo, 1958)

Sonora's original state symbol was an indigenous person standing with its arms extended outward and with the Nahui-Ollin "four cardinal directions" design on the torso, and with a triangle on each side depicting the mountain peaks. These twin peaks and Nahui-Ollin are similar to the geoglyphs found in the Lower Colorado River Valleys.

The Nahui-Ollin also symbolizes the four directions of the sun, beginning with the sunrise, high noon, sunset and midnight. In addition, humans are represented by the man of fire, located in the center of the Nahui-Ollin, symbolized by Xiutecuhtli, "The Fire Energy."

Along the Rio San Miguel north of Cucurpe is one of the most revealing images supporting Sonora's state symbol. At the edge of a canyon wall is a human shaped face, which the locals call "La Cabeza del Apache," and on top of the face is another face in the image of a skull. In addition, across an arroyo on a canyon wall there is a large petroglyph image of the Nahui Ollin, the symbol of the four directions.

The Ópatas who lived in the Moctezuma/Sahuaripa area of Sonora had a traditional New Year ceremonial dance called "Jojo" which commemorated the Azteca/Mexica migration through their land as they waited for Moctezuma to return. (Calvo, 1958)

A document in the Yaqui Museum in Vican, Sonora states that as the Nahua migration continued south. The Cahitas (Yaqui/Mayos) branched out from the Tolteca nation around the fifth century and settled permanently in the Yaqui River area, south of Guaymas, Sonora. (Fabila 1940)

When the Spaniards arrived in the 16th century the natives were organized in eight pueblos. Author Laureano Calvo, in his book "Nociones de

Historia de Sonora," suggests that the eight pueblos may have symbolized the eight nations depicted in the Boturini codices of the Azteca Migration as they left the Lower Colorado River Valleys. (Calvo 1958)

Near the end of the 12th century, the Azteca/Mexica came and settled among the Cahitas (Yaqui/Mayos). This visitation has been called the "Cuarta Morada de la Migracion Azteca," the fourth sojourn of the Azteca.

The powerful Azteca established their new territory from Guaymas, Sonora covering all of the Yaqui Valley and dominated the Cahitas. Some of them, however, left the area to escape the Azteca rule. Francisco Ahumada says that: "We now have Nahuatl geography names in the Sierra Madre mountain range among the Tarahumara, a Uto-Aztecan nation living in the states of Sonora and Chihuahua." (Ahumada 1990)

After spending time in the Yaqui Valley, the Azteca resumed their migration, passing through the Chametla/Aztlán area below Huatabampo, Sonora and Guasave, Sinaloa, passing through Culhuacan, Sinaloa, and to Piaztla, Sinaloa, originally called Piaztlan. (Buelna 1887)

In Frejes' book entitled "Historia Breve de la Conquista de Los Estados Independientes del Imperio Mexicano," he writes: "Authentic information with respect to Aztlán and the Nahua migration was preserved by being passed down from generation to generation stating that further north was a province called Aztlán. Various families from the province of Aztlán had left at different intervals and had come to settle in places such as Sonora, Sinaloa, Acaponeta, Santispac, Jalisco, Ahuatlan, Tonalan and Colima. They continued on passed the mountains of Michoacán and finally established their capital in Texcoco."

Frejes also said that a second wave of migrating nations left Aztlán and invaded the Sierra Madre, coming through the territories of Guadiana, Zacatecas, Comaja, and Queretaro, and finally settling in Lake Texcoco. The journey south then brought the Mexica to a place of many lakes such as Mexcaltitlan, Nayarit.

From Mexcaltitlan they traveled through Jalisco down to Michoacán where the Tarascos had settled after branching off from the larger Mexica group. According to the Boturini Codex glyph some of the other Nahua families went from Mexcaltitlan to Chalchihuites and La Quemada, Zacatecas, and down to the Valley of Anahuac. (Bonilla, 1942)

The importance of this archaeological area, which today is known as Chalchihuites, Zacatecas, is three-fold. First, it is the place where some of the nations that left Aztlán were unified. It's from here that the legend of the nations' search for fulfillment of the prophecy of the eagle and serpent has now gained historical credence as demonstrated by the petroglyphs and engraved images among the Chalchihuites ruins. It shows the heron, a man, an eagle and the serpent together, duplicating those found in Aztlán.

The secondly, it is the only pre-Cuauhtémoc city in which the twenty-eight moons of the lunar calendar are represented by monolithic pillars, suggesting that the nations who migrated here from the north had advanced astronomically in knowledge. Third, its most amazing architectural characteristic is the spring equinox alignment of its structures. Certain buildings were constructed in such a way that the first rays of sunlight emerging from behind the mountains enter the structure through a passage, which perfectly align all the way up to the pyramid of the Sun. The descending Sun merges with Mother Earth by its rays, creating a Serpent (Quetzalcoatl) at the house of energy (Teocalli). (Avalos, 1991)

In Chichen-Itza, Yucatan, the same phenomenon occurs during the spring equinox, as the Sun's rays create a shadow image of the sacred plumed serpent. (Kulkulcan) in Mayan. During this phenomenon the serpent enters the pyra-

mid, "El Castillo." At noon, the shadowed image of the plumed serpent emerges on the pyramid's seven levels. (Hunbatz Men, 1990)

The spring equinox phenomenon that occurs at Chalchihuites and Chichen-Itza archaeological ruins are a duplication of the equinox alignment that occurs naturally in the Palo Verde/Parker Valley. During the equinox, the sun rises in between two peaks that form the "u" in the Moon Mountains in the Colorado River Indian Tribe Reservation. The first sun ray shines on the face the mountain image of the Huitzilopochtli, looking south. In the Aztec Sun Stone Calendar, this first sun ray is called Tonatiuh, to- meaning sun, na- meaning mother earth, -tiuh meaning shining path.

The Nahua left evidence of their travels in countless places along the migration trail that eventually ended at the valley of Anahuac. One wave of migrating nations from Aztlán who ended their journey in the Valley of Anahuac did so in the following manner: "the Acolhua intermingled and stayed with the Chichimeca, eventually forming the Nation of Texcoco; the

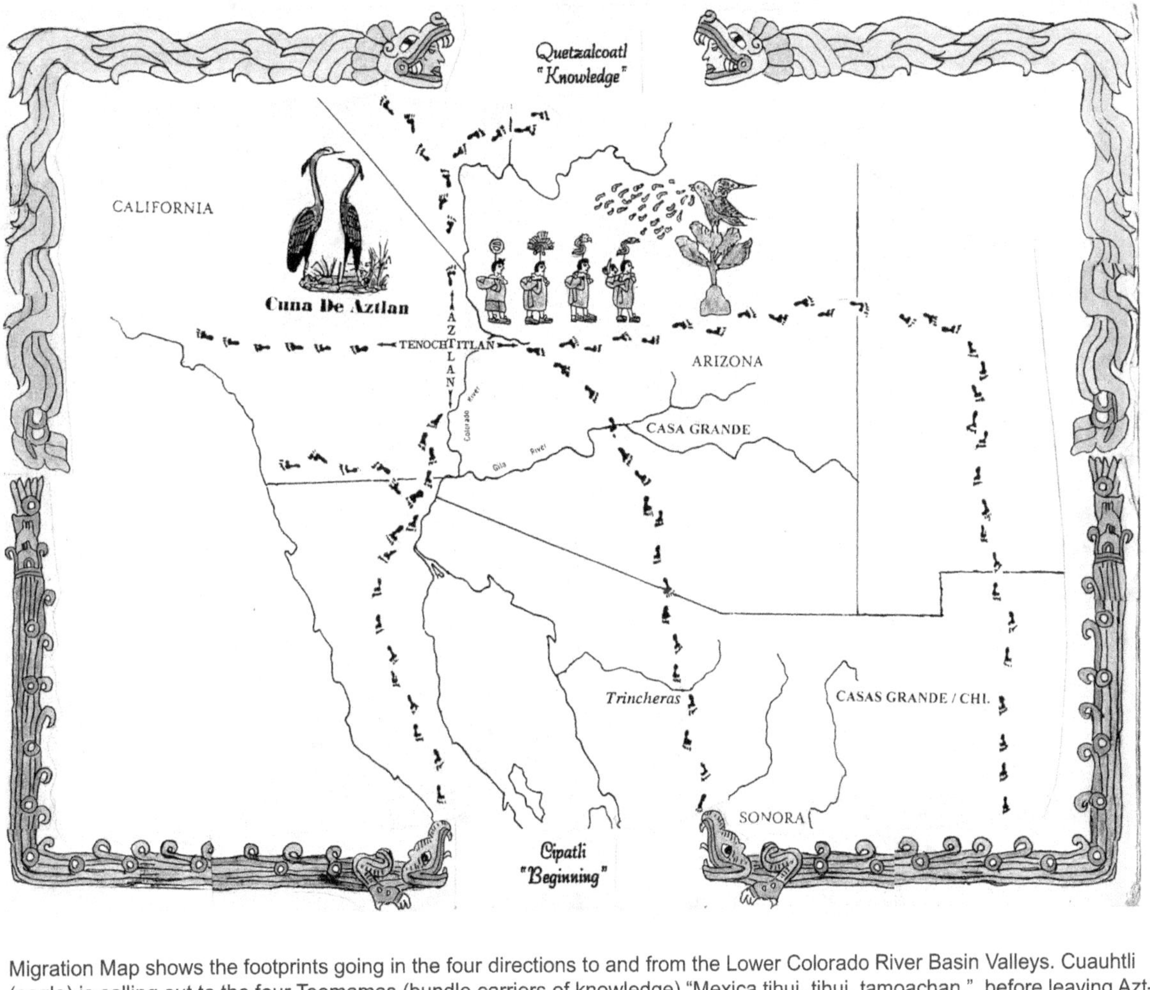

Migration Map shows the footprints going in the four directions to and from the Lower Colorado River Basin Valleys. Cuauhtli (eagle) is calling out to the four Teomamas (bundle carriers of knowledge) "Mexica tihui, tihui, tamoachan," before leaving Aztlan. From the La Cuna de Aztlan to the tomb of Cuauhtemoc migrations to and from the Lower Colorado River Basin Valleys. (Designed by Alfredo A. Figueroa)

Ancient Footprints of the Colorado River 21

Geoglyph of Nahui Ollin, four directions geoglyph found along the Colorado River, represents the base of Tamoanchan and the center of the world.

Drawing of the Sonoran State symbol. Sonoran State symbol represents the Nahua families of the Opata who settled there along the migration trail as many others who branched off their trek south. The Opata stayed in Cucurpe and Trincheras. The symbol depicts the Nahui Ollin (four directions). The twin peaks of the Cuna de Aztlan is represented by triangles with a human figure between them.

The Borgia Codex, Plate 72, the glyphs of the four directions from the left Quetzalcoatl, Xipe Totec, Tlaloc and Tonantzin. At the center of the codex is the glyph of Cicimitl and its nagualli is the horny toad.

Tecpaneca founded the Nation of Ascapotzalco; the Xochimilca settled in Xochimilco; and the Chalca settled on the banks of Lake Chalco. Not finding a suitable location in the Anahuac Valley, the Tlaxcalteca built and developed the Nation of Tlaxcala further to the east, while the Tlahuica occupied the region of Cuernavaca." (Capillio, 1965)

The consensus and the general interpretation among the Nahua scholars has been that, at the end 160 years of migrating, they arrived at their destination. Accordingly they found the signs they had been searching for; 'an eagle perched on a cactus on top of a rock outcropping located on an island in Lake Mexico.'

During the excavation of the Plaza Mayor, El Zocalo, in downtown Mexico City, the remnants of the ruins of the Twin Teocallis of Huichitlipochtli and Tláloc were found during the construction of the tunneling of the underground metro-rail system of Mexico City. These remnants were actually dated prior to 1325. This is evidence that there were structures constructed hundreds of years before 1325 by the Teotihuacans and not the Mexica. (Acamapixtli, 1992)

As more archaeological sites are excavated, new evidence of these early structures are substantiated. This new evidence challenges the norms of the years-old interpretation of the origin of the Mexica upheld by the established government.

By the time the Mexica arrived in the Anahuac Valley, the other major nations had already developed advanced civilizations. Therefore, taking advantage of their fortunate timing, they were able to absorb the advances made in the arts, sciences, mathematic, astronomy, and agricultural practices of nations such as the Olmeca, Chichimeca and Tolteca who had preceded them.

Under the leadership of Moctezuma Xocoyotzin, the Mexica organized the Confederation of Anahuac, which extended north to the Rocky Mountains of Montana and south to Nicaragua, in Central America. The word Nicaragua is derived from "Nican" (up to here) and "Nahua," representing the Nahua. Thus, Nicaragua means, "Up to here came the Nahua. (Newman 1990)

According to Mexican historian Francisco Navarette, the Mexica were attracted to the shallow, marshy freshwater lakes in the Valley of Anahuac because the surroundings were similar to those they had enjoyed in their homeland Aztlán. (Ortiz 1995)

Chapter 2.4
Mexico/Aztlán on the Colorado River and its Relationship to Mexico/Tenochtitlan

One must know how to interpret the Mexica codex and the origin of the name Mexico, to thoroughly understand the metaphoric symbolism of the Mexica creation story as it correlates with the images on the mountains, the geoglyphs on the mesas, and petroglyphs on the rocks, all in the surrounding Palo Verde/Parker Valleys.

As previously stated, the ancient island of Aztlan was in the Parker Valley, and it was surrounded by a man made lake called Mexico located directly west of two separate peaks on Moon Mountain. When seen from the California side of the river it gives the image of an extended 'u.' This 'u' represents the woman's womb.

The Vindobonensis Codex has an excellent glyph of the dried lake and the "u" in the middle of the Moon Mountain Peaks. During the equinoxes, the first rays of the rising sun 'Tonatiúh' shines directly on a peak on top of the Big Maria Mountain where it shines on the pro-

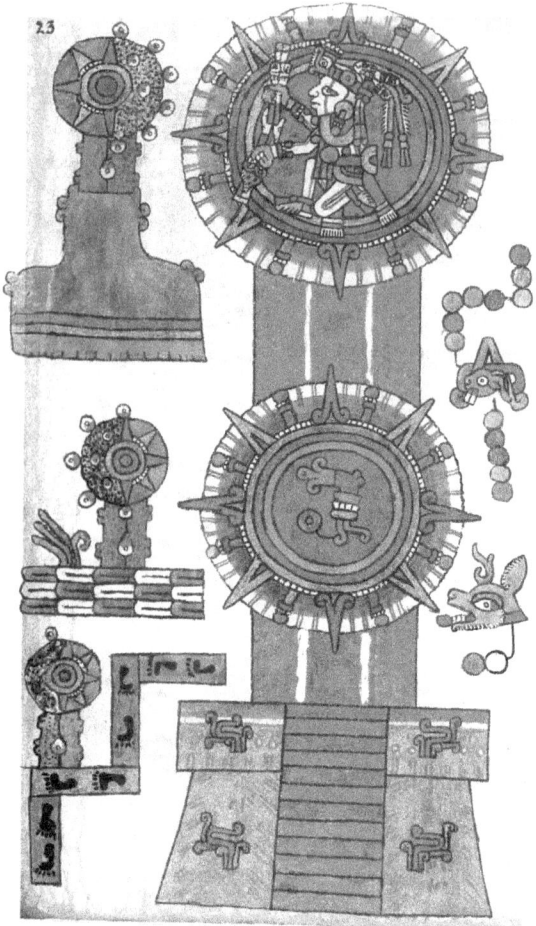

Vindobonensis Codex Fold 23.

This codex shows the equinox sunrise at the Moon Mountains, where the first sun ray, Tonatiuh, shines on the face of the Huitzilopochtli on the Big Maria Mountains.

file image of the head of Huitzilopochtli, looking south. Vindobonensis Codex fold 23 has the image of Huitzilopochtli with the sun in the background.

During the migrations from the Colorado River it was common for the Nahua to look for similar locations, geographical conditions and images and name them in honor of their place of origin. This was done so that they would remember, and fulfill the creator's principle to take this knowledge to all four directions. The names of Atotonilco, Aztlán, Culhuacan, Mexico/Tenochtitlan, and so on, are good examples of the names which were duplicated during their migrations to the four directions, according to Dr. Alfonso Caso.

An excellent analysis is given by Dr. Doris Heyden in her book "Mexico, Origin de un Simbolo," as to how the name Mexico/ Tenochtitlan came about. In her book, Heyden, explains her verbal communications with Eduardo Mateos Moctezuma who stated that: "The land under the twin-towers of La Plaza Mayor in Mexico City is all a swampland."

Heyden states that: "This discards the possibility that there existed a rocky outcropping with a cave and a spring." The swamp land at La Plaza Mayor was appropriately called El Zocalo, meaning "mudville." Zocalo deciphered Zo- from zoquete (mud), "-cal,"calli (house), "-o" (place) and all together this means "house of mud," not of rock. This evidence totally disproves the government's position that Tenochtitlan was founded on a rocky outcropping on an island in Lake Mexico. It was supposed to have been where the eagle landed on top of a nopal (cactus) that grew from a rock outcropping.

As we analyze the evidence presented here, we have determined that the name Tenochtitlan was given to the island, not based on their findings of the swampland, but on the original Tenochtitlan. The name was brought with them when they came from the Colorado River.

The origin of the allegorical meaning of Tenochtitlan comes from the Big Maria Mountain in the Colorado River. Tenochtitlan deciphered is tetl-, rock, -noch, nopalli/cactus, -ti, binding, -tlan, place, meaning "the place where the cactus grew on the rock." In the Big Maria Mountains overlooking the Palo Verde Valley is a large white limestone image of the thunderbird eagle. Its wings are spread out over a half mile aligned east and west. The head is turned facing east towards the Moon Mountains where

Diego Duran, History of Indies of New Spain Codex, Plate 4, shows the Azteca in the Palo Verde Valley, at Coatepec, Snake Mountain. Acacitli on the left has a house, (calli) flag, (panti) and a hare, (liebre) representing the old island which is now destroyed, 'El Barrio de la Liebre,' (today's El Barrio Cuchillo.) On the right is Tenoch, meaning nopal and rock.

the sun rises in CRIT Reservation. This thunderbird eagle image is seen from El Barrio Cuchillo, west of Blythe and the image of the thunderbird eagle appears to straddle a small dark peak. This is symbolic to the eagle that landed on the nopal/cactus and refers to Tenochtitlan. This image is seen today on the Mexica Flag and has been on all of their flags and banners for thousands of years to remind them of the creation story, their place of origin on the Colorado River. The only time that this image was not used was during the 300 year occupation of the Spanish invaders that lasted from 1521-1821. This image is on the artifacts that have been found while digging in El Zocalo. The importance of the thunderbird eagle is well manifested among the native art here in the United States and Mexico. The thunderbird eagle represents Cuautlehuanitl, eagle that ascends.

Eluding to the sacredness of the thunderbird eagle image on the Big Maria Mountains is the location of the ancient destroyed island of Acacitli. Acacitli means jackrabbit in the tules and was called Barrio de La Liebre by the old Spanish speaking Chemehuevi and other indigenous people. The island of Acacitli in the Palo Verde Valley was the duality of the island of the Aztlan in the Parker Valley. Today, Acacitli is called El Barrio Cuchillo in west Blythe.

In this chapter we have compelling evidence that factually challenges the accepted version that the eagle did not land in El Zocalo (mudville) in Mexico City, but landed on the Big Maria Mountains.

The origin of Mexico was on the Colorado River and was the Confederation of Anahuac, which extended from the Rocky Mountains in the north down to Nicaragua, (meaning from here came the Nahua.)

The official version of the Mexican Government states that the nation began when it became independent from Spain on Sept 16, 1821, and that the mother country is Spain, La Madre Patria Es-

Thunderbird eagle image in the Big Maria Mountains represents the national symbol of Mexico as shown on the Mexican Flag.

Fundacion de Tenochtitlan Mexico shows the eagle on a cactus on a rock, meaning Tenochtitlan.

pana. This is a "gross misinterpretation of the origin of Mexico since the origin of Mexico as a nation is deeply rooted in its cosmic traditional culture since time immemorial. Thus, it is very important that Mexico's origin be understood. As stated previously, the cosmic moral of the Mexica will be the base of all societies in the future.

Chapter 2.5
The Search for Aztlán

The first documented search for Aztlán was recorded by Fray Diego Duran, in his book "Historia Antigua de la Nueva España" (Ancient History of New Spain). Duran wrote that Moctezuma Ilhuicamina, the fifth tlatoani (spokesperson of the Mexica from 1440-1469) wanted to know the location of Xicomoztoc/Aztlán, "The Place of the Seven Caves," which was the place were his ancestors originated from.

Moctezuma called the royal historian, the elder Cuauhcoatl (Eagle Serpent) and addressed him: "Oh ancient father, I desire to know the true story, the knowledge that is hidden in your books about the Seven Caves where our ancestors, our fathers and our grandfathers lived and whence they came forth. I wish to know about the place wherein our God, Huitzilopochtli dwelt and out of which he led our forefathers."(Duran) Cuauhcoatl answered: "that our forebearers dwelt in a blissful happy place called Aztlán. They lived in leisure and had at their disposal, great flocks of ducks, of different kinds and herons, cranes, and other waterfowl."

Moctezuma was so determined to seek the land that had given birth to the Azteca people, that he sent his envoys north from the capital, Tenochtitlan (present-day Mexico City). When they returned, the envoys reported that they had fulfilled his orders and had seen the land called Aztlán/Xicomoztoc. (Chavero, 1976)

The Mexica Codex states that Huitzilopochtli was ordered by the creator Mecitli to leave Aztlán and guide the Azteca/Mexica south on a journey that took approximately 200 years. Finally in 1325, they settled in the region of the Valley of Anahuac.

After the conquest and the overthrow of the Mexica from Tenochtitlan in 1521, the Spaniards were intrigued with the rumors that they heard regarding a place called Aztlán, "A land of many riches." According to the legend, it was believed that there was a place known as the "Seven Cities of Gold of Cibola and Quivira," similar to the Mexica mystical place of Aztlán/Xicomoztoc, (located northwest of Mexico/Tenochtitlan).

Hernan Cortes was the first Spaniard who was driven by greed in search of Aztlan and its riches. He left Acapulco and travelled towards Baja California in search of his new venture. Unfortunately, Cortes only found a few pearls that he took from the natives. After Cortés's ill-fated venture to Baja California the Spaniards were still excited by the many stories told of the riches that existed somewhere in the north.

In 1540, Francisco Vasquez de Coronado set out in his expedition in search of the fabled "Seven Cities of Gold," and "El Dorado," of Cibola and Quivira. He came up from Sinaloa through Sonora then followed the San Pedro River in southern Arizona. There at the junction with the Gila River, Coronado sent his envoy, Melchor Diaz, to search for Hernando de Alarcon. Alarcon was supposed to have traveled through the Gulf of California, up the Colorado River in order to bring Coronado supplies to continue his expedition.

Diaz traveled west along the Gila River to a point where the Halchidomas Trail intersected. He followed the trail all the way to the Colorado River to a point called Weaver's Pass on the Dome Rock Mountains (overlooking the Palo Verde/Parker/Cibola Valleys.) Diaz came to the appropriately named, Cibola Valley, in search of

Ancient Footprints of the Colorado River 27

Alarcon. He then continued down the River to Quechan Territory near Yuma, Arizona. There he found a letter that had been left by Alarcon which explained that after waiting for him for a long time he decided to go back to Acapulco. Shortly after that, Melchor Diaz died of a freak accident, across the Colorado River.

Alarcon had traveled approximately 85 leagues up the Colorado River on his boat from the Gulf of California up to the area of present day Palo Verde/Parker Valleys.

In summary, Diaz and Alarcon were the first Spaniards to set foot in Aztlán, approximately 100 years after the people that were sent by Moctezuma Illuicamina.

Following the European invasion, all historical writings in Mexico required a stamp of approval from the "Consejo Real de las Indias," the Spanish administrative office for New Spain.

For three hundred years, the history of Mexico was written and rewritten under the censorship and critical scrutiny imposed by this administrative office. It followed the notorious Spanish Inquisition religious reactionary guidelines. During that time very few truthful historical writings were able to survive.

In spite of the strict Spanish reviews, there are two very well documented writings of native life in Mexico during the 16th century. Both of these writings are viewed as containing prudent pre- Cuauhtemoc historical Mexica history. At the same time, these documents had the most insidious, denigrating version of the Mexica cosmic traditions.

One of these writings was written by Fray Diego Duran's which was entitled "History of the Indias." The other writing was by Fray Bernardino de Sahagun, which was entitled, the "Florentine Codex: General History of the things of New Spain." During the Spanish Inquisition trials, Duran was a translator of Nahuatl to Spanish. Sahagun, on the other hand, was determined to convert the natives from their traditional culture to that of the European at all cost.

For years, historians continued to denigrate the Mexica and insisted on promulgating the centuries-old lies that portrayed the natives as savages, convincing the world that the Mexica practiced human sacrifices and that their cosmic traditions were evil.

Today, as researchers begin to analyze these writings related to the history of indigenous people, they are uncovering many serious misrepresentations attributable to the Hispanicized indigenous writers of the Era of New Spain (1521-1821).

According to the "Handbook of Arizona," published in 1877, a pyramid was located 50 miles above Ehrenberg, Arizona. It was built of hewn stones, and each stone was about 20-36 inches squared and was 104 feet square at the base and 20 feet high. Old timers of the area have no recollection of seeing the pyramid but had heard of its whereabouts in the valley. (Cook, 1985) The pyramid was without a doubt the one shown in the first fold of the Boturini Codex, called "Tira de la Peregrinacion" and in the Aubin Codex. Both codexes show a pyramid on the Island of Aztlán, in the middle of a lake.

Before the constructions of the dams, every summer the Colorado River would flood. The river would change its course and wipe out everything in its path. Therefore, it is logical to conclude that the pyramid was destroyed by the floods.

In relation to the floods, Fray Duran mentions in his writings that Aztlán was destroyed after the Mexica left. Today, all that is left are some of the foundations that were located on higher elevation then the old dried up lake that surrounded it. The natives of the area of the lower Colorado River Basin refer to the ancient Moon Lake as "Whalia Hanyo," and in Nahuatl it is called Lake (atezcatl) "Metztli". This dried lake is located along the edge of the mountains that have

the same name and is shown in the Vindobonensis Codex, Fold 23.

The vanished ancient island of Aztlan is located within the geographical center of the Omeyocan Diamond, "place of the two hearts." The Omeyocan is a gigantic diamond which we call the Diamond of Infinity, which encompasses most of the Palo Verde/Parker Valleys. In the Mexica Creation story, the diamond is formed by two isosceles merged together. It represents the sacred place of the origin of the duality of the energies, Ometecutli (male) in the north and Omecíhuatl (female) in the south.

In recent years we have seen a renewed interest in the whereabouts of Aztlán. The Los Angeles County Museum of Art presented a magnificent exhibition entitled, "The Road to Aztlán." The exhibit ran from May 13 to August 26, 2001 and was one of the best exhibitions ever presented in the United States by any established institution. Virginia M. Fields, writes in the text that accompanied the exhibit, The Road to Aztlan, Art from a Mythic Homeland, "...In the 1960s, the concept of Aztlan became associated with the Chicano movement for cultural affirmation and civil rights. As a Chicano symbol and allegory, Aztlan represents an ancestral homeland patterned after the mythic site of origin of the Aztecs, thought to be located in the region now known as the American Southwest. As this volume documents, the concept of Aztlan continues to have resonance for succeeding generations of Chicano and Mexican artists." (Fields, 2001)

This exhibition also coincided with the Xicano Movement's quest for Aztlán. It focused on archaeological evidence depicting the interaction between southwest United States and Mexico. It also featured many genuine artifacts including sacred stone images that were brought from Mexico's Museo del Instituto Nacional de Antropologia e Historia. The most recent research on the subject of Aztlán was also presented.

The Getty Museum in 2010 had an excellent exhibition of the Azteca. The Aztec Pantheon the Art of Empire, rediscovering Ancient Mexico has resurrected the magnificent history of the Azteca/ Mexica.

The Mexica Creation story gains momentum as the world seeks the truth about our human existence on earth.

Chapter 2.6
The Destruction of the Island of Aztlán

According to the research by Fray Diego Duran, the Azteca/Mexica destroyed the channels that surrounded the island of Aztlán when they migrated in the year 1160 A.D. This year corroborates with the investigations of the Five Suns. Similar events took place in all of the areas where the Nahua families settled and moved on continuing their journey in search of the duality of Mexico/Aztlán.

Throughout the years, the annual floods of the mighty Colorado River eventually destroyed all the ancient Azteca structures of the island of Aztlan here in the Parker Valley, 25 miles northeast from Blythe, leaving only the vestige of the foundation that are found there today. Still, the stones that were used in the teocallis were used years later to build homes for the Mexican settlers in the town of La Paz.

After Mexico lost the war with the United States in 1848, the Sonoran miners were ousted from the surrounding areas of Sonora, California, during the Gold Rush of 1849. Most miners were forced to leave their placer mines, and most of them did not have any choice but to return back to Sonora, Mexico. Most of the Sonoran miners that remained behind were killed by Anglo miners who quickly took ownership of the gold mines. This type of barbaric events brought about the rising of Joaquin Murrieta, and his

Guerilla Fighters who rose in defense of the miners and against the United States, fighting to regain California back to Mexico.

Later, in 1862, these same ousted Sonoran miners from northern California were the same miners who first found the gold that led to the La Paz Gold Rush in the Colorado River. This quickly gave way to the new Gold Rush in 1862. The area of La Paz is located 10 miles from Blythe, California, on the Colorado River Indian Tribe reservation. Among the first to find gold in the area of La Paz, were the author's ancestors, the Murrieta, Martinez and Redondo families, including Teodosia Murrieta Martinez, the author's great-great grandmother.

The town of La Paz, Arizona grew and the Mexican miners from Sonora, Mexico, gathered up the stone foundations from the ruins of the island of Aztlán, in order to construct their homes and the town of La Paz. The ruins of the island of Aztlán were approximately ten miles north of La Paz. There, from the ruins of the island of Aztlán, the miners brought the hewed stones that had been used for the teocallis in Aztlán and took them to La Paz to build the foundations of their adobe homes and buildings.

La Paz was a thriving river port town from 1862 to 1870. Steam boats from Santa Clara, on the Gulf of California would come up through the delta of the river and stop in the port of La Paz.

The Gold Rush of La Paz also opened commerce into the area and was referred to as the "Gateway to the West." This brought about steamboats on the river bringing in businesses, transporting miners, mining equipment, soldiers, and so on to Arizona, Nevada and southeast California. On the way back the steamboats would take crude ore to Santa Clara on the Gulf and from there the ocean liners would take it to San Francisco, California.

In 1870, during the height of the flood, the river changed its course and completely destroyed the adobe houses and building structures of the town of La Paz. This destruction changed the geography of the river and forced the residents to relocate to higher ground, which today is the town of Ehrenberg, Arizona.

Today all that remains of La Paz are small dirt mounds of adobe where the buildings once stood, and the stone foundations that were brought from the island of Aztlán.

Chapter 2.7
Aztlán: Consciousness in the Southwest

In reference to Moctezuma and Aztlán there is an abundance of oral and physical evidence in the Lower Colorado River Valleys. After the United States/Mexico War of 1846-48, Anglos who worked and lived in the area of the Lower Colorado River Valleys became aware of Aztlan.

Oral traditionalists of the Opatas, Pimas, Papagos and Yuman nations in Arizona and Sonora indicate that there is some traditional recollection of Moctezuma coming to their region/land and to the Lower Colorado River Valleys. This helps to confirm the lineage between most of the indigenous nations that formed the Confederation of Anahuac, as is described in the Mexica history.

After Mexico's War of Liberation from Spain in 1821, the newly formed Mexican government began an extensive effort to reclaim its indigenous roots and the search for Aztlán continued. Moctezuma's memory remained strong in history, so strong in fact that in 1827 there was a failed attempt to change the name of Alta California, to Moctezuma, which is today the state of California. (Gudde, 1959)

In the 1850s, William H. Emory of the United States/Mexican Boundary Commission who traveled the area, wrote in his survey report that:

"The name Moctezuma was as familiar to every Pueblo, Apache and Navajo as the names of the Savior or George Washington was to the Anglo-Saxon."

When the first Arizona Territory legislative assembly was held in Prescott in 1864, Governor John Goodwin's administration submitted a bill to call the new territory capital "Aztlán." It was to be located in a town to be founded: "at a point within ten miles of the junction of the Verde River and Salt River."

The bill was not approved and the town of Phoenix was chosen instead to be the capital of the Arizona Territory: "The site originally identified is within, what is now, Fort McDowell Reservation, northeast of Phoenix, seventy-five miles due south of Arizona's geographical center, Clarkdale." (Wagner 1980) At one time, Clarkdale was also called Centerville, for an obvious reason, and was also named Romita by one of the Mexican resident families from Romita, Guanajuato, Mexico. (Macias, 1954)

According to the University of Arizona Bulletin "The Arizona Place" the state's first Masonic lodge in the city of Prescott was named "The Aztlán Masonic Lodge". (1866) Continuing with the popular name of Aztlán, in 1877 there was the Aztlán Gold Mine and Aztlán Mill which was located in the surrounding mining area of Prescott, Arizona. During that time several novels were written about the "mystical" Aztlán. Continuing with the name Moctezuma in 1902, it was proposed as the state name for the combined territories of Arizona and New Mexico. (Barnes, 1960)

During the height of the Xicano Movement in the 1960-70's once again the word Aztlán resurged. Aztlán was not thought to be a mythical place but as a long lost mystical Aztlán. In their hearts, Xicanos were longing to know where Aztlán was and knew that it was here in the Southwest United States. This is why "Viva Aztlán!" became the rallying cry that motivated them to continue seeking the roots of the truth of their origin.

During that epoch many books of the Xicano struggle were written. One of the best books that briefly tells of the spiritual feeling and longing of knowing the truth of their ancestral Aztlan is "Orgullo de Aztlan"- Pride of Aztlan, by Esther Perez. Here she depicts the struggle beginning with Aztlan/Huehuetlapallan, being above the confluence of the Gila and Colorado River and the Mexica migration down to Mexico/Tenochtitlan. Here we quote her dedication to future generations that expresses her thoughts: "To the spirit of courage and nobility that has carried the greatness of our race forward from Aztlan and seen at last this proud return to ancestral soils. To the long communion of perseverance that made up our people, know patience. To the centuries of bondage which now forces us to grow more quickly, bursting with energies too long repressed and freedoms so long denied. Finally to each child of Aztlan, who looks into himself; (find) wisdom, and the knowledge to live proudly and discover an eagle's strength, our Indian presence." (Perez, 1972)

Chapter 3

The Blythe Giant Intaglios

Thousands of years ago, indigenous people living in the Lower Colorado River Valleys created gigantic figures on the mesas throughout the desert and along the river. Archaeologists call them intaglios, an Italian term which refers to an engraving process, while others called them geoglyphs, which are designs or drawings on the surface of the desert. The Blythe and Bouse figures, while technically, geoglyphs are commonly referred to as intaglios, there fore, for our purposes, these terms are interchangeable.

Blythe Giant Intaglios are ancient geoglyphs designed on the desert pavement on the mesetas. (Photo credit Alfredo A. Figueroa and Mark Day)

Most of the geoglyphs in this area were constructed on the dark gravel called "desert pavement." The small stones of the desert pavement are dark because of their manganese stain. When the desert floor is not disturbed, it looks like a blackboard when seen from above. Obviously, these areas should be respected and not disturbed because they are so fragile.

In order to create an image on the desert mesas, the small cobblestones and gravel are scraped back to expose the light colored caliche, a crust of calcium carbonate that occurs naturally in stony soil and is found in dry areas. The black cobblestones are placed outlining the image, exposing the caliche at the bottom layer, thus creating a lighter colored image.

Most of the geoglyphs along the Lower Colorado River can be found within the 200 miles between Needles, California, and Yuma, Arizona. According to Boma Johnson, retired senior archaeologist of the Bureau of Land Management (BLM) in Yuma, Arizona, there are over 275 Intaglios that have been identified up and down both sides of the Lower Colorado River. These include images of humans, animals, serpents, eagles and abstract geometric designs. The BLM believes that they range in age from 150 to 10,000 years old. These images have been found only on the Lower Colorado and Gila River Valley mesas, extending down to El Cerro del Pinacate, in Sonora. They can also be found

Ancient Footprints of the Colorado River

in the southern hemisphere near Cuzco, Peru, in the Nazca plains, where a similar method was utilized by the ancient nations.

The most famous and most impressive of these unique geoglyph formations are the Blythe Giant Intaglios (located 15 miles north of Blythe, California, off U.S. Highway 95). They are visited annually by tourists and curiosity-seekers that come to marvel and study the enormous figures. The intaglios are numbered among the world's ancient mysteries and have been featured worldwide. They were also included in the National Register of Historic Places in Washington, DC after a lengthy qualification process which first began in 1978. (Johnson 1985)

The Blythe Giant Intaglios first appeared in the London News in 1932, (Palmer 1932) and in the September, 1952, issue of National Geographic Magazine, which featured two articles, titled, "Giant Effigies of the Southwest," by Army General, George C. Marshal and "Seeking the Secrets of the Giants" by Frank M. Setzler.

We were very fortunate to have communicated with Ellis N. Palmer, George Palmer's son and he provided us with copies of the original London Newspaper articles and other material.

Since then, these famous intaglios have been featured in various journals, magazines, books, newspaper articles and documentaries. One of the most well-known documentaries is the, "Chariots of the Gods," By Erich Von Daniken. In this documentary he states: "that because the figures are best viewed from the sky, the natives perhaps were trying to communicate with people from outer space."

Von Daniken's theory was not too erroneous in suggesting that the Blythe Giant Intaglios were trying to communicate with outer space. Our research reveals that the precise placement of the human figures illustrates the duality representing humans here on earth with their cosmic counterparts or the star constellations.

There is a giant human image in the Vaticanus A Codex that represents the giants that roamed the earth during the First Sun as shown in the Azteca Sun Stone Calendar. The Sun is called Tezcatlipoca and its nagualli (animus) is the jaguar. These were the giants that were alive during that time and the old peoples' greeting was: "Don't fall, because if you fall, you fall for good." The Blythe Giant Intaglios represent the giant human image in the Vaticanus A Codex.

The Blythe Giant Intaglio site is strategically located within the confines of the Omeyocan Diamond of Infinity, place of the two hearts, which in the Nahuatl language, means "Ome" (two), and "-yo" yollotl or (heart), and "-can" (place). Omeyocan represents the place where the Nahua Creation story originated and where Ometéotl, the Creator, dwells.

The Intaglios are located off of U.S. Highway 95 on a dirt road which goes up a small grade to a

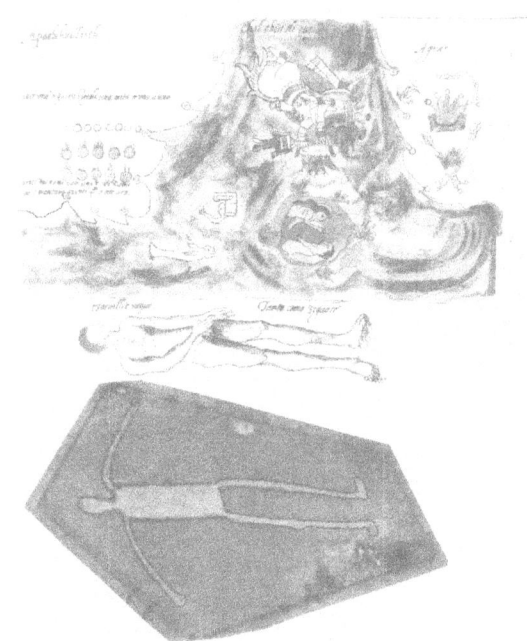

The top figure Vatican Codex A is The First Sun of Chalchiutlicue on the Aztec Sun Stone Calendar which includes the giant human figure of Ometeotl, Creator. The bottom figure is the geoglyph of Ometeotl, and is one of the world famous images of the Blythe Giant Intaglios. These giants roamed the earth during the first Sun.

small knoll, and in less than 250 yards the first of the giant figures is located. It represents the male of the three large human figures.

This male figure in Nahuatl is called Ometecuhtli, "Ome" (two) and "tecuhtli" (male). Ometecuhtli is identified by its male organ and by the geometrical position of his head towards the north and his arms extended in a form of a bow. His body therefore serves as the arrow, thus creating the bow and arrow image. Very faintly is a large circle that crosses his thighs which represents the universe. Ometecuhtli's image here on earth represents the male and his counterpart duality is the star constellation, Orion, and the line that passes through his thighs represents Orion's belt.

Southeast of the male figure is a geoglyph image of the dog, which has a long snout, pointed ears and a long neck. The dog is the nagualli (animal spirit) of the male and it represents Xolotl the twin of Ehecatl (wind) and together, they are the evening and morning star which is Venus (Quetzalcoatl). The dog's counterpart in the cosmos is "Canis Major," Orion's (The Hunter) companion. In the Mexica Creation story, Xolotl accompanies the Sun, after the sunset. The image of the dog is the one that leads human spirits through the underworld, where their spirits rest in Mictlan as referred to in the codex.

Below the dog image is a geoglyph of a double linked spiral image. The combination of the spirals symbolizes water, earth and fire, "A-tla-chinolli." atlachinolli means, A-water, -tla "talli" earth, and "-chinolli" fire. All three represent "Yeitiliztli" (The Trinity). Atlachinolli's image is beside the Eagle's beak as shown in the original Mexica Flag before the Spanish Invasion and not as it is currently shown in the Mexican Flag, with a snake in the Eagle's beak.

The small spiral of the atlachinolli image points towards the river, which extends east to the Bouse Fisherman Intaglio. The larger spiral represents fire and lies west, towards the pyramid shape of Marie Peak (in the Big Maria Mountains). Together the two spirals connected in an upright vertical position, create an image of an hourglass. The small bottom spiral is represented by a seashell which represents the ocean/earth, while the larger spiral represents the Milky Way in the cosmos.

Thus, the male human figure intaglio, the dog, and the double linked spiral, lie in a cluster on the first small knoll.

Across a wash (arroyo) there is a second large human figure that lies with another image that is on a small knoll. This is the largest of the three, measuring 171 feet from head to toe. It is the female, Omecíhuatl, meaning, "Ome-" (two) and "-cihuatl" (female). This intaglio has the similar position with the head and the arms resembling a bow and arrow as the other intaglios.

Omecíhuatl is identified by her bulging stomach similar to that of a woman that has just given birth with the placenta coming down her crotch.

Sculptures of Dog and Jaguar in Palenque and other sacred sites. On the surrounding wall of the ruins of Palenque, Chiapas, Tula and Hidalgo and many other sacred sites in Mexico, there are sculptures of a dog and cougar, following each other. The dog is the nagualli of the male and the cougar is the nagualli of the female. The cougar's tail is curled up in the form of a U, which represents the woman's womb. The dog's tail is pointing down representing the man's organ.

She is appropriately positioned with her head pointing south and with her stomach facing east towards the Moon Mountains across the Colorado River in the CRIT Reservation. Omecíhuatl represents the female here on earth, with its counterpart being the Cassiopeia star constellation in the cosmos. Cassiopeia's image is seen in the cosmos as a woman reclining in a chair and looking into a mirror that is in her hand. The constellation's main bright stars form a big "W" that is spread out and symbolizes the female's breasts. Here on earth this "W" is seen as an "M." The same image of the female breasts in the Milky Way is seen among many geoglyphs in the area that represents the woman Mother Earth.

To the south of the female figure on the same knoll, is another animal image that is "Ocelotl", which is from the cat family. It has a square head, wide-open jaw and a short neck. Its counterpart in the cosmos is the Big Dipper Constellation. The European interpretation of the Big Dipper is a bear, called "Ursa Major." However, among the Mexica it represents Ocelotl because of the black spots that it has on its body, representing the stars. The cat family is always associated with the female, while the dog is associated with the male.

Continuing west on the dirt road passing the male human figure about 200 yards on another small knoll on a higher elevation is the third human figure which lies by itself. His head is pointing southwest and his arms extend similar to the other human images which represent a bow and arrow.

This image represents Ometéotl, meaning "The Creator" in Nahuatl. This principal energy deciphered means, "Ome-" (two) and "-teotl" (Energy) or "two energies". Ometéotl represents the male and female energies combined. This figure does not have the female or male organ, but is the combination of both sexes.

The female image is southwest of the male figure which is located southeast of Ometéotl human figure, and all three form a triangle and an arrow that is pointing towards Marie Peak in the Big Maria Mountains.

The three human figure intaglios are the principal factors in the Nahua Creation Story. They are another illustration of the indigenous traditional beliefs in the importance of the three energies: Ometecuhtli, Omecíhuatl, and Ometéotl, the Creator. All together, they form "Yeitiliztli" the sacred three, in Nahuatl. This belief is similar to the Christian Theology's Holy Trinity, the Father, the Son and the Holy Spirit. However, in the Mexica Cosmic tradition, the woman is identified as one of the three main energies.

On the walls surrounding the ancient Teocalli, (temple) of Tula, Hidalgo, there are engraved images of the jaguar and dog glyphs, which wrap around the temple wall. They are shown following each other all around the temple wall and are found among many ancient ruins throughout Mexico.

The dog always has its tail down representing the male organ, and its image is formed with the tail parallel to his rear legs. The jaguar on the other hand, has an extremely long tail that loops down, then up, creating a "U-Shape." The "U-Shape" symbolizes the woman's womb and is also a glyph that represents Tezcatlipoca. (Waters, 1984)

The Blythe Giant Intaglio dog and jaguar figures originally had their tails in the same manner. However the jaguar's tail was redesigned with good intentions in 1957, but unfortunately, distorting its original formation which should be a "u" shape.

In 1957, Mr. Collis Mayflower, chairman of the Blythe Chamber of Commerce Committee, provided most of the funding for fencing and restoration of the Blythe Giant Intaglios. Mrs. Kirk Brimhall and Mrs. Wayne Dill of the Parent Teacher Association and over 15 students of the Palo Verde High School participated in this historical restoration event. Unfortunately, neither the Bureau of Land Management nor the local tribes were involved in the restoration. (Desert

Florentine Codex, Book Five, Fold 11v. "Los Gigantes," (The Giants) from the first Sun before they fell at the Blythe Giant Intaglios.

Magazine, 1957).

A Blythe teacher by the name of DeWeese W. Stevens volunteered to supervise the restoration and the students. They however, did not know that the Jaguar had a "looping tail." He and the students therefore, arranged the images according to their own assumptions, and rearranged some of the human figures feet, and destroyed part of their heads and headdresses. According to Ron Van Fleet Mojave's interpretation, the Jaguar's tail was supposed to be arranged in the form of a "U." Van Fleet, also stated that there were other programs at Palo Verde College in the early 1970s such as the Colorado River Guides, whose main purpose was to restore some of the geoglyphs west of Blythe, including the giant Kokopilli geoglyph, located west of the Blythe Giant Intaglio site, and numerous other sacred sites currently being threatened by solar power plants. It was hoped that tourist sites throughout the valleys would eventually be established and tour guides would come from the reservations.

Throughout the years many other images have been destroyed forever by careless off-road vehicles and people trampling over them because of their lack of understanding and lack of respect for these indigenous symbols that represent the Mexica Creation story.

It is very important for us to recognize and acknowledge the efforts of the people that participated in the first restoration event and the fencing of the Blythe Giant Intaglios. Without a doubt, they would have been destroyed long ago as have many of the other images. Regardless of the distortion that took place during the fencing we will forever be grateful for their dedication and involvement.

Chapter 3.2
The Bouse Fisherman Intaglio

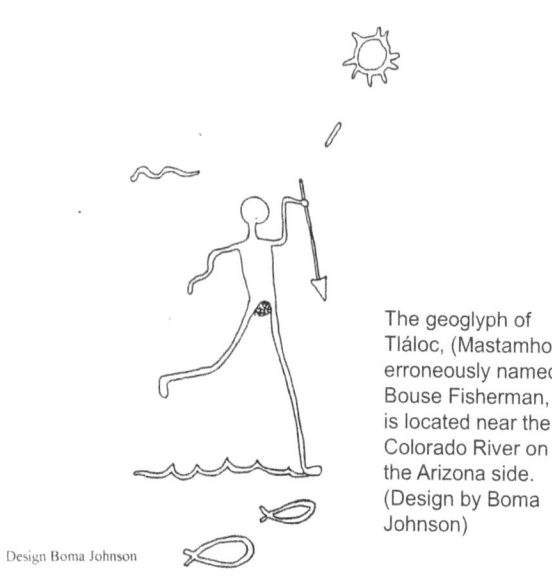

The geoglyph of Tláloc, (Mastamho) erroneously named Bouse Fisherman, is located near the Colorado River on the Arizona side. (Design by Boma Johnson)

Design Boma Johnson

The Bouse Fisherman Intaglio is a very important geoglyph of the Mexica/Uto-Aztecan and Hokan/Yuman linguistic families and is associated with the Blythe Giant Intaglios. This human geoglyph image does not represent a man, per se, but a woman. It is indicated by the crouch made of a small stone mount located between her legs. For the Mexica, this geoglyph represents Tláloc, the female and mother earth. Tlaloc is the duality of Huitzilopochtli, the male, the cosmic father.

To the Hokan linguistic families of the Colorado River, the geoglyph represents Mustamho to the Mojaves and Kumustamho to the Quechans, similar to the painting that they have in their museum.

When the site was first revealed to the non-indigenous public there was confusion and speculation in terms of what it meant and what it represented. Why was there an image of a spearman in the middle of the desert so far away from the water? There was no research in existence, as far as the Anglo was concerned, on this intaglio. Therefore, those who saw it did not know what to make out of it.

The geoglyph resembles a human figure thrusting a spear into the water with two fish images below. This intaglio was erroneously named by the Anglos, "Bouse Fisherman," because that is what they assumed it was since they lacked the knowledge of the indigenous significance of the surrounding areas and of the Mexica Codex.

Above the human figure's hand is a line that connects the sun with the spear. The spear in his hand is thrusting down towards the wavy line that represents water and earth. The two fishes represent Pisces in the zodiac signs. The Era of Pisces started during the first Sun as shown on the Azteca Sun Stone Calendar.

The Spear represents lightning, rain, fertility and the communicator between humans, cosmos and mother earth. The Sun image is communicated by a small line that goes from the top of the spear to the Sun.

The point of the spear is a triangle made of quartz stones representing the "Crystal of the Cosmos," as symbolized by the Omeyocan Diamond here on Earth. The triangle symbolizes the three energies, Yeitiliztli in Nahuatl.
The faint "M" above the figure's head on the left represents Cassiopeia in the Milky Way and the woman's breasts on earth.

Some of the Colorado River Basin nations still have Lightning Clans which continue to sing the songs in remembrance of the Creator.

This intaglio depicts the creation story that associates the cosmos, humans, and earth, and represents Tláloc in the Mexica creation story.

The ancient tlaquilos (sculptures/writers) with the Creator's calling, strategically and mathematically constructed the Bouse Fisherman Intaglio site to form the eastern boundary of the

Omeyocan Diamond and what we call the Diamond of Infinity. It is the only man-made component of the four corners that outline the boundary of the huge diamond that encompasses the Palo Verde/Parker Valleys.

Tlaloc-Ixtlilxochilt Codex shows Tláloc's image in a glyph which represents Mother Earth, fertility and water. Tláloc is shown with the staff that represents lightning and creates life. Tlaloc unites the cosmos, humans and earth.

Tlaloc-Ixtlilxochilt Codex shows Tláloc's image in a glyph which represents Mother Earth, fertility and water. Tláloc is shown with the staff that represents lightning and creates life. Tlaloc unites the cosmos, humans and earth.

Chapter 3.3
Omeyocan: The Diamond of Infinity

The Lower Colorado River Valleys begin at Spirit Mountain, north of Needles, California, continue south to the confluence of the Colorado and Gila Rivers, further south to the Gulf of California. This is an area that has an abundance of over 275 intaglios and evidentiary natural formations. The confluence of the Colorado and Gila Rivers are as historically important to our indigenous people as the Tigris and Euphrates Rivers are to western civilization.

The indigenous traditionalists of the Lower Colorado River Nations have direct linkage with the ancient Mexica families that left here thousands of years ago. The mountain ranges surrounding the Palo Verde/Parker Valleys are comprised of sacred sites which are the center of all spiritual significance. One of the most topographical phenomena that has confirmed the identification and location of the long-sought mystical Island of Aztlán in the Palo Verde/Parker Valleys was the identification of the geographical boundaries of Omeyocan, the Diamond of Infinity.

The Island of Aztlán was located approximately in the center of the diamond. This diamond is called "Omeyocan" in Nahuatl and its geographical revelation validates the superior knowledge and wisdom possessed by our indigenous ancestors.

The diamond is the symbol of infinity for all the Lower Colorado River and Uto-Aztecan nations, and is the most prominent symbol emblazoned on native traditional dress and artifacts. The Diamond of Infinity "Omeyocan" is the place of the two hearts that illustrates the creation story and represents the crystal of the cosmos and the thirteenth level of knowledge. It is where the duality Omecíhuatl (female) and Ometecuhtli (male) reside and their images on Earth are the Blythe Giant Intaglios.

In the Mexica Creation Story, the Omeyocan Diamond is formed by two-isosceles (triangles) combined together to form the sacred place of Omeyocan.

The Uto-Aztecan Nations never disassociated

themselves from their cosmic rituals. They were deeply rooted in the most profound human subconscious as the result of their involvement with Mother Earth and Father Cosmo.

In the native traditional creation story, they never constructed any architectonic structures without a meaning or symbolic abstract concept. It was all based on physical, geometrical, cosmic phenomenal events, natural formations and surroundings. (Acamapixtli, 1989)

The ancient cosmic observation involved the participation of all elements in the universe, in continuous unison and harmony. Through their observations and studies of the movement of the celestial bodies, they were able to coordinate and elaborate links to create such a precise recording indicated on the Azteca Sun Stone Calendar. This calendar was used to guide their everyday lives. They knew and were convinced that as humans they were an integral part of the universe with the cosmos and conformed to all forces of nature. Thus, they maintained a harmonious equilibrium from the day they were born to the day they died with all the elements, including the cosmos, earth, night and day, light and dark, good and bad, female and male -- all were seen as one entity: humans, creator, environment, tradition, and science.

The Mexica believed in applying the principles of archaeoastronomy. As a result, we can see how the majestic diamond formed by two isosceles triangles joins together. This formation is based on specific peaks and other geographical mountain locations that outline the image of the Diamond of Omeyocan in the Palo Verde/Parker Valley and their surrounding areas.

Of the two triangles, the northern triangle is the largest, which is why it represents the male duality. The northern point of the diamond image is the mountain peak which is called "Ipalnemohuani" in Nahuatl meaning: "the giver of all life, the divinity."

Christian Theology makes reference to a similar image called "God's Eye," which is a human eye inside a triangle. In the old churches, this image was placed above the main altar, and in both cases, this image represents the creator.

The southern isosceles triangle point represents the female duality, the Mother "Tonantzin." It is located approximately 50 miles south from Ipalnemohuani's mountain image.

During the winter solstice, the metamorphosis of Tonantzin is formed and is one of the most outstanding phenomena in the Palo Verde/Parker Valleys. In the late afternoon, a shadow on a peak forms the diamond image shadow which is created by two mountains in the foreground overlapping and forms a v-shape.

The western point of the Omeyocan Diamond is the head image of Huitzilopochtli on the top of the Big Maria Mountain.

The Bouse Fisherman Intaglio (Tláloc) forms the eastern point of the Omeyocan Diamond, which is on the desert pavement.

Aztec Sun Stone Calendar, Tonalmachiotl, the great venerable mechanism where the movement and measurement of the cosmos is recorded.

In Mexica tradition, the Huitzilopochtli and Tláloc pyramids (Teocalli) were always together. All the dual teocallis are based on similar positions as the Omeyocan Diamond. Both teocallis were the main temples and center of all Mexica culture and tradition as they are located in El Zocalo in Mexico City.

The dimensions of the entire diamond are as follows: from the north point to the south point, approximately 50 miles, from the east point to the west point, approximately 32 miles. The line connecting the east and west point is where the Ipalnemohuani and Tonantzin isosceles meet.

During their migrations from the Lower Colorado River Basin Valleys, the Aztecas sought sites and geographical formations similar to those within the Omeyocan Diamond and its surroundings. Many times they attempted to duplicate them. This was done to remind them of their place of origin. Some of these locations can be found in Cucurpe, Sonora, which was the center of the Opata nation. Three peaks outline the north, west and south points and a cave representing a woman's womb which is in the eastern boundary, representing Tláloc, similar to the Omeyocan Diamond.

When the early Nahua migrations got to the area of modern day Mexico City, they duplicated the Omeyocan Diamond. The north part of the Diamond is a mountain called Coatepec and the western point is Malincalco, the eastern point is Tepotztlan and the southern tip of the Diamond is Xochitlcalco. Altogether they outline the Diamond similar to Omeyocan here in the Palo Verde/Parker Valley.

Anahuac, Teotihuacan, which was located northeast of Mexico City, was one of the seven most sacred cities in the world during the last days of the Mexica rule. According to the astronomical concepts, its layout and parameters are terrestrial images of stellar constellations. The twin teocallis in the twin cities of Tenochtitlan and Tlatelolco were constructed based on the same astronomical concept.

At the temple site in the ancient Mayan City of Uaxactun, Guatemala, an overlaid Diamond forms during the spring equinox when the rays of the rising sun enter the structure and align with a nearby observatory. During the summer and winter solstice, the rays of the rising sun form the diamond's northern and southern boundaries. (Millon, 1973)

The construction of El Castillo teocalli in Chichen-Itza, Yucatan, Mexico was also based on the same calendar concepts. During the spring equinox, an image of the snake "Quetzalcoatl" is formed by the shadows on the seven isosceles on the side of the teocalli. (Hunbatz Men, 1990)

In the Lower Colorado River Basin Valleys, the Omeyocan Diamond's geometric boundary overlaps most of the old CRIT Reservation boundaries when it was formed in 1865. The top point of the Omeyocan Diamond is approximately at the same latitude as the top point of the Reservation. The southern part of the CRIT Reservation boundary extended to the base of where Tonantzin, the southern point of the Omeyocan is located. We are very thankful to our elders that envisioned the protection of the Omeyocan Diamond boundaries.

Chapter 3.4
The Mule Mountains/Cicimitl and Kokopilli/Quetzalcoatl

According to most of the Hokan/Yuman and Uto-Aztecan linguistic families, Spirit Mountain, located northwest of Needles, California, is the genesis of their creation stories. In the Hokan/Mojave Creation story, it is said that in the beginning it was all black and there was a big void. Chaos followed, then the creation, and from the union of earth and sky the Great Spirit

Map of Omeyocan Diamond

The Omeyocan Diamond, over laid in the Palo Verde/Parker Valleys shows the west point as the head of Huitzilopochtli on the Big Maria Mountains and the east point as the Bouse Fisherman, Tlaloc. The destroyed island of Aztlan is in the center of the Blythe Giant Intaglios and the Moon Mountains in the CRIT Reservation. Designed by Alfredo A. Figueroa and drawn by Victoria Aguilera

Matavilya was born. (Hinton, 1984)

As time passed Matavilya prepared himself to teach the people who would later inhabit the universe, what they needed to know about their world. But before he could do so, his sister, Frog Woman, killed him. It was then that his little brother, Mastamho, took responsibility for the world and its people. (Kerober, 1976)

Ron Van Fleet describes part of the oral creation story and states that Mastamho, with his magic wand, stirred the contents of a three-legged pot, or molcajete. He threw the contents behind him, thus, creating the Milky Way, the entire universe, water, and air. When he was finished, he placed the empty pot upside down on the earth, with the three legs up, therefore, creating the three peaks of "Hamock Avi," the Mule Mountains, fifteen miles southwest of Blythe.

He then struck four times with his magic wand (Provo) and every time he struck it, he made a different kind of being, until he finally created all living things. With his wand, he then poked into the earth and drew a line, creating the Colorado River. After all was created, he went to his house "Ava Thupo" (Mojave), Tlalocan (Nahuatl), at Spirit Mountain "Avi Kwame." This was the first house on earth, the dwelling of the Spirit Mentor, creator of all things.

This is where the creation story of the Lower Colorado River Hokan/Yuman and Uto-Aztecan linguistic families' originated and it is from here that they migrated to and from at various times.

When the nations migrated, they went to the four directions, "Nahui Ollin," meaning the four movements in Nahua. The Mexica were the last to leave of the Uto-Aztecan and they went south. The Knowledge Keepers took with them their traditions "Huehuetlatolli," (the old knowledge), to remind them of their past dwelling on the Lower Colorado River Valleys. The Four Knowledge Keepers are shown in the Boturini Codex leaving Aztlán and are represented by four mountain peaks in the Big Maria Mountains going south.

When the Nahua left their area of origin, they began to use three-legged molcajetes in daily food preparation and also, as part of their burial rituals in order to send their spirits back to their house, "calli," the three peaks of the Mule Mountains, overlooking the Palo Verde Valley, and fifteen miles southwest of Blythe, directly west of Ripley, California. The evidence of the beginning of the participation of the Mexica migrations and Creation story are the Mule Mountains. The Mule Mountains represent the third glyph, "calli," meaning earth/house on the Azteca Sun Stone Calendar and is found going counter clockwise within the 20 day glyph.

The "three legged molcahete" is the most popu-

lar in the southwest and in Mexico today. After the conquest, the Spanish Conquistadores brought with them indigenous slaves. They were mostly Tlaxcalteca. The Spaniards brought these indigenous slaves to help them settle the new conquered lands. The slaves brought with them the three-legged molcajete and introduced it to California and the rest of the southwest.

The indigenous families along the Lower Colorado River Basin Valleys continued to use the flat oblong metate (mortar). They did not need to be reminded of their spiritual resting place because they were living in the area where the Mule Mountains, three-peaks, are located here in the Palo Verde Valley. The three-peaks were also depicted at the bottom of the original Mexica Flag that was used by Cuitlahuac, the 10th Mexica Tlatoani, when he defeated Cortes on June 30, 1520, also referred to as "La Noche Triste," by Hispanicized historians. On the contrary, this date was a victorious event to the indigenous people.

Jairo Rodriguez del Olmo, son of the 12th descendant of the Cuauhtémoc Dynasty, Dr. Salvador Rodriguez Juarez, relates that in ancient times, Chontal natives living in Ixcateopan, Guerrero, would place the charred remains of their deceased in urns, or ollas. At the time of the burial, a three-legged molcajete would be placed upside down over the opening of the burial urns with the charred remains.

Rodriguez confirmed that this was done to return the spirits of the deceased to their place of earthly origin, the three peaks of the Mule Mountains. When the remains of Cuauhtémoc were being uncovered in 1949, a molcajete was found on top of the remains of his burial urn, which is on exhibit at the Ixcateopan Museum.

This same burial tradition was also found in Caborca, Sonora, located on the Mexica Migration Trail going south. Benjamin Celaya Crespo local well-known, amateur archaeological enthusiast, of Caborca, Sonora, has found over fifteen burial mounds near Caborca. These mounds include molcajetes or metates (with three legs) upside down over ollas with ashes inside of them. Caborca is one of the main stops of the Mexica migration route.

To further substantiate this burial tradition, it is important to note that the Mayan section of National Museum of Anthropology in Mexico City houses an exhibit of this ritual showing the upside-down molcajete on top of a burial urn containing a child's skeleton. Nearby is an adult skeleton flat on its back, an up-ended, saucer-shaped molcajete stands near its head, (resembling a hat).

According to Boma Johnson, retired archaeologist of the BLM, it is common to find burial mounds containing fragments of metates throughout California and the southwest, but they are not found in the Lower Colorado River Valleys.

In the Mexica tradition, when the body of person dies the spirit goes to the four directions in four days, until it goes to "calli" (house), which is the three-peaks in the Mule Mountains. There at "calli," the Great Spirit, "Cicimitl" takes the spirits to one of the four final resting places all based on how the person died and how they lived during their life. By Spanish speakers, Cicimitl, is commonly referred to as 'cucuy,' (pronounced coo-coo-y) 'the spirit of the night.' It is a giant geoglyph which is directly magnetic north from the Mule Mountains next to the Kokopilli geoglyph. Cicimitl is the duality/twin of Kokopilli. Most of the spirits go to Mictlan, the "Topock-Mystery Maze," where the spirits repose, near Needles, California.

Years back, the Mule Mountains were referred to as the Upside Mountains, and were known as the Molcajete, Calli Mountains in Nahuatl. In the Cahuilla language they are referred to Mul-al similar to Molcajete in Nahuatl, hence the name Mule Mountains.

Located at the crossroads of the area's major north, south, east and west trails, the Mule

Mountains have always been held sacred by the indigenous people. Their story is included within the folklore of almost every indigenous nation and the hundreds of historical petroglyphs and geoglyphs found within the area and on the Mule Mountains themselves.

Kokopilli/Quetzalcoatl Geoglyph Image

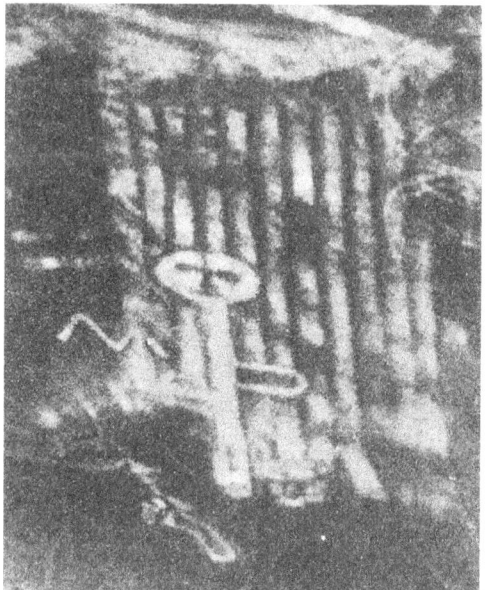

Cicimitl

Cicimitl Geoglyph is the Great Spirit that takes the human spirits to Mictlan. Cicimitl means compass in Nahuatl and in this geoglyph he is shown as a skeleton. It is geographically located in line with the Mule Mountains, calli in the south, and his head is pointing to magnetic north that terminates at the Topock Maze, 10 miles southeast of Needles, CA.

Cicimitl Magliabecchi Codex is in the Nazional Centrale Library in Florence, Italy. Here Cicimitl was painted like a skeleton, full of hearts and hands around the neck and head. Around the hearts there are 11 flags, which the Mexica call Pantli. It is represented in the original Mexican Flag before the European invasion during the battle of Cuitlauac and Cuauhtemoc in 1521.

This Kokopilli image is one of the most popular icons of the Creator known throughout the southwest. In this giant geoglyph, and in most of the images, Kokopilli/Quetzalcoatl is drinking the pulque with a popote/ straw. This straw also represents the flute which creates wind. This image represents Quetzalcoatl's travels to the west during the different Suns as documented in the Five Suns of the Aztec Sun Stone Calendar.

Directly north of the Mule Mountains, is the location of the giant geoglyph image of the world famous icon, Kokopelli (Kokopilli) and represents Quetzalcoatl. This giant geoglyph is approximately 200 ft. long and is facing west. His giant image has a road running through its back and head. This road was made when it was used as an off road race way. The Kokopilli geoglyph is facing west because it is departing with the sunset at the end of the 3rd Sun. When Quetzalcoatl left he promised to come back during the end of the 4th Sun which ended in 1483 and the 5th Sun began in 1535.

Quetzalcoatl is known among the Hopis and other nations as Kokopelli, the hunchback image playing the flute.

In the Azteca/Mexica creation story, Kokopilli (spelled with an 'i' instead of an 'e') is also Quetzalcoatl, the creator. Kokopilli is deciphered as "Koko," which means "Hurt in the crown of the head" and "-

pilli" means "Our Lord," and all together it means, "Our Lord is hurt." As we enter the new era of Aquarius, the Creator, Quetzalcoatl, is leaving at the end of the era of Pisces.

Kokopilli/Quetzalcoatl is manifested in the glyphs of the Florentine Codex. In Chapter 4, Illustration 11, you see an old bearded/bladed man who is Huemac and he is offering Quetzalcoatl a drink of "Pulque" and he says… "My Lord, drink of this, because if you don't drink it afterwards you will desire it. At least sample it with your little finger."

Kokopilli is hunchback because he has all the knowledge of the world on his back. This knowledge is depicted by the seven lines on his back and these same lines also represent the harmonious balance (equilibrium) of the world. His image is seen on hundreds of petroglyphs along the migration routes in the four directions out of the Colorado River area as depicted on the Nahua Codex. In the Codex, the hunchback is called "Teomama-Huehuetlatolli" meaning "The Bundle Carriers of Knowledge." Kokopilli's five feathers on his head represent the communication from the center of the earth to the cosmos. His upper body is of a bee and the lower portion is that of a human, which demonstrates human association with all living species.

Mexica Flag that was used by Cuitlahuac before the invasion. The 11 Sun Rays surrounding the eagle on the flag Cuitlahuac and Cicimitl represent the sun spots and sun flares that erupt every 11 years when the sun's magnetic field flips over. It takes two flips to complete a cycle. Scientists predict the next flip will occur May, 2013. (Astronomy Magazine)

Mule Mountains

The original image of Cicimitl appears on the Mule Mountains, "calli" meaning house in Nahuatl. Calli is the first syllable where the name California originally derived from. Cicimitl is referred to as E.T., extraterrestrial. His face is on the peak on the right. The human spirits all go to 'calli' and from there Cicimitl takes them to magnetic north to the Topock Maze.

Chapter 3.5
The Return of Quetzalcoatl To La Cuna de Aztlan

Quetzalcoatl is the most frequented personality in the Nahua/Mayan pantheon. No other image or energy reached its fame during the pre-Cuauhtémoc civilization. According to the Legend of Quetzalcoatl in the Mexica Codexes (Ancient Books), Quetzalcoatl departed toward the sunset, to Tlapallan-Tlillan (the ancient reddish-black land) and died approximately, in the year Ce-Acatl 947 AD.

The return of Quetzalcoatl was determined by Xuihmolpilli. The Azteca/Mexica binding of the nine-52-year-cycle measurement of time known as Xiuhmolpilli, was derived from the traditional 52-year New Fire Ceremony. Xuihmolpilli also prophesized the return of Quetzalcoatl from

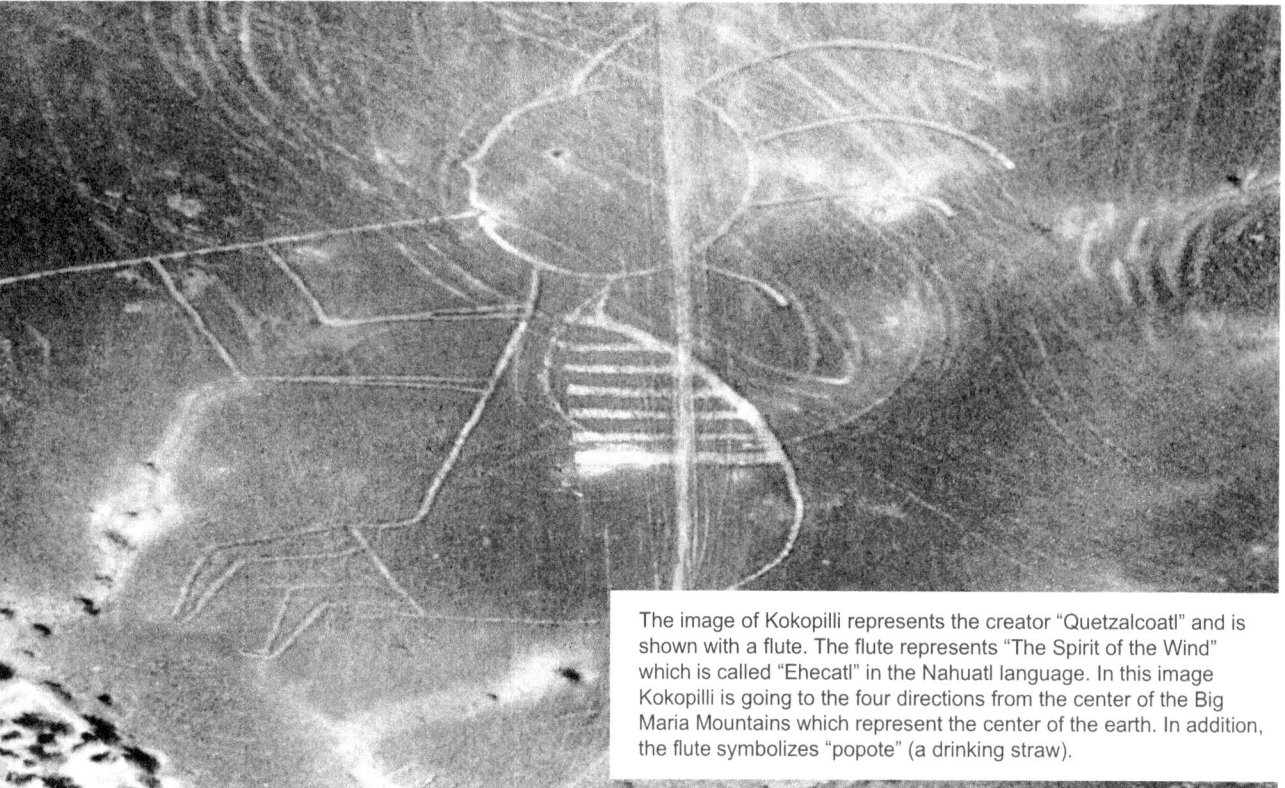

The image of Kokopilli represents the creator "Quetzalcoatl" and is shown with a flute. The flute represents "The Spirit of the Wind" which is called "Ehecatl" in the Nahuatl language. In this image Kokopilli is going to the four directions from the center of the Big Maria Mountains which represent the center of the earth. In addition, the flute symbolizes "popote" (a drinking straw).

the distant east, and thus, one day, full fill the prophecy of the cyclical repetition of the measurement of time.

Quetzalcoatl is commonly referred to as the plumed serpent. In Nahuatl, Quetzal refers to the Quetzal bird of the Mayan highlands. Quetzal also means precious. Coatl means serpent and twin. Quetzalcoatl's image is manifested in various forms, metamorphoses, and has many personalities. The cross image of Quetzalcoatl has existed for millenniums here in La Cuna de Aztlan in the Lower Colorado River Basin Valleys and throughout the Western Hemisphere. Quetzalcoatl is the spirit within all humans, among nature and the cosmos. He created everything. The creator is "he who has no name yet has all the names." The Nahuatl speaking nations have known of his knowledge for thousands of years. The knowledge of Quetzalcoatl is manifested on the Tonalmachiotl, also known as the Azteca Sun Stone Calendar.

Quetzalcoatl is referred to in many terms. In the Nahuatl language, he is known as Topilzin, our Venerated Lord, Ce-Acatl, our origin/beginning, Nahui Ollin, the four movements, Xuitechutli, the Lord of Fire, Ehecatl, the Venerated Wind, and Xolotl, the Dog, etc. Ehecatl and Xolotl are the twins that represent the duality of Venus as the morning and evening star, respectively. The cosmic constellation of Gemini represents the twins and man and woman.

Quetzalcoatl came at the beginning of the 5th Sun as prophesized, but in the form of a blonde bearded Christopher Columbus in 1492 and twenty-seven years later in the form of Hernan Cortes in 1519. Thus, the greatest devastation and genocide of a civilization the world has ever experienced was the European invasion of Anahuac. The return of Quetzalcoatl is forthcoming, but this time he will come from the west.

Quetzalcoatl The Creator's image as the bearded Quetzalcoatl when he cremated himself, and the lava and flames consumed his body and turned into doves that flew straight to the planet Venus, becoming Ehecatl, the morning star and Xolotl, the evening star. The cremation site is an extinct volcano in the Lower Colorado River Basin. (Codex Magliadecchi, Fray Bernardino de Sahagun.)

Ancient Footprints of the Colorado River 47

Chapter 4

The Pleiades and the New Fire Ceremony: Measurement of Time

The rising of the Pleiades (Seven-Sister Constellation) to its zenith every 52-years constituted one of the most important and sacred days for the Mexica/Mayan culture. It marked the end of a phase in their lives and the renovation of a new one. This was called "Xuihmolpilli," the compiling or the binding of the years.

The Mexica/Mayan people used two main Calendars; the Lunar which marked 260 days and the Solar Calendar that marked the 365 Solar days which corresponds with the seasons of the year.

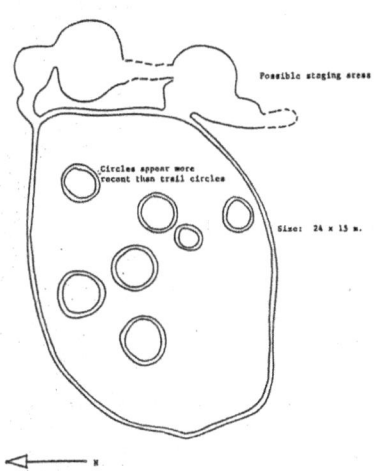

During the rising of the Pleiades, the two calendars met and synchronized in opposition on a certain date every 52 years. At that time it was thought that the world would terminate and a new one would begin.

After the passing of the Pleiades at midnight and the world continuing on its course, the Mexica began the celebration of the New Fire Ceremony.

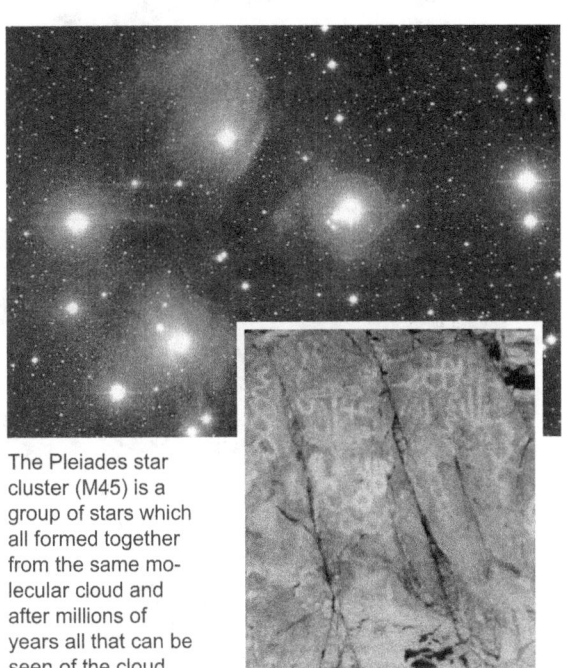

The Pleiades star cluster (M45) is a group of stars which all formed together from the same molecular cloud and after millions of years all that can be seen of the cloud are little wispy filaments around the stars. (http://schmidling.netfirms.com/m45.htm, July 16, 2004.)

Petroglyph of the Pleiades Star Cluster at the base of the Tonantzin shadow image in the Dome Rock Mountains during the Winter Solstice. (Picture taken by Alfredo A. Figueroa, Alfredo M. Figueroa, Jr.)

The last 52-year New Fire Ceremony was celebrated in 1483. It took place at Huixachtlan or Cithaltepetl (Cerro Estrella/Star Hill) the suburb

Codex Telleriano-Remensis of New Fire Ceremony-The codex shows the rising of the Pleiades and the New Fire Ceremony. The date, 1524 is crossed out and the date shown is 1507. Both are incorrect yet historians continue use 1507 as if it were factual.

of Iztapalapa, located southwest of downtown Mexico City. The hill is located in the middle of the Valley of Anahuac, and during the celebration a large bonfire was lit for this important event that could be seen for miles around.

The position of the Pleiades determined the day of the ceremony. The day before the ceremony, all the fires in the valley were extinguished and all household goods, "ollas" (cooking pots) and "metates/molcajetes" (three-legged grinding stones) were broken and thrown away. As a traditional ritual, homes were swept clean and at dusk, everyone would climb to the rooftops to wait for darkness and the commencement of the arrival of the rising of the Pleiades to its zenith.

The De Solei Codex depicts an excellent picture portraying the priest patiently looking up towards the cosmos in expectation of seeing the Pleiades rise to its zenith at midnight.

In the Palo Verde Valley there are numerous archaeological sites that show evidence of the same ritual that took place when the Mexica lived in the area, coordinating the ceremony with the movement of the Pleiades.

During the ceremony, the knowledge-keepers (priests) would dress in ornaments that had images of Huitzilopochtli, Tláloc, and Quetzalcoatl. As the Sun began to set, they proceeded from the east to the top of the "Teocalli" (pyramid-shaped temple) located on top of El Cerro Estrella. They would walk

in solemn procession and in full observance pacing themselves with the travel of the Pleiades. This was why the Mexica called them "Teonenemi" which means "they travel like the cosmic energies" because they were emulating the rising of the Pleiades from the east to its zenith in the cosmos.

When the Pleiades were in the correct geometrical position and had passed its zenith, the knowledge-keepers then knew that the world was going to continue and they started the New Fire as part of the celebration. The priests lit four bundles, each with 52 sticks and runners would carry the lighted torches from the ceremonial fire to the four directions and to "El Templo Mayor" (Zocalo). In El Zocalo, the new fire was ignited at Huitzilopochtli's Teocalli, heart of the Mexica tradition and culture. This was the symbol of the beginning of a new life, prompting a cry of relief and joy throughout Anahuac. (Day, 1992)

The Mexica would celebrate the New Fire ceremony here on earth in conjunction with the cosmic counterpart to honor the Creator. In its cosmic counterpart, it is celebrated by the "Leonides," "The Shower of Stars." The Leonides are seen every November 16, and they have a unique role after the rising of the Pleiades, which verified that the world would continue on its course.

The Mexica continued with their tradition as shown in the Boturini codex. The codex shows the new fire symbols/glyphs nine times, from the beginning of their migration from Aztlán. (Carpania)

These New Fire symbols/glyphs are shown in the outer circle of the Azteca Sun Stone Calendar, and we can find them in dozens of archeological sites in the southwest United States and in northwest México.
According to the Mexica/Mayan tradition, since time immemorial, the rising of the Pleiades to its zenith at midnight every 52 years, marked the universal time or the point of departure. This crucial mathematical breakdown of cosmic measurement of time has totally been rejected or left in obscurity by the European historians/invaders. Only recently, have astronomers began to accept the fact that there is not a beginning or ending in the universe, giving acknowledgment to the Mexica/Mayan cosmic tradition. (Astronomy, 2009)

The last 52-year rising of the Pleiades to its zenith occurred on November 14, 2003. (Stardate University of Texas, 11-14-2003.) According to our mathematical breakdown, 52 years form a cycle, and nine 52-year cycles equals 468 years, which in turn makes one Mexica Sun. This mathematical break down is shown in the Five Suns of the Aztec Sun Stone Calendar.

As a result, if we subtract 468 years from 2003, we get the year 1535, which was the year of the conquest of México/Tenochtitlan.

The year 1535, also marked the end of the Forth Sun and the beginning of the Fifth Sun, which ended in 2003. 2003 began the transition of the end of the fifth sun. We are currently living in the last year of the 9 year transition. End of the Fifth Sun will be 2012.

One era is comprised of five suns. Mathematically, five times 468 years equals 2340 years, which takes you back to the year 338 B.C., which was the beginning of the Era of Pisces. The Era of Pisces is characterized by the dominance of religion and will end in 2012. The symbol of Pisces is the two fishes as shown in the Bouse Fisherman intaglio group. The ending of the Era of Pisces will mark the end of the Fifth Sun, and will then revert back to the First Sun with the beginning of the Era of Aquarius. The majority of the anthropologists and historians have not taken in to consideration the measurements of the Suns recorded by the Azteca Sun Stone Calendar. Instead, they have included in their writings the theory of a mythical Sixth or Seven Sun which is totally erroneous.

(The following is a personal account of the rising

of the Pleiades by the author.) The last rising of the Pleiades to its zenith was a memorable and phenomenal event that was witnessed by Michelle Leivas-Kristman, Demesia Figueroa, and my self, the author, Alfredo A. Figueroa. The three of us were vigilant during the night from the front patio of our house, in El Barrio of Acacitli. We patiently watched as the Pleiades traveled to its zenith which began in the east at sundown and continued through midnight.

We had prepared ourselves to observe this sacred event because earlier that morning the news on KERU's Radio Bilingue program from Fresno, California announced this very important cosmological event. The program was from the McDonald Observatory of the University of Texas, which mentioned that at midnight the Pleiades would rise to its zenith.

The news took us completely by surprise because the majority of the investigators, including their advisors of the Mexica culture, thought that the last time the Pleiades had risen to its zenith was in 1507, before the European Conquerors prohibited the celebrating of the ceremony. Obviously, with the rising of the Pleiades on November 14, 2003, there was a huge mathematical error in the Telleriano-Remensis Codex that depicts the last Mexica New Fire Ceremony taking place in 1507. With this new information, the mathematical calculations are hereby corrected and the appropriate adjustments made to give them the correct date of the last time the Pleiades rose to their zenith before 1521.

It is now known that the date 1507 was erroneous because we had personally witnessed it and applied our own mathematical breakdowns in order to correctly identify the date based on these new facts. This deception was first conceived by the European conquerors who wanted to keep these sacred events from being known to the world. The European conquerors deliberately distorted the date of the Pleiades rising to its zenith to eliminate the traditional ritual of the New Fire Ceremony.

The Telleriano-Remensis Codex was painted by the "Mexica Tlacuilos", but scrutinized by the despot Spanish Priests, who wanted to convert the indigenous to the Catholic religion at all cost. In the codex, the date on top of the image of the New Fire Ceremony is 1524, but the 1524 has been crossed-out and the date 1507 is written.

As a result, we can now verify that both dates where erroneous. This error continues to this day and is believed by investigators, anthropologists, and writers of the Azteca/Mexica culture, because they all base their studies on the year 1507 instead of the actual day, 1535. (Figueroa)

This error caused major detriment regarding the facts of our cosmic indigenous traditions for more than 500 years.

One of the first things that the European invaders did was to destroy the Twin Towers of El Zocalo, in the center of Mexico/Tenochtitlan. The Twin Towers symbolized the Teocallis of Huitzilopochtli and Tláloc which respectively represented the Father Cosmo and Mother Earth.

The Teocallis also represented the Sacred Spiritual Heart and the center of all the power of The Confederation of Anahuac, extending from the Rocky Mountains in Montana in the United States down to Nicaragua in Central America.

Fray Joseph de Acosta's book entitled "Natural and Moral History of the Indies," confesses that the priest had to lie in order to comply with the teaching of the Church, such as shown in the Telleriano-Remensis Codex. Acosta states: "the reason we were forced to say that the men of the Indias were European or Asian, was so as not to contradict the Sacred Scripture, that clearly shows that all men descend from Adam, and thus we cannot give another origin to the men of the Indias, because the same Divine Scripture also says to us that all the earth, beasts and animal perished, but those that reserved for propagation of their breed in Noah's Ark." Acosta also

stated: "it is a false opinion of those that say that Indios descend from Jews." (FCE, 1940)

In the surrounding areas of the Colorado River, particularly, in the Palo Verde Valley, there are numerous archeological sites that have an abundance of broken ollas (clay pots), molcajetes (grinding stones) and other household artifacts. These artifacts are semi-buried along the side of the Colorado River and on the edge of its mesas, alluding to the rituals of the New Fire Ceremony.

These ruins clearly indicate that the 52-year New Fire ceremony was, among other things, an impetus for resuming the periodic search of the Mexica people for a place to renew there lives.

Here in the Colorado River Valleys, among the Intaglios and geoglyphs, are the symbols of the Pleiades. According to Boma Johnson, there is also a petroglyph with the Seven Sisters constellation at Sears Point, on the Gila River. It has seven clustered dots, ¾" wide, just above a horizontal line, which illustrates the eastern skyline on the horizon as the Seven Sisters constellation rises.

Continuing south, to Sonora, Mexico you will find at La Sierra La Provedora, located 5-miles west of Caborca. There are hundreds of petroglyphs in La Provedora. Here you will find three petroglyphs that are together: The Heron, Turtle and Pleiades image. This culmination of these three images signifies that the people from the land of the herons, met in Caborca (meaning "Turtle Shell") during one of the 52-year cycles when the Mexica left from Aztlán on the Colorado River. Petroglyphs of the Pleiades cluster appear all along the migration routes.

The ruins of the great population centers of Mesa Verde (Colorado), Chalco Canyon, Aztec Ruins (New Mexico), Tuzigoot, Snaketown, Pueblo Grande, Casa Grande (Arizona), and in Mexico, Trincheras, Rayon (Sonora), Casas Grandes (Chihuahua), Chalchiutes, and La Quemada (Zacatecas), reveal a great deal about this native tradition that had been with them throughout the migrations.

Archaeological theories attribute that the mass movement of migrations was due to epidemics, droughts, and warfare. This theory is now being debated by new scholar investigations, revealing that the 52-year New Fire Ceremony tradition was the driving force behind the migrations. Archeologist Stephen Lekson studied one of the sites of the ruins in Arizona and wrote that: "Almost every house had grinding stones and other utensils broken." Why did they suddenly leave knowing they would never return? There was plenty of water nearby."

After researching the ruins at Chalco Canyon and Casas Grandes, Lekson told the American Archeology Society that all the sites mentioned were constructed in a straight line by the same people moving south at different intervals. Boma Johnson also stated that the Mimbres Culture which is located on the Mimbres River in southwest New Mexico is also on the same straight line as mentioned by Lekson.

The Nahua nation was predestined by the Creator to start their pilgrimage, at the culmination of every 52 year cycles. They would settle and rebuild at different locations similar to the Island of Aztlán in the Colorado River. They would build barriers, plantations, fisheries, and "chinampas" (plantings along the waterways), similar to Xochimilco, in Mexico City. That is why you can find numerous sites named Aztlán along the migrant trails throughout the continent.

According to the traditional cosmic beliefs, upon descending from the cosmos, the Creator "Mexitli," told the Aztecas that they would no longer be called Azteca but Mexica. This is why the name was changed to Mexica. Therefore, it was their duty to take the Creation Story from the Colorado River to the four directions, (nahuiollin). The migrations were predestined as demonstrated by the Boturini, Siguenza, and Aubin Codex's, which show the "Teomamas"

(Knowledge Keepers) with bundles of knowledge and Huitzilopochtli on their backs.

After one hundred sixty years of migration, the Mexica nation settled permanently in the Valley of Anahuac in present day Mexico City. The 52-year ceremony continued to be celebrated, which adopted the element of destroying the old to make way for the new. Therefore, instead of leaving the valley of Anahuac, they stayed permanently and constructed new additions on top of the old teocallis in reference to the 52-year ceremonies.

In 1978, while excavating El Zocalo, in downtown Mexico City, investigators uncovered the Twin Teocallis. They uncovered nine separate layers of structures below the existing Teocalli giving credibility to the fact that they were modified at different intervals. This proves that the founding of México/Tenochtitlan was not in the year 1325, but in fact, hundreds of years before. (Day 1992)

Currently, in Mexico, the 52-year fire ceremony of the Pleiades has continued to prevail since ancient times. In order to emulate the 52-year ceremony a danza called "Los Voladores de Papantla," is preformed by the native "Totonacas" of Veracruz, Mexico.

According to Fray Clavijero, "The pole in the ceremonial solar danza and ritual represents the binding between the cosmos and Mother Earth. In this ceremony five men climb to the top of a pole wearing eagle, guacamaya (similar to the parrot) or butterfly costumes. One of the men stays on top of the pole waving a banner representing the cosmos (pantli), while playing a flute which symbolizes the wind (ehécatl). On top of the pole there is a small rotating square platform which has 4 long ropes that tie each of the four men that will descend to the ground after turning 13 times (4x13=52), as they form an imaginary pyramid, which concludes with the cosmos descending to earth." (Clavijero, 1982)

In 1519, the Confederation of Anahuac was at the height of its existence and was led by the Tlatoani Moctezuma Xocoyotzin of the Mexica. The Mexica were the supreme power of all the continent of Anahuac. When Cortes conquered Mexico/Tenochtitlan, one of the first things that he did was to destroy the Twin Towers "Teocallis" of El Zocalo that represented the power of the Confederation of Anahuac. The conquering of Mexico/Tenochtitlan was the end of the Fourth Sun which brought about complete devastation of native culture, language, traditions, and obscurity for all natives of the continent for 500 years.

The Fifth Sun began in 1535, and will end in 2012. There is a similarity in the destruction of the Twin Towers of the World Trade Center in New York City on September 11, 2001 and the destruction of the Twin Towers of El Zocalo. The Twin Towers of the World Trade Center represented the power of the capitalist world and the Twin Towers of El Zocalo represented the power of Confederation of Anahuac.

Today, people are concerned about what will happen in 2012. Mayan expert, Jose Luis Romero Rivera, states that the archaeological chard on the stella known as the Monument Six does not predict the end of the world nor does it mention a tragedy. This stella, recently found at Tortuguero Mountain in Tabasco, Mexico, only predicts the end of the time period of the Mayan Bactum on December 23, 2012, the end of an era. (Jornada Newspaper, March 29, 2011)

No one can predict what will happen in 2012. One can only look back in the past and reflect on the atrocities committed by the Spanish Invaders. What happened to the millions of indigenous people of the Confederation of Anahuac at the end of the Fourth Sun? No one knows for sure what the end of the Fifth Sun will bring.

Chapter 5

Movement and Measurement: The Mathematical Symbolism of Time

The Mexica utilized mathematics in all phases throughout their lives. This included science, architecture, social events, sports, traditions and beliefs with a symbolic meaning that was attributed to certain numbers.

The Mayan "Hunab K'U" and the Nahuatl word "olmeca" mean the same, (movement and measurement). Olmeca is derived from "ollin", meaning (movement) and "meca" from "mecatl" meaning (rope and measurement). Everything in the universe is based on movement and measurement. The best example is the Mexica/Mayan Sun Stone Calendar which represents measurement and movement and symbolizes the universe.

Zero, "0" represents the Creator, the one who has no name and has all the names. Its image in the cosmos is the Black Hole, the center of the spiral of the Milky Way.

The zero represents the beginning, the end, chaos, and the infinity. Thousands of years before the European invasion, the indigenous people of Anahuac were fully aware and were guided by the concept of the "0" and the use of the decimal point. That is why the Mexica/Mayan calendar is more precise then the European Gregorian calendar. Furthermore, European math began with the Roman numeral one "I" and did not even acknowledge the "0" at all.

One, "1" is after zero. The number one signifies the light, life, and God's eye or "Ipalnemohuani" in Nahuatl, which is the top corner of the Omeyocan Diamond at the thirteenth level of knowledge.

Two, "2" represents duality in the cosmos and is manifested in the Gemini Twins, when they descend on the peak of Tamoanchan forming the letter "X." The duality relates to all aspects of the Creation as represented by Ometecutli (Male), Omecíhuatl (Female), Father Sun/Mother Earth, Huitzilopochtli/Tezcatlipoca, Night/Day and so on.

Three, "3" represents the triangle of the arrowhead. The front tip represents Ometéotl and the two bottom tips represent Ometecutli (Male) and Omecíhuatl (Female).

Four, "4" represents Nahui-Ollin, four movements, four directions, swastika, four seasons, and the four energies: Xipitotec, Huitzilopochtli, Quetzalcoatl, and Tezcatlipoca.

Five, "5" represents Quincunx, the four dots in a circle or square that has a dot in each corner and one in the middle. The middle dot represents "Xuitecutli" (Man of Fire). It also signifies the Five Suns, and represents the Creator's image called Tloque-Nahuaque, the image with the symbol of the open hand and its five fingers, meaning "Among all, we do all for the benefit of all, like the fingers in the hand all different shapes, all different sizes but all together in the palm of the hand."

Six, "6" represents the six points of merging of the two triangles, Mictlan and Tonalan, which form a star with six points. It is also the four cardinal directions with the zenith and nadir.

Seven, "7" represents Xicomoztoc, the place of the womb of Mother Earth where humanity was born and the seven organs of the female's reproductive system. 7 also represents the Pleiades, Seven Sisters constellation and the number of equilibrium.

Eight, "8" represents the merging of two squares in the inner part of the Mexica/Mayan Sun Stone Calendar. One square indicates the four cardinal directions and the other square is the four Astros that are interrelated into the four cardinal points. The Astros points represent the Sun, Earth, Moon and Venus, and all together form the image of 8 triangles.

Nine, "9" represents transition and the nine months of a woman's pregnancy cycle.

Thirteen, "13" represents the 13th level of Omeyocan where Ometéotl resides. This level is achieved by humans who have committed themselves to Mother Nature's requirements and traditional ways.

The number 13 also represents the 13 moons that currently exist. This totally contradicts the 12 months of the Gregorian calendar. Thirteen represents the 13 constellations and discredits the 12 constellations currently used in horoscopes zodiac signs. When you multiply 13 by 4, you get a total of 52, signifying the beginning and ending as manifested by the rising of the Pleiades to its zenith every 52 years. It is the measurement of time since time immemorial. Only recently, has the 13th constellation been mentioned and explored.

Also, the number fifty-two, "52," was the number of members of the Tlatocan, the Supreme Senate Council of the Confederation of the Anahuac. It was the ruling body of most of the continent of Anahuac. On this council there were 26 women and 26 men. The spokesperson for the women was called Cihuacóatl and the spokesperson for the men was called Tlatoani. Both males and females had equal voices on the council.

Unfortunately, with the invasion by the Europeans, the concept of "machismo" came with them. The male "machismo" philosophy dominated and imposed the male influence throughout society with their titles of nobility, "kings" and "emperors." Religion played a role as well in the diminished importance of equality. They totally ignored the role of the woman, Cihuacoatl, and the duality-based traditions of the indigenous community that had been practiced and had flourished for thousands of years.

In many nations, the female is still given her rightful place. Throughout the centuries among traditional indigenous people, when a person reaches the golden age of fifty-two years, they are enrolled in the Circle of Elders, honored and respected.

The Mexica were never disassociated from the cosmos because everyday had a cosmic meaning. They always knew that which we are barely beginning to understand: The true meaning of our existence here on earth. Who are we? When did we come to this earth? Why are we here? Where did we come from? These are the questions that anthropologists have longed pursued.

The Mexica did not invent anything! They observed their natural surroundings. They knew their past history and studied the cosmos. They knew that the measurement of time was based on the 52 year cycles, and the Five Suns, as shown in the Azteca Sun Stone Calendar. Cuauhtémoc knew what he was talking about when he issued his last decree.

The Mexica knew about the cosmic events because they based everything on the principle of "Neltiliztli" meaning: "To seek the roots of the truth."

Chapter 5.2
Comparing Symbolic Illustrations

Part of our field investigations within the Palo Verde/Parker Valleys have included the process of cross referencing the geoglyph, petroglyph and pictograph symbols, with the images/glyphs depicted on the Mexica Codices. These symbols and images represent ancient Mexica thought and belief relevant to the Colorado River.

When the Mexica knowledge keepers, "tlamantinimis," migrated from the Lower Colorado River, they took with them all their knowledge, beliefs, thought and tradition. They left behind primitive symbolic manifestations of their presence in the stage that was reflective of their tradition at the time of their departure. They left behind thousands of geoglyphs, petroglyphs, pictographs, wind-rowed designs and so on.

As they migrated south they were able to incorporate other cultures and develop new techniques for documenting and memorializing the creation story. This eventually evolved into the codex, a form of recording history. They painted glyphs and carved stone sculptures like the Azteca Sun Stone Calendar in order to preserve their culture and tradition.

Included on this page are 2 images that have crossed-referenced with the Colorado River culture and the ancient codices.

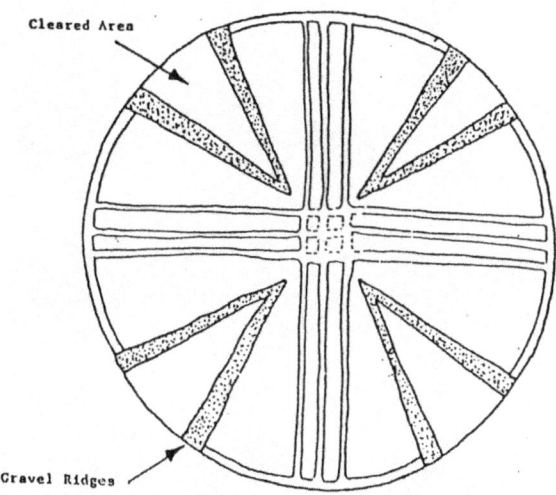

Quetzalcoatl's cross geoglyph in the Colorado River is an interpretation of Quetzalcoatl's travels to the four directions and is centered on the Colorado River. The image is that of what is known as the Maltese cross. (Designed by Boma Johnson)

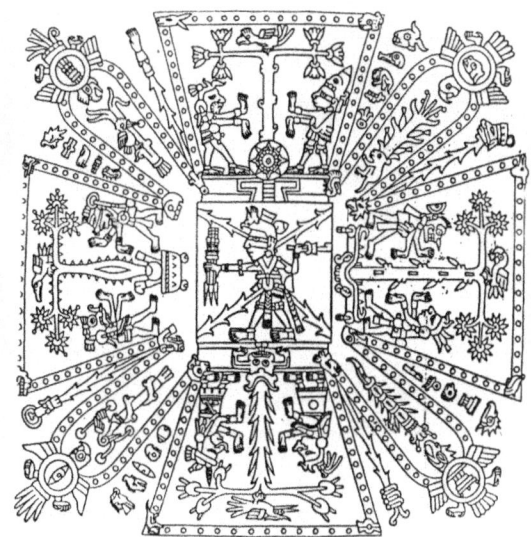

XIUHTECUTLI

The center of this codex is of Xuitecutli/Quetzalcoatl and it is the Aztec Calendar in a different image. The codex represents the geoglyph of Quetzalcoatl's cross.

The Fejervary-Meyer Codex is one of the few pre-Cuauhtémoc codices. It belongs to the Borgia group of Codex and is located in the Liverpool, England Museum. The information in the codex is authentic because it was painted by the Mexica tlaquillos (codex artist) before the Spanish priest imposed their distortions on the codices.

Chapter 6

Cuauhtemoc: Symbol of Liberation

Cuauhtemoc is one of the most proclaimed heroes of all time among the Spanish speaking natives of the southwest and Mexico. In the Confederation of Anahuac, Cuauhtemoc was the 11th Tlatoani, (spokesperson).

Cuauhtémoc's history in Mexico has been totally distorted, deliberately obscured and ignored by the Hispanicized government policies and imposed their views. Mexico is a nation whose people, to this day, are uninformed of their indigenous cultural heritage and the truth of their origin, even though many possess a strong sense of pride in their indigenous culture and hunger to learn the truth of their origin.

On August 13, 1521, Hernan Cortes sieged Mexico/Tenochtitlan. This was an infamous day in the Mexica history, marking the beginning of the 500 years of suppression and destruction of indigenous knowledge, language, customs and traditions. As a result, the Mexica and all indigenous people of Anahuac would be kept in darkness for centuries.

Consequently, the majority of Mexica do not understand the significance of their ancestor, Cuauhtémoc. He is, for the indigenous people in Mexico and throughout the continent, the truest symbol of liberation.

However, now the five hundred years of darkness are over and we are beginning to spread the word of the New Knowledge that is so necessary for the unification of all indigenous people.

Therefore, in order to understand the Mexica history and the name of Cuauhtémoc, you must also know the origin of the name: How, when, where and why, Cuauhtémoc?

The name Cuauhtemoc originated in the Mexica creation story. As you may know, there are numerous legends that tell about the creation of the world. The one that we relate to, herein, is found in the book, "Historia de los Mexicanos por sus Pinturas." We have included it due to its evidentiary findings about the creation story. It explains that the earth was created from the body of the dragon/alligator, in the cosmos, and its head was called "Cipactli." The story says that Cipactli came down and formed the earth, and brought the sky down with it after the cosmological event referred to as the "Big Bang."

In his book, "Tamoanchan Tlalocan: Places of the Mist," Alfredo Lopez Austin quotes: "Having seen…the sky fall upon earth…they ordered all four of them to make four paths through the center of the earth in order for them to enter and to lift up the sky. And they created four men to help them. One was called Cuauhtemoc, another Itzcoatl, another Itzmalli and the other one, Tenexuchitl. After these four men were created the two gods, Tezcatlipuca and Quetzalcoatl, made themselves into large trees, Tezcatlipuca was the tree they called Tezcacuahuitl, which means mirror tree, and Quetzalcoatl's tree was called Quetzalhuexotl. Men and trees and gods raised the sky with its stars where it is now." (Austin, 1997)

As we read the above creation story, we know that one of the men that helped raise the sky was Cuauhtémoc. This is the origin of the name, Cuauhtemoc. The four men were the four poles and they are the base of what is called Tamoanchan, the hour-glass image formed like an "X" meaning, "Tata (grandfather) that descends to his House, earth "Nana" (grandmother)."

Along with this allegory interpretation of the origin of the name of Cuauhtemoc, the evidence found in the surrounding mountains of the Palo Verde Valley confirms that the name Cuauhtemoc originated in this area and is related to the creation story.

This investigation included deciphering the petroglyphs, located in the Eagle Mountain range located within Joshua Tree National Park, about 60 miles west of Blythe, California off Interstate-10.

Throughout the centuries, numerous mountain ranges in the surrounding areas of the Palo Verde/Parker Valleys have kept their original names and meanings despite the differences in the native languages. For example, the name of the Eagle Mountain Range has changed, but its meaning has remained the same.

In the Mojave language, Eagle Mountain is called "Amat Avi Aspa" meaning place of Eagle Mountain. The Chemehuevi and Cahuilla also have their names for Eagle Mountain. Our Chemehuevi and other indigenous Elders have always regarded Eagle Mountain as very sacred place. When the Spaniards came to this area they called it "La Sierra de la Aguila," and when the Anglos came, the name was changed to what it is today, Eagle Mountain.

Through our investigations, we have deciphered and cross-referenced some of the petroglyphs, and other symbols found on these mountains, with the Borgia Codex. We have also conducted field studies during the solstices and equinoxes confirming the authenticity of the allegorical name of "Cuauhtémoc."

In the Nahuatl language, the name Eagle Mountain refers to Cuauhtémoc and is derived from the word "Cuauhtli-" meaning (eagle) and "-temoc," meaning (descends) confirming that Cuauhtémoc, means "Descending Eagle".

The "V" of Eagle Mountain facing Blythe.

The sun setting on Eagle Mountain. The manifestation of the metamorphosis of Cuauhtémoc takes place when the Sun (Eagle) descends on a most distinct "V" formation on the mountain range during the Summer Solstice. Thus, the origin of the name of the range, Eagle Mountain, meaning 'where the sunsets.' This event can be seen from the Palo Verde Valley in the east. (Photo taken by Alfredo A. Figueroa)

In the Mexica codex, all of the energies have a spiritual animus/nagualli or symbolic animal representation. The eagle is one of the naguallis of the Sun, and represents the sun during the summer solstice at 9:00 am and 3:00 pm. Therefore, Cuauhtémoc represents the sun as it begins to descend on the Eagle Mountain Range.

The manifestation of the metamorphosis of Cuauhtémoc takes place when the Sun (Eagle) descends on a most distinct "V" formation on the mountain range during the Summer Solstice. Thus, the origin of the name of the range, Eagle Mountain, meaning 'where the sunsets.' This event can be seen from the Palo Verde Valley in the east.

When members of the Figueroa family were growing up, they would always wonder why the Eagle Mountain Range was called Eagle Mountain. Danuario Figueroa, father of the author, had worked during the 1930s at the Black Eagle Mine and he never mentioned seeing any eagles.

Continuing with our investigations throughout the years, cross-referencing the Borgia Codex with our local indigenous names, we were able to determine why the mountain range was called Eagle Mountain.

Cuauhtemoc means 'descending eagle.' The eagle is the nagualli of the setting sun. The picture represents the sun descending on Eagle Mountain where it got its name and the teocalli is Tamoanchan, Acacitli, Blythe, CA. (Painting by Jesus Herrera)

Other mountain ranges in the area have also kept their native names, such as the Chuckwalla Mountain Range south of Eagle Mountain located near Desert Center, California. Chuckwalla means "Cuetzpalin" in Nahuatl and in Spanish it means "lagarto" or "lagartijo" and in English it means lizard. There is a small mountain ridge outcropping in Desert Center which is called Alligator Ridge and is derived from its original name Chuckwalla. Cuetzpalin is the forth image of the 20-days on the Aztec Sun Stone Calendar.

Cuauhtémoc, was born on February 23, and is believed to have been born in the year of 1496 in the town of Zompancuahuitl, Guerrero. He was the son of Ahuizoto, who was the son of Ahuizotl the eight-Tlatoani of the Mexica.

Cuauhtémoc was the grandson of Ahuizotl, the Tlatoani and not his son as mentioned by many historians. This is the reason why critics say that the investigation by Dr. Salvador Rodriguez Juarez, the 12th descendant of the Cuauhtemoc Dynasty, was not true; that Cuauhtémoc's mother, Cuayahuitl was a Chontal, daughter of Cuayautitla the Tlatoani of Zompancuahuitl and the surrounding Chontal territory.

When Cuauhtémoc was 15 years old he was sent to Mexico/Tenochtitlan to live with his father Ahuizoto and go to school. There he enrolled in the Calmeca institutions of higher learning where he became a warrior and after his training he returned to Zompancuahuitl with his mother.

In 1515, he was elected "Tlacatecuhtli", (Supreme Commander) of Tenochtitlan's twin city, Tlatelolco because of his bravery and knowledge of warfare. He was at Tenochtitlan when the Tlatoani Moctezuma Xocoyotzin, was killed by Hernan Cortes in 1520. Cuitlahuac was elected Tlatoani of the Confederation of Anahuac after the death of his brother Moctezuma. It was during the reign of Cuitlahuac that Cortes and his allies were defeated on June 30, 1520.

The Spaniards and the Hispanicize Mexican Government refer to that day, as "La Noche Triste cuando lloro Cortes," (the sad night when Cortez cried). For all indigenous people, however, this was "La Noche de Triunfo," (the night of triumph).

After the defeat of Cortes by Cuitlahuac, Cortes and his allies went to Tlaxcala to recuperate with his principle ally, Xicotencatl. There they were able to recuperate and prepare, as well as organize more allies to attack Tenochtitlan again.

Cuitlahuac ruled for only five month and on December 3, 1520 he died of smallpox, a disease brought over by the European invaders.

On February 1, 1521, when Cuauhtémoc was still in his twenties, he was elected to become the 11th Tlatoani of the Confederation of Anahuac. On the same day, he married Tecuichpoch, daughter of Moctezuma Xocoyotzin. He immediately began to organize the defense against Cortes and his allies, who had held Tenochtitlan under siege for 80 days with a complete blockade around the island city.

Cuauhtémoc tried to rally other nations that were friendly with the Mexica, but his attempts were futile because all of his warriors were exhausted. Famine was rampant, as was the horrible plague of smallpox that had killed Cuitláhuac.

Cuauhtémoc's mother, Cuayahuitl, organized an army of new recruits in Guerrero to help end the siege. She came from the south, through Malinalco and Cuernavaca, but her troops were routed at both places by the Spaniards and their allies.

Even the Texcocanos, longtime allies of the Mexica, were now in the Cortes camp. They were the ones who helped build the thirteen "bergantines" (boats) that were instrumental in the defeat of Mexico/Tenochtitlan and the capture of Cuauhtémoc and his followers on August 13, 1521.

Statue of Cuauhtemoc at Ixcateopan Plaza
(Photo taken by Alfredo A. Figueroa, in 1996.)

Though some of his former allies deserted him, some remained faithful to Cuauhtémoc. A message was sent to the allies of the Confederation of Anahuac and nations from the Lower Colorado River Valley area to help fight the Spaniards. According to Ron Van Fleet, the Mojave's oral history explains that they traveled great distance to Mexico/Tenochtitlan to help in the fight. Mojave warriors would later face the Spaniards once again in 1680, when they helped the Hopi and Pueblo oust the Spaniards from Santa Fe and all of New Mexico.

Cuauhtemoc was the last defender of Mexico/Tenochtitlan. After having endured eighty days of fierce fighting, completely surrounded by the invaders and allies he knew that the end was near. On August the 12th 1521 he issued a final decree: "Our sun has concealed itself; our sun has gone from our vision, the invaders have left us in total darkness. We know that our sun will return again to shine upon us, but meanwhile, it will remain in the house of repose, Mictlan. Let us unite, concealing in our hearts all things that we love. We must conceal our temples, our schools, our courts of ball playing, our singing houses; and we shall leave our streets deserted and seclude ourselves in our homes. Our homes shall be our temples, schools, ball courts, singing and traditional studies." "From this day forth until now, it will be our beloved Anahuac. With the protection of our creator and as a result of our traditions, our education that our ancestors instilled in our parents, and with all the persistence and emphasis that they instilled on us, that we do not forget to tell our children that one day it shall be that Anahuac shall rise again and reach its zenith of power and we shall fulfill our Great Destiny."

Cuauhtemoc finally surrendered on August 13, 1521. The indigenous world that had flourished in the Anahuac continent for thousands of years came to an abrupt end when Cuauhtémoc was captured by Captain Garcia Holguin, an officer in Cortes' army. This infamous day in Mexica history marked the beginning of the destruction of the indigenous role in the world that had existed for thousands of years. This included the indigenous knowledge, languages, customs, and cosmic traditions. The indigenous way of life was kept in darkness for 500 years.

At the time of his capture, Cuauhtémoc and his family were taken prisoners and brought before Hernan Cortes. In a gesture that earned him the admiration of the conqueror, Cuauhtémoc pointed to the dagger of Cortes' and said, "Oh, Malintzin, take that dagger and kill me. I have done all I can in defense of my people and now I'm your prisoner."

When he was first captured, Cuauhtémoc was treated with consideration and Cortes allowed him to continue governing the city. But when Cuauhtémoc refused to reveal the location of the treasures of the Mexica, Cortes gave the order to torture Cuauhtémoc and Tetlepanquetzal, the Tlatoani of Tlacopan and a member of the "Triple Alianza."

On October 15, 1521, Captain Julian Alderete, a royal tax collector of the Spanish King, tortured the two prisoners by burning their feet. It is written that Tetlepanquetzal cried out to Cuauhtémoc: "Tell Cortes where the treasure is hidden because I can no longer withstand the pain." Cuauhtémoc quickly responded, "A caso estoy en un baño de temaxcal?" (Do you think I'm in a sweathouse?) This phrase has been repeated through the centuries as an illustration of the strength of Cuauhtémoc's resistance.

This strength and resistance has made him the absolute leader of the Mexica/Xicano/Indigenous Movements (Movimiento de Mexicanidad e Indiginista). He serves as an inspiration to millions of Mexica and other suffering and oppressed indigenous people, and is an example for those who would resist efforts to obliterate their place in history.

Cuauhtémoc and the rest of the Tlatoanis from the Triple Alianza were kept in prison for more than three years. Finally on October 12, 1524, Cortes was called to Honduras because one of his followers had rebelled against him. As he was departing, his advisors told him that there was going to be an uprising by Cuauhtémoc's followers during his absence. Cortes then decided to take the prisoners along with him.

While on the road to Honduras, Cortes' followers told him that they were going to pass through Chontal territory and that the Chontales were waiting to ambush Cortes in order to free Cuauhtémoc. Cortes then decided to hang the

prisoners. In the morning of February 28, 1525, near a place called Izancanac today's Tenosique, in the state of Tabasco, Cortes hung Cuauhtémoc and 13 other Mexica leaders.

Tctzilacatzin, a friend of Cuauhtémoc who had also been held prisoner but who had managed to escape, was able to recover Cuauhtémoc's body. He took the body back to Zompancuahuitl the town of his birthplace that was later renamed Ixcateopan, Guerrero. Tctzilacatzin, like Cuauhtémoc was a Chontal, from a town near Ixcateopan. His bravery during the defense of Tenochtitlan is documented in the Florentine Codex.

The exact location of Cuauhtémoc's tomb was kept a secret among the descendants of the dynasty, until February 2, 1949, when the secret was finally revealed.

Today, the world again is reminded of the ancient prophecy of Cuauhtémoc. The Spanish conquest began the era of 500 years of darkness that fell upon the indigenous world. Today, at the end of the era of darkness, the indigenous world is awakening and realizing the truth of their heritage, the origin of their ancestors and greatness of their culture, traditions and beliefs. This awakening is the only solution to the salvation of the indigenous people, the return to their roots!

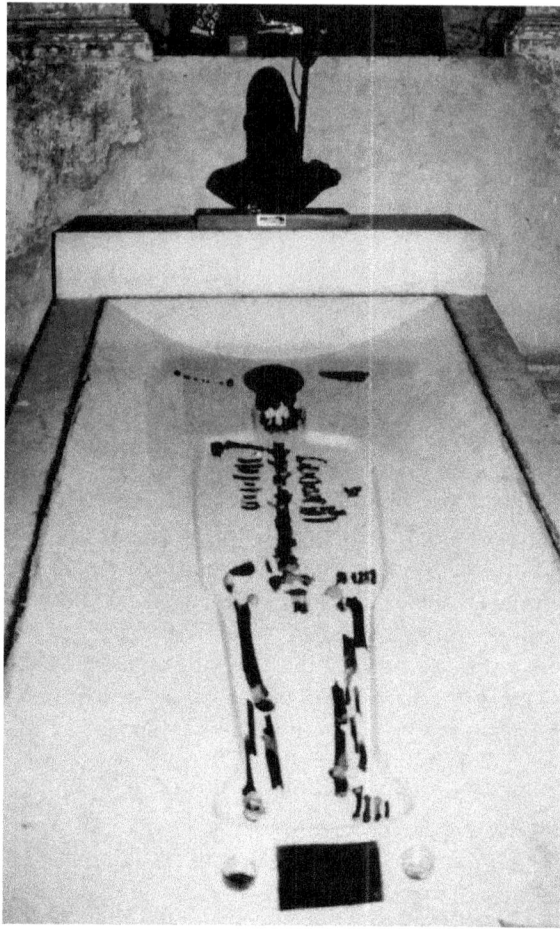

The tomb of Cuauhtemoc, at the site of the Church of Santa Maria de Asuncion, Ixcateopan, Guerrero. Cuauhtemoc is the Symbol of the Mexicanidad; The Birth of the New Knowledge, today known worldwide. (Photo Credit Jairo Rodriguez del Olmo)

Chapter 6.2
Revelation of Cuauhtémoc's Tomb

The remains of Cuauhtémoc were secretly guarded at his mother's house in Ixcateopan, Guerrero, for four years until 1529, when Fray Toribio de Benavente (Motolinia) came to Ixcateopan looking for the whereabouts or remains of Fray Juan de Tecto. Fray de Tecto was with Cortes on his trip to Honduras, when he took Cuauhtemoc with him. Fray de Tecto, was very sympathetic to Cuauhtémoc and his followers and when Cortes killed Cuauhtémoc on the route to Honduras he also killed Fray de Tecto. When Cortes got back from Honduras, he lied and reported to church officials in Mexico City that Fray de Tecto had died of starvation on the way to Honduras and his remains where left there.

Cortes had hung Fray de Tecto because he did not want him to denounce his (Cortes) crimes and atrocities he had committed against the natives to King Charles V. The Codex of 1528 shows both Cuauhtémoc and Fray de Tecto hanging from a tree.

As a result of Fray de Tecto's disappearance, Fray Bernardino de Sahagun had sent Fray Toribio de Benavente and Juan Juarez to investigate the truth of Fray de Tecto's whereabouts. King Charles the Fifth was Fray de Tecto's good friend and was concerned about his disappearance. Both investigators traveled through the states of Morelos and Guerrero until they came upon the town of Zompancuahuitl, today's Ixcateopan de Cuauhtemoc, Guerrero.

Fray Benavente was called "Motolinia" by the natives and was very well liked because he walked barefooted and wore ragged clothing and would not abuse nor mistreat the natives like the other Spaniards would.

While in Ixcateopan, the descendants of Cuauhtémoc told Motolinia that the remains of Fray de Tecto and Cuauhtémoc were at his mother's house. Motolinia knew that the Spanish government wanted to kill all of Cuauhtémoc's descendants and destroy all remembrance of Cuauhtemoc. They also feared an uprising led by the Chontales and other allies against them. Therefore, Motolina had the remains of Cuauhtemoc and Fray de Tecto buried under the Chontal "momoztli," (altar). In 1529, Motolina had a small "Capilla" (Chapel) built on top of the Altar.

Afterwards in 1539, the small capilla was destroyed and the actual Santa Maria de Acension Church was built leaving the altar in the same place where Motolina had instructed the descendants to leave Cuauhtémoc's remains. According to the laws of the Church, you had to either be a king or pope in order to be buried under a Church's Altar. The church still remains today and serves as a mausoleum and museum of Cuauhtémoc.

Cuauhtémoc's tomb was kept a secret for more than 420 years by Cuauhtémoc's descendants through "La Carta Viva" (Oral History) and other documentation that had been gathered throughout the generations. Cuauhtemoc's original descendants vowed to be quiet about the burial place and were committed to preserving Motolinia's secret and this commitment was passed on for 12 generations. The old name of "Zompancuahuitl" was changed to the name of "Izcatiemoteopan" which means "place where the spirit of Cuauhtémoc lies in cotton."

The secret of Cuauhtémoc began when Motolinia drew a sketch of its exact measurements where his remains were located. He left the descendants these documentations and writings. He warned them to conceal the secret because he did not know when the hostile government positions were going to cease. The secret of his burial was not to be revealed until these hostilities ceased.

According Dr. Salvador Rodriguez's oral family tradition, they were not to reveal the location of Cuauhtémoc's tomb: "Until Cuauhtemoc was remembered in five-values, until his heroic deeds were cherished by the government in control and until his descendents were no longer persecuted."

The natives of Ixcateopan also swore to preserve the Chontal language but learn the Nahuatl as a cover up of their Chontal language. From that day forth, Nahuatl became the official language of the natives of the area.

Jose Amador was the original descendant of Cuauhtémoc who began the centuries-old oral tradition transmitted from generation to generation. The name of Jose Amador was the family name given to the descendants, besides their given name. The tradition continued throughout the centuries, which also included some of the family members becoming priests who would feign in accepting the religious doctrine, to protect the secret.

The main purpose of becoming priest was to be able to read and write their genealogy and traditions. During this period there were very few people that could read and write Spanish, with the exception of the religious institutions.

Part of Dr. Rodriguez' documentation came from old bibles and other books in which the writings were along the edges and blank pages. According to Dr. Rodriguez, each descendant left their children the documents that each had received from his or her parents and they would include their own personal recommendations. They would also emphasize the oral history and had them sworn to continue the pledge until the proper time came to reveal the tomb. Most of our indigenous oral history traditions come from our elders and have been passed on for generations through the chants, and songs.

According to Dr. Rodriguez, his maternal grandfather, Don Florentino Juarez, wrote in his documents that all the information was to be given to Jovita Juarez. This information would be given to the following people upon her death: "And my aunt Maria Ines Juarez received the documentation from Jovita. When I was a young man my Tia Ines told me that I was to receive the commission next in line, heir of the secret of Cuauhtémoc's tomb. My aunt died in 1943, and I received everything. The documentation remained a secret so that there would not be any alterations to the history of our nation. I was a young man when I received this commission to further my knowledge of our indigenous background. My aunt told me that I had to go to Europe to study the many codexes that had been stolen from our beloved Mexico and were exhibited in many different museums and universities."

Jario Rodríguez del Olmo, the son of Dr. Salvador Rodríguez, is now the 13th descendent of the lineage of Cuauhtémoc. According to Jairo Rodriguez, his father had indeed, been sent to Europe by his grandfather to study the codexes that had been stolen from Mexico. He went to Paris, France, Florence, Italy, and Vienna, Austria in search of the codexes.

When Dr. Rodriguez came back from Europe he was able to put together the 420 years of his family's written and oral history that had been handed down to him. He was able to cross-reference and verify his genealogical lineage of the dynasty of Cuauhtémoc. This is how he knew the truth about how deep the remains of Cuauhtémoc were buried under the altar of the Church of Santa Maria de Asuncion.

According to Jario, Dr. Rodriguez became very enthusiastic with his investigations and even went to study the Nahuatl language in order to fully understand the codexes. At that time he was associated with the very well renowned philosopher, and anthropologist of Mexico, Professor Alfonso Caso. Dr. Rodriguez received his diploma as an investigator of Artistic Monuments and History, continued his investigations from Ixcateopan, and at the same time, continued his medical profession. During that time, he found out, among other things, that the Rodriguez family was of the Moctezuma Chimalpopoca lineage.

The secret of Cuauhtemoc's tomb was kept throughout the centuries with strict disciplinary devotion, always waiting patiently and longing for the coming of the "Five Values;" these values which were originally set as the time limit for revealing the truth of Cuauhtémoc.

Finally, in 1947, during the Presidency of Miguel Aleman, the Mexican government issued a "5 Peso" coin with the image of Cuauhtémoc. It was then that Dr. Rodriguez became apprehensive yet excited because he felt "una corazonada, (a gut-feeling)" and knew that the time had come to reveal the truth and not to fear any retroactions by the government or other agencies.

Prior to February 2, 1949, the historian Saturnino Tellez Reyes found a codex that strongly supported Dr. Rodriguez in his interpretations of the oral history and the written documentation of the authenticity of Cuauhtémoc's remains. (Reyes 1979).

On February 2, 1949 Dr. Rodriguez told the local parish priest that Cuauhtémoc's tomb was located under the Altar of the Church of Santa

Maria de Asuncion. The priest, David Salgado, informed the city officials of Ixcateopan and they contacted the governor of the state of Guerrero. General Baltazar Leyva, the governor at that time, then advised President Miguel Aleman Valdez of their request to proceed and get permission to further research Dr. Rodriguez's claims. He then informed the National Institute of Anthropology and History (INAH) in Mexico City of the situation. Professor Alfonso Caso head of INAH, sent the renowned anthropologist Señorita Eulalia Guzman as Chief Paleographic Investigator, to study the documents that were in Dr. Rodriguez's procession and check their authenticity to the 16th century.

Eulalia Guzman went to Ixcateopan and had many heated debates with Dr. Rodriguez concerning the government's position of the official story of Cuauhtémoc's remains. She argued that according to the government's official history, Cuauhtémoc was a native of Tenochtitlan and son of the tlatoani Ahuizotl and his remains were left somewhere along the way to Honduras where Cortes had killed him.

After Dr. Rodriguez revealed the location of the tomb of Cuauhtémoc, negative publicity and controversy arose throughout the Mexico. As a result, hundreds of people including scientists, journalist and traditionalists became curious and sought more information.

The investigations and meetings between Dr. Rodriguez and Eulalia Guzman lasted nine months. Finally, Señorita Guzman was convinced that the documentation that Dr. Rodriguez had in his possession was true. She then petitioned Governor Leyva to proceed with the necessary excavation of the altar in the church which was coordinated by INAH. The Catholic Church also granted permission to INAH for the excavation.

It was a historical day in the history of Mexico and in the entire world, when the tomb of Cuauhtémoc's remains was uncovered. The stones from the old teocalli and the church were identified as being of antiquity having been constructed in 1529. All those present were amazed except for Dr. Rodriguez who saw that the burial urn (olla) was in the exact spot as written in the documentation that was handed down to him by his ancestors.

On top of the burial urn was an upside down three-legged molcajete (grinding stone) which was placed on top of the urn as part of the tradition in the Chontal culture. This was done in order to remind the spirits of their place of origin. The upside down molcajete placed on top of a burial urn is symbolic to many of the tribal customs that the nations took with them when they left the Lower Colorado River Basin area The three-legs of the molcajete represent the three-peaks of calli (house) which are located 15 miles southwest of Blythe, California, and have erroneously been called The Mule Mountains. (Alfredo Figueroa)

Together with the urn at the tomb were other items such as a copper plate that said "Rey Coatemo" meaning King Cuauhtémoc. This revealing caused great controversy among many anthropologists and historians around the world. Señorita Guzman's group authenticated the artifacts. Because of her intervention, Guzman was the one who received the credit for revealing the remains of Cuauhtémoc, instead of the direct descendents who knew all along where the remains of Cuauhtémoc were for 420 years, but who had waited until the right time to reveal the location of the tomb.

The descendants invited people from Europe and all over the world to examine the remains in order to satisfy and calm the critics. This examination also included Dr. Rodriguez's documentations of his lineage to the Cuauhtémoc Dynasty, the location of the tomb and vintage construction of the church. Most importantly, however, was the scientific study of Cuauhtémoc's burnt bones. This study concurred that the bones from the feet of the skeleton were severely burnt. As a result, no one refuted the story of the torment that Cuauhtémoc suffered

when his feet were burned and killed by Cortes.

Even though, some critics still deny the authenticity of Cuauhtémoc remains, the government of Mexico officially proclaimed the old church and the mausoleum "Altar de la Nacion", (the Altar of the Nation). This altar was converted into a National Historic Museum, and brought forth "The Birth of the New Knowledge," which had also been buried for 420 years.

Before the revelation of the tomb of Cuauhtémoc, Dr. Rodriguez led a humble servant's life in his town of Ixcateopan. After all the commotion and publicity was over, Dr. Rodriguez was able to negotiate the construction of a paved highway from Tasco, Guerrero to Ixcateopan throughout the extreme mountainous area. The government also made many improvements to the town and built a new Catholic Church, schools and soccer fields. The name of Cuauhtémoc was also added to the town, "Ixcateopan de Cuauhtémoc."

Through his generosity, General Lazaro Cardenas, ex-president of Mexico, paid for the construction of a 40-foot bronze statue of Cuauhtémoc, which sits on top of a marble pyramid that was constructed at the entrance to the town.

This true story of Cuauhtémoc, as revealed by Dr. Rodriguez, has not received its due credit in history books or movies. However, here in this book, this dynasty is presented as one of the greatest revelations of all times.

During the three hundred years of Spanish rule which ended in 1821, August 13 had been imposed on the Méxica by the Spaniards as the most important holiday of the year. It was to be a reminder to the Méxica that they were a conquered people. It was also an attempt to eradicate all indigenous traditions and force them to assimilate into the European religion and society.

Today, in Mexico City, there is a large sign in Tlatelolco, Plaza de la Tres Culturas, which is located on the site where Cuauhtémoc was captured. The signs says the following: "El 13 de agosto de 1521 heroicamente defendido por Cuauhtémoc cayo Tlatelolco en poder de Hernán Cortes, no fue triunfo ni derrota, fue el doloroso nacimiento del Pueblo Mestizo, que es el México de hoy." "On August 13, 1521, heroically defended by Cuauhtémoc Tlatelolco fell to the power of Hernan Cortes, it was not a triumph or a defeat, rather a painful birthing of the Mestizo nation which is today's Mexico."

This again is an attempt to continue the oppression and distortion of indigenous history. This is an excellent example of one of the biggest mockeries toward the indigenous communities by the Hispanicized Mexican government and evidence that this mentality prevails today despite the ousting of the Spanish in 1821.

This true story of Cuauhtémoc, as revealed by Dr. Rodriguez, has not received its due credit in movies or books. However, here in this book we present this dynasty as one of the greatest revelations of modern times.

The revelation of Cuauhtémoc's Tomb heralded the spiritual and philosophical birth of the modern-day Xicano Movement, and all indigenous people. This demands justice and dignity for all as they reclaim their indigenous roots. As Cuauhtémoc's decree stated, "The time will come when our Sun will shine again."

Chapter 6.3
Homage to Florencio Yesca

Florencio Yesca, the Gran Maestro of "La Danza Explendor Azteca," was sent to the United States by Dr. Salvador Rodriguez from Mexico City, in the early 1970s to pave the way for the coming of the Cuauhtémoc Spiritual Pilgrimage in 1985.

Yesca's overall mission was to teach the Danza Azteca to all the Xicanos in United States. The danza is without an exception one of the movements that has a tremendous impact on the lives

Florencio Yescas, Died July 5, 1985
Painting by Annika Lambert

"Loor eterno en memoria a la voz reveladora en el desierto, enseñando y educando a los Xicanos con las danzas y del reencuentro con nuestra cultura, preparando el camino de la Nueva Sabiduría."

"Eternal remembrance and thanks to the memory of the voice that came to the desert, bringing forth education and teaching to all Xicanos, the danza and reencounter with our traditional culture, that is preparing us for path of the New Knowledge." (Figueroa)

of Xicanos, who, for years, have been seeking the truth of their Mexica roots.

Yesca organized and informed Xicanos about the greatness of our indigenous traditions and culture. He also introduced to them the "Birth of the New Knowledge" which is the revealment of Cuauhtemoc's Prophecy.

In the early 1970s, Yesca came to San Diego and Los Angeles, California, and he met for the first time in "El Centro Cultural" in San Diego with the Xicano community to discuss and share some of the research concerning La Cuna de Aztlán. He was very receptive and fully agreed with the revelations concerning the findings in La Cuna de Aztlan and offered his full cooperation and wanted to visit Blythe, California.

In his trip to the United States, Yesca was accompanied by one of his students, Lazaro Arvizu, who organized Danza groups in Southern California, while Yesca traveled all over the United States teaching the Danza Azteca.

Dr. Salvador Rodriguez giving instructions and final blessings to Estrella Newman and Hunbatz Men while Don Salvador's daughter, Maria Alberta del Olmo, looks on, at the beginning of the Cuauhtemoc Spiritual March in December, 1985, in Ixcateopan, Guerrero. (Photo by Darline Burns)

After touring the United States, Yesca finally came to the Palo Verde Valley to educate the community and prepare them for Cuauhtémoc's Spiritual Pilgrimage, which was in its planning stages. Yesca felt honored to visit Blythe. He informed them that they should be very proud to live in the center of Aztlán. He made reference to the indigenous culture in the Lower Colorado River Valleys and of the Nahua migrations south to Mexico City. He cited the information from traditionalist oral history, which stated that the Mexica came from Aztlán, a place on the Colorado River north of the confluences with the Gila River. Maestro Yesca urged the building of a cultural and educational center in Blythe, acknowledging that this was indeed Aztlán.

Maestro Yesca was one of the most knowledgeable danzantes that memorialized the migration period of the Azteca/Mexica history through his danza. One of the oldest works performed by his danzantes honors the journey of the indigenous people from Aztlán which is called: "La Migracion de Los Chichimeca," (The Chichimeca Migration).

Yesca was dedicated to his culture. He was one of the first Mexica historians who supported the research confirming that La Cuna de Aztlán was in the Lower Colorado River Basin Valley. He knew that his time was limited to fulfill his commitment to Dr. Rodriguez, to prepare for "The Cuauhtémoc Spiritual Pilgrimage" that was forth coming.

Maestro Yesca was in his late fifties when he came to the United States and that is why he

anxious to extend his travels and dedicated his time teaching others La Danza. During this time he was able to travel through the Pacific Northwest, Colorado, Arizona, New Mexico, Texas, Kansas, Illinois and as far as New York City, and finally settling in California at "El Parque de la Raza", in Los Angeles where he made his headquarters.

Throughout his travels he was able to establish and organize different danza groups that have gained considerable momentum throughout the years.

Yesca began participating in la danza at the age of four, and his first ritual was performed at the shrine Virgin of Guadalupe, which is located in Mexico City. This shrine is a Sacred Site of the Mexica which is called "Tonantzin-Tepeyac" in Nahuatl.

He continued with the danza until he died in his mid-seventies in San Juan, in the state of Mexico, on July 5, 1985. He had spent over fifteen years in the United States, but unfortunately, did not get to see the Cuauhtémoc Spiritual Pilgrimage. It began on December 7, 1985, in Ixcateopan, Guerrero and ended in Los Angeles, California February 23, 1986, which was Cuauhtemoc's birthday.

Florencio Yesca's journey to this country fulfilled part of the prophecies stated in Cuauhtémoc's decree, on August 13, 1521 which briefly stated: "Our Sun has gone from our vision and we will soon be in the dark, but the time will come when our sun will shine again. Then we will again build our schools (calmekas), and cultural centers (kuikakaltin) of danza and song, and demanding justice and equality."

Florencio Yesca's return to Aztlán was the last leg of his journey on the Road to Aztlán, fully completing the circle of the Mexica migration.

The Mexica migration that had once left Aztlán on the Colorado River in 1160 was now returning to break ground for the Cuauhtémoc Spiritual Pilgrimage that was coming from Ixcateopan.

Today in Mexico City and in the United States, the Azteca Danza is one of the fastest growing movements, and danzantes can be seen all around the city in different parks and especially in the downtown. The Danza Azteca is one of the most popular traditional and educational movements in all of the Xicano Movement. In Mexico City, at El Zocalo, the danzantes continue to pay their respect to the Creator.

Chapter 6.4
Cuauhtémoc Spiritual Pilgrimage

According to Cuauhtemoc's descendants, the revelation of the location of Cuauhtemoc's tomb in Ixcateopan, Guerrero, was a sign that the age of darkness, imposed by the Spaniards, was ending.

Cuauhtemoc's descendent, Dr. Salvador Rodriguez was aging and his life was coming to an end, he could no longer see and was in poor health. Still, he was determined to continue and fulfill Cuauhtémoc's prophecy: "that our Sun would shine again." Therefore, he ordered the revival of "La Ceremonia de Fuego Nuevo," (The New Fire Ceremony).

The New Fire Ceremony was initiated with the Cuauhtémoc Spiritual Pilgrimage that was to end on Cuauhtémoc's birthday on February 23, 1986 in Los Angeles, California.

The director of Mexico City's, Taller Escuela Julian Carrillo, Estrella Newman, leader of the Mexicanidad Movement and Hunbatz Men, a Mayan shaman and traditional leader, were chosen to organize the journey that would bring the "Sacred Fire" (The Lighted Torch) from the tomb of Cuauhtémoc back to Aztlán, on the Colorado River.

Dr. Rodriguez gave his final blessing to the participants of the Cuauhtémoc Spiritual Pilgrimage. In Ixcateopan, Guerrero, he lit the eternal torch on December 7, 1985, at the end of the New Fire Ceremony, the Sacred Fire, which was due arrive in Los Angeles on Cuauhtémoc's birthday, February 23.

The pilgrimage was composed of native traditionalists, and people of various religions and faiths. Among them was a Buddhist monk from Japan who was inspired by the similarity between his beliefs and those of the Nahua.

After the participants left Ixcateopan they arrived in El Zocalo in Mexico City, where they were greeted by thousands of school children, and a large group of danzantes, as well as the president of the Universidad Nacional Autonoma de Mexico, Dr. Jorge Carpizo, who gave them the official welcome. Together they participated in "La Ceremonia Del Fuego Nuevo." The participants then continued on to the Teocalli Del Sol in Teotihuacan, where the ancient rites were performed in their honor on top of the Teocalli del Sol. (Pyramid of the Sun)

Chief Victor 'Sky Eagle' Lopez, of the Chumash, is pictured standing outside of Joaquin Murrieta's house in Santa Barbara, California, February 23, 1986. There was a major concentration of Chumas located near Santa Barbara, and they all supported Murrieta's cause. (Photo credit Amelia Lopez, widow of Sky Eagle)

The historical journey continued north to Cuidad Juarez, Chihuahua. In El Paso, Texas, however, the participants clashed with modern reality. They were unable to cross the border, like their forefathers the Azteca/México had hundreds of years before. They were required to present a visa or post a $1,000 dollar bond to be able to cross the International Border created by the United States in 1848. This was a sad reminder of the changes that had taken place over the past century when indigenous people were free to traverse throughout the continent.

After crossing the artificial border that bifurcates the indigenous blood heritage, the few participants who were able to post bond, took the message of Cuauhtémoc to a number of reservations in the southwest, among them the Hopi, Pueblo, and Navajo. (Hunbatz Men)

Finally they arrived at Parker, Arizona and the elders greeted the participants when they arrived at the Colorado River Indian Tribe Reservation (CRIT). This meeting became more rewarding at the realization that they had reached the ancient land of Aztlán. This joyful

1985 Cuauhtemoc Spiritual Pilgrimage participants on the road from CRIT Reservation to Escuela de La Raza Unida in Blythe, CA. Pictured left to right, Japanese Buddhist Monk, Junji Shimanulo, Felipe Villanueva, Humbatz Men, Alejandro Tarahumara. (Picture from Palo Verde Times, credit Elva Garza)

encounter included the singing of bird songs, stipulating the migration of the natives from Aztlán to the four directions that took place for thousands of years.

The participants of the pilgrimage were bringing to fruition the oral history that speaks of the descendants of Moctezuma and Cuauhtémoc returning to Mexico/Aztlán, their place of origin, where they had lived for centuries. (Gilbert Levias)

Cuauhtémoc's parents were descendants of the Lower Colorado River area. His mother was Chontal, which is a member of the Yuman/Hokan linguistic family and his father was Mexica, member of the Uto-Aztecan, Chemehuevi and Hopi linguistic family.

The next stop of the pilgrimage was La Escuela de la Raza Unida (ERU) in Blythe, California. There at La Escuela a large crowd gathered to welcome the group. Although the group did not know of Dr. Salvador Rodriguez, the reverse was evidently not true because when the participants arrived at ERU, Hunbatz Men said: "We are looking for the people of Aztlán, and we are bringing them greetings from the descendant of Cuauhtémoc." The crowd at ERU was overwhelmed when they realized that their school was known in southern Mexico.

During their short time in Blythe, the pilgrimage participants gave informative lectures about Cuauhtémoc prophecies, explaining the significance of the pilgrimage and the history of the New Fire Ceremony. At the same time the Sacred New Fire rituals were preformed.

Upon leaving to continue the pilgrimage, Hunbatz Men invited ERU students and personnel from Blythe, to join the group at Lincoln Park in Los Angeles, in order to participate in Cuauhtémoc's birthday celebration on February 23, 1986. La Escuela took a large group of students and personnel to participate in the event that took place in Los Angeles. It was a memorable event, where over 500 Mexica danzantes and "matachines" performed danzas and other traditional ceremonies.

During the final celebration of the pilgrimage at Lincoln Park, Chief Manuel Rocha, (now deceased) of the Gabrilenos of Los Angeles and Chief Victor "Sky Eagle" Lopez (now deceased) of the Chumash addressed the audience. Chief Lopez told the crowd: "Cuauhtémoc, to the indigenous people, represented George Washington and Abraham Lincoln all rolled into one." The Los Angeles celebration, permeated in spirit, pride and joy the centuries-old quest to return to Aztlán was completed.

Cortes may have killed Cuauhtémoc in 1525, but his spirit will continue to live forever in the minds and spirits of the Xicano/Indigenous people.

Chapter 6.5
From the Cradle of Aztlán To the Tomb Cuauhtémoc

After the Cuauhtémoc Spiritual Pilgrimage event in Los Angeles, California, Hunbatz Men and Felipe Villanueva came to visit the Blythe Giant Intaglios and other Sacred Sites in Palo Verde/Parker Valleys.

Many blessings resulted from the 1985 Cuauhtémoc Spiritual Pilgrimage besides returning the Sacred Fire to Aztlán. Ties were established with the descendants of Cuauhtémoc in Ixcateopan, Guerrero. After the Pilgrimage, correspondence was received from Dr. Salvador Rodriguez Juarez, who invited the group from Blythe to visit Ixcateopan and the tomb of Cuauhtémoc.

Four years later, a delegation from Blythe, took a trip to Mexico City. They were able to visit Dr. Rodriguez in Ixcateopan, Guerrero on December 7, 1990. They presented him with gifts and greetings from the Colorado River Indian Tribes Reservation.

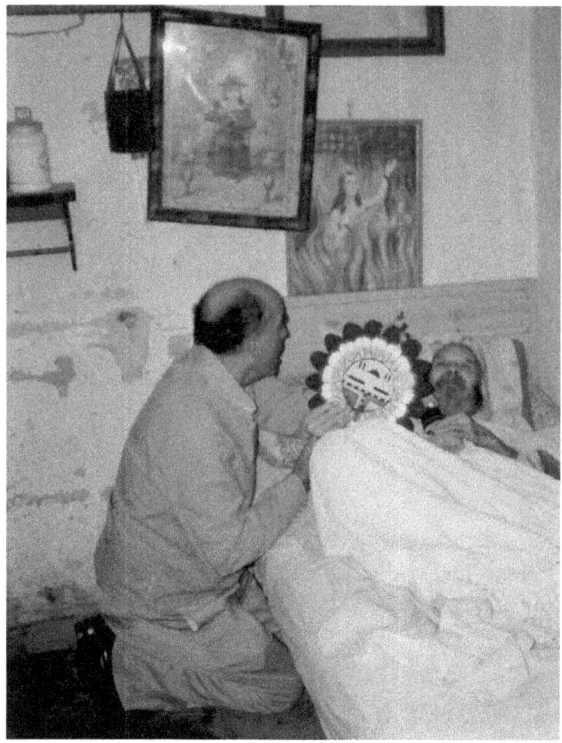

Alfredo Figueroa with Dr. Salvador Rodríguez in his death bed, December 9, 1990. Alfredo finally met Dr. Rodríguez in Ixcateopan, linking the historical lineage of the Colorado River nations from the Colorado River to the Tomb of Cuauhtemoc. (Photo credit Martín Martínez)

The following is a personal account by Alfredo A. Figueroa, the author, of his visit to Mexico City. Upon arriving in Mexico City, the author contacted his colleague, Estrella Newman, and she sent Felipe Villanueva and Professor Ricardo Lopez Alvarado to meet with them at the hotel. The following day was indeed a memorable and exciting experience because the author and his wife had never been in Mexico City. As a result, the delegation was able to tour the Zocalo, the INAH (Instituto Nacional de Anthropologia Historia) and other historical sites that had been one of their long desired dreams.

On December 9, together with Ricardo Lopez Alvarado and Felipe Villanueva who served as guides, the delegation went to Ixcateopan, Guerrero to meet with Dr. Rodriguez. That morning they took a bus from Mexico City to Tasco and from there they were going to be transferred to a shuttle van that would take them to Ixcateopan, (a 26 mile drive through the mountains). As it turned out the shuttle van was not in service. Fortunately, Professor Alvarado decided to speak with the Mayor of Tasco for assistance. However, the Mayor was not there because he had been kidnapped weeks earlier. Taking the mayor's place was the vice-mayor who was a very proud Zapoteca. He greeted the delegation warmly and they were able to sit with him and explain the motive of their trip. The vice-mayor was amazed that they had traveled more than 2,000 miles from Aztlán on the Colorado River to visit Dr. Rodriguez and the tomb of Cuauhtémoc.

Fortunately, the vice-mayor agreed to provide transportation for the group to travel to Ixcateopan the following day. This rewarding meeting and interview were well documented as the vice mayor was very knowledgeable of the Mexica and Zapoteca history and of their origin in Aztlán. In addition, he knew about the significance of the revealing of the Tomb of Cuauhtémoc and we documented the meeting and interview.

As it turned out, it was very gratifying because the delegation was able to tour and spend the night in Tasco, the silver capital of the world. The following morning, true to his word, the vice-mayor had a police pick-up truck waiting for them in front of the hotel with a driver and an armed policeman to accompany us.

The trip to Ixcateopan was breathtaking. The scenery and the majestic mountains provided the group with an overwhelming view of green luscious landscape. A beautiful cascade caressed this semi-jungle environment with an abundance of poinsettias "noche buenas" blanketing the sides of the mountains. At one point the group stopped at a vista point on the side of the road to get a view of Tasco that was not far, even though they had been on the road for an hour. There, they were able to get a view of Igualla, Guerrero and the surrounding valleys. After sightseeing they came upon two ladies that had

been gathering "aguardiente" from the agave plant. They offered to buy some aguardiente to taste it because it was the first time that they had the opportunity to see it being gathered in the mountain sides.

As they continued on the road, the church steeple of Ixcateopan came into view. They arrived just before sundown and were thrilled to be there at this time because the name Cuauhtémoc means "Eagle that Descends" (Sun Descending). At the entrance to the town, they stopped to admire the 40-foot statue of Cuauhtémoc which stands on top of a small marble pyramid greeting at those who arrive to Ixcateopan.

They were taken directly to the only motel in town, and Ricardo immediately went to look for Jario Rodriguez del Olmo, son of Dr. Rodriguez. Ricardo returned with bad news and said that Dr. Rodriguez had been bedridden for over three years, and was blind, hard-of-hearing and very sick. Fortunately for them, Jario was available to meet with them down the street. The group met with him and told him what their mission in Ixcateopan was and the author showed him the letter of invitation sent to him by Dr. Rodriguez.

Jario did not give them any guarantee but he said that he would go and talk to his father. A few minutes later he came back and told us that it was okay to visit his father but not for long because of his deteriorating health.

Upon arriving at his house, Jario told his father that the people whom he had invited to come were there and that they had a delegation from Aztlán in the Colorado River. There the group entered a small room, where, in the corner of this old adobe house, in a small wooden cot, laid Dr. Salvador Rodriguez Juarez, a great legend and the 12th descendant of Cuauhtémoc.

Dr. Rodriguez called out to Jario, "?Aqui estan?" (Are they here?), and Jario responded "Si." (Yes), and then he said "Dile que venga aca." (Tell him to come here). The author immediately kneeled by his side to hold his hand and present him with the gifts that had been sent from the Colorado River Indian Tribe (CRIT) and Vice-Chairman Mona Polacca and then began telling him the story about how they had came from Aztlán and of their connection to Cuauhtémoc and his name on the Colorado River.

Sadly, Dr. Rodriguez could not hear and the author's voice started breaking up because of the emotional event. They did not have much of an interchangeable conversation until he told Dr. Rodriguez, in a loud tone, "Dame un mensaje para llevarselos a la gente del Rio Colorado." (Give me a message, so that I can take it back to the people of the Colorado River).

Dr. Rodriguez responded, "Quiero agradecerles por todos sus esfuerzos por venir desde tan lejos y que reciban todas mis bendiciones." (I want to thank all of you for all your efforts and for coming from so far away, you receive my blessings).

The meeting with Dr. Rodriguez was one of the most spiritual and emotional encounters that the author had ever experienced in his life. Here they were in the presence of this great man, this legend, whose family had kept secret, for 420 years, the location of the tomb of Cuauhtémoc. This historical revelation opened the door to the splendors of unknown history to the world. This event brought forth the Birth of the New Knowledge and was instrumental in the movement of regaining our Xicano roots which flourished during modern day Xicano Movement.

Most of our delegation together with Jario, had tears in their eyes because this was indeed one of there most emotional experiences that they had also encountered. Jario told us that we had come so far just to visit and learn from his father while people from the surrounding communities did not appreciate his father's great knowledge.

The visit to Ixcateopan gave the delegation the opportunity to form a friendship with the direct descendants of Cuauhtémoc which had great personal significance. It also served as affirma-

tion of what we knew was the truth about the Mexica Migrations from Mexico/Aztlán on the Colorado River to the founding of Mexico/Tenochtitlan, present day Mexico City.

While in Ixcateopan, the delegation also received a special tour from Jario, who took them to the Tomb of Cuauhtémoc and the museum. In the museum he showed them the "olla" (burial urn) where the burnt bones of Cuauhtémoc were placed inside and had an upside down 3-legged "molcajete" placed on top of the olla before it was buried.

Jario del Olmo also explained that the upside down molcajete was placed on top of the olla so that their spirits would go to their resting place, the mountains with the three-peaks. When Jario was talking about this it further confirmed the ritual of placing the upside down molcajete on the burial urn. Throughout our research in following the migration trails through the state of Sonora, Mexico, there had been many findings of burial urns with molcajetes placed upside down on top of them. However, the author had never heard of this practice taking place this far south. After ten days in Mexico City, visiting Teotihuacan, the Instituto de Anthropologia Museum, etc., the delegation returned home really energized as they knew that the trip was a like a dream come true. Six months after this historical encounter with Dr. Rodriguez, the author received the sad news of his passing. On Sunday, July 7, 1991, Dr. Salvador Rodriguez Juarez died. Jairo, Dr. Rodriguez' son, called the author at 4:30 am that same day and told him that his father had just passed away two hours ago. The author and his family were the first people outside of his immediate family to be notified. The author immediately notified Estrella Newman in Mexico City and she called the press and other friends in Mexico.

Dr. Rodriguez was buried the following day as is customary in the Mexica culture. His son, Jairo assured that all of the people close to his father were notified of his passing and he was buried in the presence of many friends and admirers that came from Mexico City and the surrounding areas.

Before Dr. Rodriguez died he had expressed a desire to die during the total sun eclipse that he knew was forth coming. The oral history of Cuauhtémoc stated that he was born during a total eclipse. Dr. Rodriguez died on July 7, 1991 and the total Sun eclipse occurred on July 11, 1991, passing directly over Ixcateopan, Guerrero.

Dr. Rodriguez devoted his life to his family and to the Spirit of Cuauhtémoc and waited for the right time to reveal the truth of the location of the tomb of Cuauhtémoc. The dedication of his life without a doubt was one of the most significant happenings that contributed to the fulfillment of the prophecy of Cuauhtémoc.

On August 6, 1991, Dr. Rodriguez was honored and given a respectful place in the world history during his birthday festivities. The festivities were a memorable event in Ixcateopan with people coming from all over Mexico to pay homage and respect to this simple humble man, who was true to his convictions. He brought to Mexico the Birth of the New Knowledge, and was a true Tlatoani, a servant of his people.

His son, Jario, is now in charge of the converted museum where the remains of Cuauhtémoc and other artifacts are housed. Jario Rodriguez del Olmo is now the 13th direct descendent of the Cuauhtémoc's dynasty! Is this "fate or consequential?"

The author and his wife were very grateful to have been invited by Dr. Rodriguez to visit Ixcateopan. The fact that they were able to talk to him before he passed away proved to be one of the most memorable and spiritual encounters that they have ever had in all their involvement in social justice causes. This experience was forth coming in the New Sun shining again. This encounter fulfilled the long sought connection, "From the Cradle of Aztlán to the Tomb of Cuauhtémoc." "Desde la Cuna de Aztlán hasta la Tumba de Cuauhtémoc!"

Chapter 7

Peace and Dignity Journey of 1992

In 1990, as the Christopher Columbus Day Quince-centennial festivities were rapidly approaching, the Indigenous Alliance of the Americas of 500 Years of Resistance organized an event to counter/protest these upcoming festivities. The Indigenous Alliance of the Americas of 500 Years of Resistance met in Quito, Ecuador on July 20, 1990. They met with over 120 international indigenous nations and fraternal organizations from all over the continent and issued the Declaration of Quito.

The main purpose of this declaration was to demonstrate emphatic rejection of the forthcoming Columbus Continental Quince -Centennial celebration. The declaration read: "We shall utilize that date as an occasion to strengthen our process of continental unity and struggle towards our liberation, and to affirm our decision to defend our education, culture and traditions. It is as fundamental to our identity as people, reclaiming and maintaining our own spiritual and community life."

The main priority of the Alliance was to counter the Quince-Centennial festivities with an event that would also take place all over the continent. It was decided that it was necessary to create an event that would give indigenous people the opportunity to honor and recognize their struggle and survival throughout the last five-centuries of the dark ages. This event was called "The Peace and Dignity Journeys of 1992."

This continental spiritual journey put into action the ancient prophecy of our ancestors who poetically envisioned the unification of the Eagle from the north and the Condor from the south. This was a continental feat that would unite the indigenous people. The theme of the event was:

"One People, One Continent"
"Una Raza, Un Continente"

Indigenous people have been taught that running is a vital part of their life, connecting with Mother Earth and helping them communicate with the cosmos. The connection humans make with Mother Earth as they run in Nahuatl is called "Tepecyolotl" (The Heart beat of Mother Earth). This is similar to a beat of a drum. As their feet elevate they are making contact with the cosmos and when their feet hit the ground they make a connection with Mother Earth. Thus, this repeated cycle is reinforcing the unity of spiritual running, symbolizing a harmonious equilibrium among all people, Mother Earth and the cosmos.

The Peace and Dignity Journey Run rekindled the runners with the old Confederation of Anahuac which extended from the Rocky Mountains in Montana in the north, down to Nicaragua in the south.

Under the direction of Chief Gary Harrison, of the Alaska's Athapaskan Nation, on May 2, 1992, indigenous runners left simultaneously from Tok, Alaska in the north and from Argentina in the south. After a 6 month journey, the runners met in the sacred city of Teotihuacan, Mexico on October 12, 1992. This date coincided with the so-called 500 year anniversary of what the United States and European governments referred to as the "The discovery of America by Columbus."

The Peace and Dignity Journey was organized in order to heal and reconnect all nations across the borders. Taking place throughout the continent,

north, central, south, this journey was to embrace all nations and strive for a peaceful coexistence with everyone in the entire world.

When the Peace and Dignity Journey runners came down the Pacific Coast route, and entered California, they went down the coast through San Francisco, Los Angeles, and San Diego. A tributary route passed through San Bernardino, California following Interstate-10, passing through Blythe, California and meeting with the main route again in Phoenix, Arizona.

When the ERU Support Committee first heard that one of the Peace and Dignity stops would be in Blythe, and would take place on August 13, they became very excited. As stated before, this day is the most sacred day of the year. In one of the 20-day calendars of Aztec Sun Stone Solar Calendar, August 13th is the thirteenth day of the thirteenth month in the eighteenth month calendar. The 13th month is called Teotleco, meaning the "Coming of the Energies, the Great Spirit."

The Peace and Dignity run left Nuñez Park in San Bernardino, California, on August 8, 1992 after receiving special blessings from their Indigenous Elders. The runners then passed though the Soboba, Santa Rosa, Morongo, Cahuilla, and Torres Martinez Reservations. The Blythe representatives, including the Colorado River Tribes, were the organizers of the Peace and Dignity Run from Desert Center, California to Quartzite, Arizona.

On August 12, 1992, the runners arrived in Desert Center where they were welcomed by members of the five Colorado River Reservations. Environmental activists, Donna and Larry Charpied of the "Stop the Eagle Mountain Dump Organization," were the hosts of the event.

During the afternoon the participants were able to enjoy the many festivities and spiritual encounters. The evening became a rewarding event for those in attendance. There were native dances and singing as well as lectures and native story telling concerning the sacredness of Eagle Mountain and the Chuckwalla Mountains.

The runners left the following morning on August 13, at sunrise after receiving blessings from the Elders. There was a concern because August 13 is one of the hottest days of the year, and no one knew if the runners would be able to run the 48-mile journey to Blythe in 110 degree heat. As a precaution, the Blythe Ambulance followed them throughout the route.

However, around 8:00 am, a heavy overcast appeared and lingered throughout the day making it pleasant for the runners to continue onto Blythe. In fact some of the runners ran all the way without relaying with others. At that point, they knew that the creator, Ometéotl, was looking over them and had given them a special blessing. Today, they know, Desert Center is one of the most Sacred Sites as recorded in the Azteca Sun Stone Calendar.

Once the runners arrived in Blythe, there was a large crowd of people awaiting their arrival at Todd Park. Representatives from all the reservations and City Mayor Tom Farrage, were there to welcome and honor them with a City of Blythe Resolution, which proclaimed August 13, 1992 as "Peace and Dignity Journey Day," in Blythe, California.

During that evening, there were many native groups performed bird songs and for the first time the bird songs and their meanings were interpreted to the public by the singers. This was indeed a very memorable day for all, especially for La Escuela de la Raza Unida Support Committee because they did not have any input in the scheduled date of the event nor had they participated in the planning of the night-stops of the Tributary Run. The Run coincided without deliberate planning with this historical day, August 13th. As previously stated, this was the date Cuauhtémoc was captured in 1521, which is the most sacred day of the year for the indigenous people.

The runner's route that passed through Blythe reenacted the hundreds of indigenous migrations that had come and gone, for thousands of years, to and from the Colorado River, including the last Mexica Migration that took place in 1160 AD (as shown in the Boturini Codex). As the Mexica before them, they left the Colorado River, and took their knowledge of the Creation Story all the way to Mexico/ Tenochtitlan.

Mohave Spiritual runner and CRIT Reservation coordinator, Ron Van Fleet, had planned to run from Desert Center, California to Phoenix, Arizona, a total of 205 miles. However, Ron became so emotionally involved in the spiritual aspect of the journey that he totally committed himself to participate in the run to its entirety. He continued all the way down to the final destination in Teotihuacan, arriving two months later. Soon after, Van Fleet became one of the main spiritual leaders, always there to assist Gustavo Gutierrez during the many stops of the journey.

assembled in front of the Quetzalcoatl Teocalli. The main sacred staffs of the eagle and the condor carried by the runners were placed at the north and south end of the makeshift bow with the rest of the community staffs, creating an outline of the half moon. The staffs from the north were adorned with eagle feathers, while the south staff was adorn with condor feathers. This was an amazing and historical event.

1992 Peace and Dignity Journey Runners being received by the Mayor of Quartzite, first stop from Blythe, CA. Left to right, Gustavo Gutierrez, Mayor Richard Odham, Ron Van Fleet.

1992 Peace and Dignity Journey, Colorado River Organizing Committee in Desert Center, CA, July 27, 1992. Pictured left to right Alfredo A. Figueroa, Donna Charpied, Ron Von Fleet and David Reyes. (Photo credit Gustavo Gutierrez)

Once the runners and participants arrived in Mexico City, on October 11, 1992, they went to the sacred city of Teotihuacan (place of the energies) where the Pyramid of the Sun, Moon and Quetzalcoatl are located. The participants then

The Sacred Fire was lit in the middle of the circle formed by all the participants that came from all over the United States, Mexico and South America. Wallace Black Elk, a Sioux Traditional Leader, led this historical and spiritual ceremony. All those present received the traditional cleansing and blessings by this Sioux leader as well as by other traditional leaders of the different indigenous nations from Mexico.

The following day the Sacred Bundles were formed. These bundles contained animal relics, (bird feathers, claws, bones etc.) which had been given to the runners by the Elders along the route so that they could take them to Teotihuacan. All staffs and other sacred objects were put together in bundles to later take them to Ixca-

teopan, Guerrero. Afterwards they would be taken to the different indigenous gatherings as a symbol of remembrance of this historical day. This was in remembrance of how our Knowledge Keepers brought with them their Bundles of Knowledge to the Valley of Anahuac from the Colorado River.

A spirit of brotherhood prevailed throughout the two-days in Teotihuacán. Augmenting to the fervor was the singing of the Bird Songs by 22 Cocopah Traditional Bird Singers lead by Tribal Chairman Dale Phillips. The Bird Songs were sung in the ancient language which makes reference to the Nahua and the rest of the native nations' migrations to and from the Colorado River. This was one of the most inspirational highlights of the entire event. It was memorable and breathtaking to see the Cocopah nation, the Guardians of the Colorado River Delta paying homage to the ancient Nahua people and singing in front of the teocalli of Quetzalcoatl.

Upon the completion of the run at Teotihuacan on October 12, 1992, the participants went to Ixcateopan to pay homage to Cuauhtémoc. There they were welcomed by the Mayor of Ixcateopan and by Jairo Rodriguez del Olmo (the 13th Descendent of the Cuauhtémoc Dynasty).

The Peace and Dignity participants led by Ron Van Fleet, the author, and the delegation of Mexico City, had the privilege to visit the tomb of Cuauhtémoc in Ixcateopan, Guerrero. They all came to pay their respects and to rekindle the fact that a new cycle had begun, and that the 500-year-old struggle would continue.

On December of the same year, the organizers of the Committee to Stop the Construction of the Proposed Ward Valley Nuclear Toxic Dump (near Needles, California) traveled to Mexico to get the support of the government in order to stop the proposed dump. The group included Chemehuevi Chairman Matthew Leivas, who was accompanied by Mojave Council Member Steve Lopez, Environmentalist Jane Williams, and the author. Together, they revisited Ixca-

teopan in order to reaffirm the historical cultural linkage between the Lower Colorado River Valley Nations and the Dynasty of Cuauhtémoc in Ixcateopan. This further solidified the connection between Blythe, California and Ixcateopan, Guerrero which were formally established as sister cities in 1993.

Chapter 7.2
The Second Peace and Dignity Journey 1996

When the Peace and Dignity Journey of 1992 was over and all the participants had gone home, they analyzed the huge success accomplished by the PDJ. This was the first time in modern history that thousands of participants collaborated together up and down the continent unifying the spiritual awakening of "One People, One Continent Movement."

The Peace and Dignity Journey, (PDJ) was a colossal event and quite an achievement for all the participants and runners. This journey took them all on a 6-month, 10,000 mile run throughout the continents. Although the run began with very little money, it gained momentum and was a huge success. The Peace and Dignity Journey was supported mostly by donations from the participants and by individuals, as well as by sponsors who provided contributions for lodging, food, and gas. These contributions were received as the runners passed through the different reservations and communities.

After the excitement of the 1992 Peace and Dignity Journey had settled down, a group of activists got together in Phoenix, Arizona, under the leadership of Gustavo Gutierrez and decided to continue the continental event every four years and began planning for the next run in 1996. This time the theme of the run was to continue organizing the different indigenous groups and organizations as well as to venerate our elders, the guardians of our Indigenous traditions and to honor and teach our children the tradi-

1996 Peace and Dignity Journey organizer Gustavo Gutierrez and runners, including Richard Windchell, Richard Yassi, Jesus Figueroa, and Hector Santiago in front of Alfredo A. Figueroa's house in Blythe, CA.(Photo credit Alfredo A. Figueroa)

tional way.

On April, 1996, Gustavo Gutierrez and two other participants from Phoenix, Arizona, stopped in Blythe on their way up to Alaska to organize the route. In Blythe, Jesus Roman Figueroa, son of the author, joined Gustavo and continued contacting people all the way up to Alaska.

Once again the Peace and Dignity Journey began on May 1, 1996 in Chickaloon, Alaska, with Chief Gary Harrison of the Athapaskan Nation as host. In "Tehuantinsullo" (South America) the run began simultaneously in the town of Villa, Argentina, with Francisco Melo at the helm, Margarito Ruiz coordinating the Central America section and Alfonso Perez Espiñdola coordinating in southern Mexico.

The run began on May 1, 1996 and Jesus Figueroa thought that he was just going to assist Gutierrez and drive the van that followed the runners. However, to his surprise Gutierrez told him to get out of the van and join the run.

Once again the runners arrived in Blythe on August 13. The Mojave runners from Needles, under the guidance of Steve Lopez and Victor Van Fleet arrived there as well. From the south in Yuma, Arizona, came Phil Emerson and his Quechan group. During the time of the Journey, we were at the height of the struggle against the purposed Ward Valley Nuclear Toxic Dump site, near Needles, California. The organizer of Green Peace, Bradley Angel and a group of environmentalist joined us by bringing a bus. Together, we all went down to Yuma to meet with the tributary runners from Baja California that had passed through the indigenous communities. Then Phil and Chris Emerson lead the group from Yuma to Phoenix, and all the way to Mexico City.

When the runners left Blythe, a staff with the image of a heron on top was entrusted to Jesus for him to present to the Cuauhtémoc Dynasty and was to be placed among the offerings at Cuauhtémoc's tomb. The heron is the image that represents Aztlán, "Land of the Herons," "Lugar de las Garzas."

The 1996 route was re-routed in order for the runners to pass through Ixcateopan before going to Mexico City to meet with the southern route.

By this time, Jesus, the Blythe native, had become an inspiration to the runners by singing the different songs and native chants that he learned throughout the route, and from stopping at the different reservations along the way.

The runners and their supporters traveled to Ixcateopan. Upon their arrival, the interim mayor and Jairo Rodriguez del Olmo, Cuauhtémoc's descendent, greeted them at the site of the 40 foot statue of Cuauhtémoc, located at the entrance of the town. The mayor then escorted the runners to four historically significant sites including Dr. Salvador Rodriguez Juarez' house and his tomb; the ruins of the house where Cuauhtémoc was born and the Altar of the Nation that contained Cuauhtémoc's remains.

At each stop, the historical background of the location was explained and group members sang traditional chants and blessed the site. At the final stop, the Altar of the Nation, the mayor, placed the La Cuna de Aztlán staff among the offerings that adorn the tomb of Cuauhtémoc,

October, 1996, Peace and Dignity Journey Runner Jesus 'Chuy' Figueroa, presenting the Mayor of Ixcateopan, Guerrero with the heron (symbol of Aztlan) staff representing La Cuna de Aztlan, after running from Chickaloon, Alaska to Teotihuacan, Mexico. (Photo credit Alfredo A. Figueroa)

together with a plaque that has the following inscription:

"Peace and Dignity Journey, 1996: La Cuna de Aztlán, Blythe, California - Tomb of Cuauhtémoc, Ixcateopan, Guerrero." "This Journey embraces our reencounter with our roots from the Cradle of Aztlán to the Tomb of Cuauhtémoc, following the ancient migration of the Nahua, and in honor of the last Tlatoani (Spokesperson), absolute symbol of the 500 years of resistance of the occupation of Anahuac. Ixcateopan, Guerrero, the Cradle of Mexicanidad, Altar of the Nation. Also, in honor of all the participants that started this journey in Chickaloon, Alaska, on May 1, 1996, and simultaneously in southern Argentina, culminating in the sacred city of Teotihuacan, on October 12, 1996."

The Peace and Dignity Journey participants brought the message of peace and dignity to all the Indigenous communities and other groups that seek their roots. They also promoted unity among the continents by unifying the eagle from the north and the condor from the south. This encounter was celebrated on October 6, 1996, at Ixcateopan, Guerrero, at that time it had already become the sister city of Blythe, California.

The Peace and Dignity Journeys were life-changing events for many of the runners and others who participated because they helped re-connect today's indigenous communities with their forefathers. On October 9, 1996, just before the completion of the second Peace and Dignity Journey, at El Cerro Estrella, in the Valley of Anahuac, the Journey runners participated in another historic ritual, which was the rebirth of the ancient New Fire Ceremony.

That afternoon the City Fathers of Iztapalapa came to the Civic Auditorium where the runners were lodging and where they had an official welcoming to the city as guest of honors for having organized this historical and unique event that was the first of its kind in modern history. After the function they were taken in police cars and escorted to the top of El Cerro Estrella where they witnessed one of the most spectacular sacred ceremonies they had ever experienced. There was loud chanting of hundreds of participants, drum beating, "concha" reverberation, with the climax of the event being the reenactment of the sacred 52-year New Fire Ceremony.

At the top of El Cerro Estrella, the Elders lit four bundles each containing 52 sticks similar to what is seen in the glyph of the Borbonico Codex. As they gazed all around El Cerro Estrella they could see the lights of one of the largest metropolitans in the world. They all transported themselves mentally and recon-

nected with the last New Fire ceremony celebrated in Mexico/Tenochtitlan in 1483, before the European conquest. This is especially important since the sacred ceremony was prohibited in 1535, after the invasion.

This exciting and dramatic event included runners from different communities carrying a torch and running down the trail from El Cerro Estrella. They took the torch to their different communities and most importantly to El Zocalo at La Plaza Mayor.

After relay running for 6,000 miles the following runners all ran the full distance. They were Jesus Figueroa, Richard Yassi, Ruben "Mo" Gonzales, Gustavo Gutierrez, Antonio Chavez, Hector Santiago, and Rick Windchell. These runners started on May 1, 1996 in Chickaloon, Alaska and six-months later arrived at El Zocalo in the heart of Mexico City, on October 12, 1996, ending the Second Peace and Dignity Journey.

Chapter 7.3
Blythe, California & Ixcateopan, Guerrero: Sister Cities and the 500th birthday of Cuauhtemoc

The Cuauhtémoc Spiritual Pilgrimage of February 1986 brought Blythe, California and Ixcateopan, Guerrero together for the first time. The second time that these two cities connected was on December 9, 1990, when a delegation from Blythe was invited to visit Dr. Salvador Rodriguez. This relationship was strengthened with the 1992 Peace & Dignity Journey.
The two cities maintained constant communication, and formed strong ties and a bond throughout the history of both cities. There was a strong spiritual calling because of Cuauhtémoc's lineage in the Colorado River.

Finally in 1993, the two cities officially became sister cities when the Blythe City Council accepted Ixcateopan, Guerrero's approval, that was also officiated by the Mexican Consulate of San Bernardino, California.

During the 500 year anniversary of the birthday of Cuauhtémoc, the city of Ixcateopan invited us as guest of honor. Among those attending and accompanying the author to these festivities of February 23, 1997 were Ralph Caldera, Hector Cerda, Marcos Aguilar, Jesus Figueroa.

From February 21 to February 23, dozens of native delegations came from the surrounding communities to pay homage to Cuauhtémoc. They were joined by groups from the cities of Santa Rosa, San Jose, Fresno and Los Angeles, California. They also came from Albuquerque, New Mexico, and from all over Mexico and Guatemala.

This was a very exciting and emotional event because the Blythe delegation the guests of honor together with all the elders of Ixcateopan on this historical day.

During the festivities, the Blythe/Ixcateopan Sister City banner hung from the portal of the courtyard of the Altar of the Nation where the remains of Cuauhtémoc lay. Hundreds of danzantes performed continuously inside and out the main plaza. Day and night there thundering drums could be heard from miles away.

One of the highlights of the celebration was the presentation and blessing of the Sacred Peace and Dignity Journeys staffs that had been on tour in Mexico since October 12, 1996. Jesus Figueroa of Blythe presented the Mayor of Ixcateopan and Jario Rodriguez del Olmo with the special staff that represented the eagle from the north. Likewise Moises from Uruguay presented the family of the indigenous nations the staff that represented the condor from the south. Xolotl, from Mexico City, presented the Cuauhtémoc family staff.

A special television program featured the events, as did Radio Bilingual, transmitting throughout the United States and Mexico. These festivities were filled with unity and harmony, and were a huge success. No one wanted to leave because of the spiritual atmosphere that energized all the participants.

Following the anniversary celebration, the city of Tenosique, Tabasco had invited the city officials of Ixcateopan to join them in their annual celebration in commemoration of Cuauhtémoc. Marcos Aguilar from the Blythe delegation and some of the danzantes journeyed southeast to the city, of Tenosique to participate in the celebration.

At the base of the Giant Statue of Cuauhtémoc, in Tenosique, Marcos Aguilar placed the Blythe/Ixcateopan Sister City Banner. This banner highlighted the historical linkage of the trinity that was formed with La Cuna de Aztlán, Place of Cuauhtémoc's ancestors; Ixcateopan, Guerrero "place of his birth;" and Tenosique, Tabasco, "place where he was killed."

During this time, an idea was proposed to establish a cultural center in honor of Dr. Salvador Rodriguez Juarez. The center is to be called Centro Cultural Dr. Salvador Rodriguez.

In the future, a more permanent educational and cultural center will be constructed to recognize the Cradle of La Mexicanidad, "Birth of the New Knowledge." In this center, students from every place in the world will learn the truth about the greatness of their indigenous heritage and of Cuauhtémoc.

In Blythe, California, similar plans have been made to construct a La Cuna de Aztlán Historical Cultural and Educational center built by La Escuela de la Raza Unida in the Palo Verde Valley.

Chapter 8

The Eradication of Our Indigenous Roots; Why We Don't Know Our Indigenous Roots

One of the most heinous crimes committed by European invaders against indigenous people was the destruction of nearly all indigenous culture, beliefs, language and tradition. A destruction of this magnitude had never taken place in the world. This destruction also completely destroyed Mexico/Tenochtitlan. With the annihilation and suppression of the indigenous culture, the European invasion created confusion within the indigenous nations regarding the truth of their origin, their language and their identity.

Christopher Columbus gave birth to this massive confusion and distortion regarding the true identity of the indigenous descendants in the western hemisphere when he "discovered" America. Columbus arrived in the Caribbean islands October 12, 1492. He mistakenly called the natives "Caribe Indians." Columbus thought that he had found the route to India, where its inhabitants were called "Indians." Since then, indigenous people throughout the western hemisphere have been referred to as Indians. Today we know for a fact that Columbus did not discover America and the natives from the Caribbean were not Indians, yet the confusion continues, as indigenous nations are referred to as Indians.

The malicious eradication of indigenous roots was extensive. An example of this eradication was documented in the confession of Fray Juan Zumarraga, the first Bishop of Mexico. In his writings, he boldly states with pride that he was personally involved in the destruction of over fifteen thousand codexes from the library of Texcoco. These codexes contained the Huehuetlatotli, the ancient sacred stories of the Nahua Creation story based in Texcoco. (Westheim, 1965)

Fortunately, here in the Lower Colorado River Basin, we still have our sacred intaglios, petroglyphs, pictographs, sacred mountain images that tell the creation story of our human existence here on earth and our connection with the cosmos. These sacred sites were not destroyed by the Spanish invaders because the Spanish never saw the connection of the geographical surroundings of the southwest with the indigenous nations residing in the area. The Spanish influence in this area consisted of their search for precious treasures and temples such as those they had seen in Mexico/Tenochtitlan. The lack of these similar structures disinterested them. However, today, we are in the verge of losing our ancient sacred sites forever, due to the massive destruction taking place in the southwestern deserts by mega-solar power projects. Unfortunately, the general public who support these projects lack the knowledge to appreciate these ancient footprints left on earth by our ancestors.

After intense studies conducted within the area, and after years of research, many facts and revelations about this great civilization are slowly surfacing. This ancient civilization has now began to speak through the sacred drawings on the mesas, canyon walls, and rocks, which are fulfilling what the ancient prophecies stated: "The time will come to tell the truth, when the monolithic petroglyphs rise by themselves, our sun will shine again and speak about the greatness of our traditions."

The Spanish imposed a sixteen level caste system on the natives of Mexico. (This painting by an anonymous painter is oil on canvas from the 18th Century, in the Los Angeles County Museum 1980 exhibit. Rights reserved, M. Knoedler and Co. Inc., New York.

The Europeans set out to suppress and reshape the culture of the conquered people by forcing them to assimilate to their own ideals, customs, culture, religions and language in order to maintain their dominance.

The indigenous traditions were deliberately reinterpreted and their beliefs were denigrated. For example, at the fall of Tenochtitlan, revisionist historians began to change the image of Huitzilopochtli. His image was changed from that of a positive energy of the Mexica tradition, the origin of all good, to the god of war, the devil, who demanded human sacrifices. This complete distortion of the Mexica tradition was even more appalling since traditional indigenous people did not have any gods or devils within their culture. Indigenous nations believe that the cosmos and the creator are related to every living thing on earth: all humans, animals and plants. This belief is in total contrast to European religion and belief. Europeans forcibly imposed their religious beliefs on indigenous people. They also deliberately misinterpreted the Mexica cultural beliefs as they replaced Mexica energies with gods and devils as a way to annihilate them from their cultural roots, traditions, and belief systems. It was this type of destruction that enslaved and oppressed indigenous people for hundreds of years as they were forced to denounce their traditions and beliefs. To this day, indigenous people continue to be oppressed and persecuted throughout the world by dominant European governments.
After the conquest of Mexico/Tenochtitlan and Spanish rule was secured, the Spaniards changed the name of Anahuac to New Spain. The Hispanicized indigenous writers and artists who created the Post-Cuauhtémoc Nahua codex were coerced to falsify the story of their culture of their own people by the religious zealots.

One of the most damaging and falsified myths of the history of the Mexica, has been the lies about human sacrifices and indigenous offerings to the gods. According to most European chroniclers, sacrifices were a common practice throughout Anahuac. This malicious lie was based on testimony told by one Spaniard. To this day, the atrocity of this lie prevails among historians and scholars who have written about Mexica history. This lie has been a huge obstacle in promoting the truth about indigenous culture. (Romero Vargas, 1981)

Dr. Ignacio Romero Vargas Yturbide, professor at the University of Michoacán in Morelia was one of Mexico's most renowned historians of the Nahua Culture. He said that the historians of the Mexica culture were just "repeaters of the lies" (repetidores de mentiras) that had been written in the post-Cuauhtémoc era after the conquest. Dr. Romero Vargas also stated in his writings, that: "Europeans were low class humans, who did not have any respect for life, culture, laws or private property." It is up to indigenous historians to rewrite the truth of their own history.

Even though Europe had suffered thousands of years of war, never in the world had any civilization or cities been destroyed to the extent that Anahuac had been destroyed by the European invaders. What was not destroyed by the sword was destroyed by the lies that Frays wrote. The three tactics that the Europeans used to conquer the indigenous people were: lies, treason and deceitfulness, "mentiras, engaños, y traiciones."(Hunbatz Men, 1990)

The well documented and excellent research of Dr. Peter Hassler of the University of Zurich, Switzerland entitled: "Human, Sacrifice among the Mexica and other Indian Communities: Reality or Fantasy?" is a great example of the blatant lies Europeans conquerors wrote as a means of justifying the massacres they committed against indigenous people. Dr. Hassler researched over 450 books, codices, and anthropological studies, before disclosing the results to his study. His conclusion stated "that there were never any human sacrifices." He also stated that there was "no offering of the human hearts to the Sun" nor was there any form of cannibalism as often portrayed in the Post-Cuauhtémoc codices.

Dr. Hassler makes reference to the book of

Bernal Diaz del Castillo: "Historia Verdadera de la Conquista de la Nueva España." In this book, Castillo states that the Spaniards "witnessed" the human sacrifices and rituals performed by the Mexica to their comrades. Today, research shows that Castillo, a loyal Cortes follower, fictionalized his account to substantiate the atrocities committed against the indigenous people.

According to Dr. Hassler, Castillo was the only eye witness testimony that had ever been recorded in all the books printed during the Spanish Conquest. Castillo states in his book, that it was during the defeat of Cortes by Cuitláhuac on June 30, 1520: "Cortes and his men were resting at what is called "El Arbol de la Noche Triste" and Sandoval and Francisco de Lugo and Andres de Tapia were with Pedro de Alvardo at Tlacopan, he said that they heard loud sounds of "Caracoles" and "Tambores" and saw when the captured Spanish soldiers were led up the stairs of "Ulchllobos" (Huitzilopochtli) temple when they were placed facing up on top of a flat stone and their hearts were cut out with a obsidian knife and offered to their "Malditos Idolos," the Sun. Then their bodies would be thrown down the temple where the people would then chop their arms, legs to be taken and eaten."

Dr. Hassler reports that: "Tlacopan is 6 to 8 kilometers (4 miles) from El Zocalo, where the Twin Temples are located and that it would be impossible for them to have seen any human sacrifice. Furthermore, Bernal Del Castillo was very old when he told his story."

In addition, Hernan Cortes stated in the second letter that he wrote to King Charles V, that: "He was with Montezuma when he forbade them moreover to make human sacrifices to the idols as was their want, because besides being abomination in the sight of God it is prohibited by your majesty's laws which declare that he who kills shall be killed. From time henceforth they departed from it, and during the whole time that I was in the city not a single living soul was known to be killed and sacrificed."

Ironically, Cortes, himself, was responsible for the massacres of millions of indigenous people who refused to conform to the new form of Spanish government and practice their religious rituals. If any one had witnessed "human sacrifices," it would have been Cortes when he ordered the deaths of millions of indigenous people. He would travel extensively throughout Anahuac, conquering and destroying indigenous civilizations. Cortes never saw an indigenous sacrifice another human because it was not part of the indigenous culture to sacrifice humans. Cortes made sure that the natives who were not killed by the sword were killed by the cross. The Spaniards forced them to reject all their traditions, culture and language or be put to death. Therefore, they had no other alternative but to assimilate to Spanish rule and religion.

One of the most infamous priests who vehemently repeated these lies about the indigenous people was Fray Diego Duran, who wrote the "The History of the Indies of New Spain." Fray Duran was the official translator from Nahuatl to Spanish for the notorious Spanish Inquisition orchestrated by the Roman Catholic Church tribunal, for the examination and punishment for heretic. The Inquisition was responsible for hundreds of thousands of deaths of indigenous people.

Fray Duran said that during the rule of Ahuitzotl, "It was found that there where 80,400 men to be sacrificed in the dedication of the great temple of México, Tenochtitlan. Duran said that "Ahuitzotl sat upon the royal throne displaying to all the nations his grandeur and the magnificence of his kingdom and the courage of his people." Unfortunately, these atrocious lies written by Duran are still being repeated and have been accepted as the official version of our indigenous culture beliefs and tradition.

In the recent 2007 film, "Apocalypto" produced by Mel Gibson, thousands of Mayan prisoners are sacrificed one after the other. The prisoners'

hearts are cut out and offered to their gods. This fictitious interpretation was an abomination and extremely demeaning to indigenous people. In today's society, indigenous people respect each other's culture, traditions and customs. They are, as a people, more open-minded and vehemently denounce these absurd lies.

What was even more incredible was that Mel Gibson was also able to recruit hundreds of Mayans and other indigenous people to participate in such a movie that is based on all the lies that have been perpetrated for centuries about indigenous people. There is no doubt that Gibson must have read Duran's book.

For the past 40 years, the resurfacing of the term "Hispanic" has also contributed to the misidentification of indigenous people. This term has been cast as the preferred term when referring to the Spanish surname and Spanish speaking populations of the United States.

The United States government is one of the main culprits of the use of the label Hispanic. Mainstream media has picked up the label, including the Spanish/English media (television, internet, radio, newspapers, etc) reinforcing the usage of the term Hispanic on a regular basis. The term has also been supported wholeheartedly by the emerging majority of the Spanish speaking community in the United States. This is another historical abomination imposed by the European conqueror.

Dr. Rodolfo "Rudy" Acuña, prominent writer/historian makes reference to the term "Hispanic" in his classic book, "Anything but Mexican." Acuña defines this term as "The Pendejo Factor" for those who have been corralled by the manipulation of words and identity. He explains the term "Hispanic" was deliberately imposed politically on the Spanish speaking communities during the Mexican American Political Association (MAPA) endorsing convention held in Pico Rivera, California in 1972. At that time, MAPA was the most influential Xicano political organizations in the United States. During the convention held in Los Angeles/Pico Rivera, the Republican National Committee's "Hispanic" representatives wanted to get MAPA's endorsement to support President Richard Nixon re-election.

Nixon's representatives offered MAPA delegates, a briefcase filled with money in exchange for their support for Nixon. However, the MAPA delegates rejected the outright blatant bribery, which was "la brava." The MAPA delegates instead supported the democratic ticket of Hubert Humphrey for president.

As it turned out the Republican National Committee, was very disappointed by the results. However, they had already recruited a large constituency among Anti-Castro Cuban "gusanos" from Florida and the right winged "Hispanics" from Texas, New York, and Central and South Americans. Therefore, in "one scoop" they lumped together all the Spanish speaking surname people and labeled them Hispanic. As a result, through this gross political manipulation, the RNC was able to lure in the Hispanics and demonstrate to the media that the "Hispanic" community was supporting Richard Nixon's re-election.

Indigenous communities must return to their indigenous roots and over turn these imposed labels that seek to keep them from their true identity. The Mexica fought the Spanish for three-hundred years from 1521-1821, until they were able to over throw the Spaniards and regain their original name "Mexica" and their country "Mexico." These names had been given to them by Mecitli, when the Creator changed their name from Azteca to Mexica. Yet, in one fell swoop, all of a sudden through Nixon's presidential campaign, we all became Hispanics.

Overwhelming obstacles have been put in place to keep the indigenous from taking pride in their culture. For example, during the occupation of Spanish rule in Mexico, a caste system was implemented, and was referred to as a "Castes Society," which had sixteen categories.

The first category is the term "Mestizo," imposed upon the conquered indigenous population, which classifies the child of a Spaniard and an indigenous woman. This is the true Mestizo. The second is "Castizo", which is the child of a "Mestizo" and a Spaniard. These categories continue until the fifteenth which is called "Tente en el Aire" (Stand in Mid-air), which was the child of a "Mulata" with a "No te Entiendo (I Do not Understand you)." Finally, the sixteenth caste was named "No te Entiendo", which was the child of an "India" and "Torna Atras" (Turn Back). Therefore, in what category would the indigenous people be today?

Throughout the 300 years of Spanish rule in Mexico, less than 130,000 Spaniards came to what they called New Spain. According to Manuel Gamio, there were approximately 10-15 million natives in Mexico. As a result, most of the Mexica are indigenous instead of Spanish. It is no wonder that so many indigenous people today, suffer from a disorder referred to as Personal Identity Disorder, or PI, as it is called by the Xicano activist here in the United States and in Mexico by the activist of "El Movimiento de la Mexicanidad."

Along the same lines and ideology which adds still more confusion regarding indigenous identity, is the concept depicted on a mosaic that is on the wall of a building located in the Universidad Nacional Autonoma de Mexico in Mexico, which has the image of 3-heads. One of the heads has the image of the Spanish conquistador. The second head on the opposite side is a Mexica face. The third head in the center is what is called the Mestizo. This 3-headed image is supposed to represent the Mexica that we are today. Unfortunately, this notion has misled the indigenous people to believe they have more Spanish blood than they is really possible. In fact the majority of the people in Mexico and in the southwest United States are indigenous. (See Chapter 9)

The indigenous communities throughout the world must join forces and demand that historical records be corrected and rewrite their own history for the benefit of future generations. Unfortunately, these distortions and lies are still being repeated by "los repetidores de las mentiras" that Romero Vargas quoted.

Still, throughout, the centuries, in spite of the dominance of the European conquerors, pockets of indigenous people and traditional elders in Mexico, know the truth of their origin and have passed their oral history on to their generations. They have persistently clung on to their culture and traditions and have served as the Teomamas (Knowledge Keepers) bundle carriers in bringing forth the truth.

According to Hunbatz Men, the Mayan preserved their culture because the Mayan practiced the process of "huanche" which meant, "to hear but do not listen, to see but do not observe." Therefore, these brave indigenous nations did not allow themselves to become brainwashed by the European religious zealots. For generations, the Mayans have continued to live in their own traditional ways.

A Mexica proverb says:

"They cut off our fruit, broke off our trunks, but they have not been able to destroy our roots."

⦿⦿⦿⦿⦿

Chapter 9

Xicano!

Left to right: Students carrying La Virgen de Guadalupe and the Mexico and United States Flags; Alfredo Ruben Figueroa, Sally Vasquez, Manuel Sanchez, Jose Burrola, Rafaela Bustamante, Salvador Garcia, Raymundo Luna, Lorenzo Romero, Jose Quintero, Carmela Figueroa, Ruperto Garnica, Jorge Guillen, Feliciano 'Chano' Gaytan, Lupe Cisneros. (Photo credit Baldemar Sauceda)

Xicano (Chicano) denominates the person who defends their culture and seeks their indigenous roots. Chicano is derived from the Nahuatl word "chix-zanotl," that was modified to "Xicano" and means "the man of the fertile valley." The "Xix-zanotl" was a segment of the elite of the elders called "Pipiltín", "whose main function was the defense and protection of the culture of the Mexica nation." (Dominguez)

The Xix-zanotls were organized by the tlatoani Netzahualcoyotl and were the personal guards and escorts of Cuauhtémoc until his defeat on August 13, 1521.

The word Xicano is herein written with the letter "X," because "X" represents the merging of cosmic Father and Mother Earth. It also symbolizes the true meaning of those that have lost their culture and are seeking to regain it as shown in the Mexica Codex.

The consonant-blend "ch" has always been the common form of spelling the word "Chicano," which is from the Spanish language. In every Nahuatl word that has the sound of "sh" or "ch" in the beginning, the Spaniards added the "ch" in place of the Nahuatl "x." This again, was another tactic used to take away the true meaning and importance of how to decipher the words such as Xicano, Xicomozstoc and Xapultepec.

After of 300 years of Spanish rule, Xicanos serving under the command of the priest Miguel Hidalgo were distinguished by their patriotic fervor and valor. Their "civil rights movement" sparked the beginning of the struggle of Xicanos to fight against the dominant Spanish yoke.

Finally in 1821, the Xicanos/Mexica defeated the Spaniards and rejected the name "La Nueva España" for their nation and regained their authentic name of Mexica and Mexico. When the United States invaded Mexico in 1846, Xicanos once again rose under the banner of the Netzahualcoyotl Society, and were the major opposition in the signing of the Treaty of Guadalupe Hidalgo on February 2, 1848.

Student picketing Palo Verde Unified public schools in Blythe, CA, 1972, Left to right, Demetrio Pecina, Jose Quintero, Manuel 'Teddy Bear,' Alfredo M. Figueroa, Jr., Ricardo Davila and Gilbert Castro. (Photo credit Palo Verde Times, by Elva Garza.)

During the Mexican Revolution of 1910, Xicanos of the Netzahualcoyotl Society, under the leadership of Carlos Madero, brother of Francisco L. Madero, fought to overthrow the dictatorship of Porfirio Diaz. In addition, the personal guards of Emiliano Zapata, were called "Los Coroneles Xicanos," and together with "Los Dorados de Pancho Villa", were the main forces that defeated

Left: ERU students, late 1970s, front cover of the 'Militant Magazine.' Students, Estella Navarro, Maria "Machi" Figueroa (Rivera), participated in a United Farmworkers demonstration against the Agricultural Labor Relations Board in Riverside, California. Middle: Pictured here is Bert Corona speaking at a conference at the University of California, Riverside. Bert was instrumental in the development of La Escuela de la Raza Unida. Right: Cesar Chavez, speaking at Ruth Brown Elementary auditorium during one of his many trips to Blythe, CA. He provided the union office as a temporary administrative office for ERU.

and ousted Porfirio Diaz. (Dominguez)

During Mexican Revolution, thousands of Mexica immigrated to the southwest United States and most of them entered the state of California. These immigrants brought with them the vernacular manner of speaking and introduced the word "Xicano." In California, the word Xicano was mentioned in many "corridos," and as a result, the word Xicano became popularized. The corridos are the main form of entertainment for the Xicanos because they tell a story. In the 1920s the word Xicano was popularized by Spanish speaking radio programs, that played Xicano music as was the case of Pedro J. Gonzalez of "El Trio Los Madrugadores." (Figueroa)

At the height of the Xicano Movement in the 1960s and '70s, the pride of the Xicano militants was their struggle to regain their indigenous and cultural roots. After years of suffering blatant discrimination at the hands of the Anglos, Xicanos began to challenge the racially biased systems, at the local and national level. Xicanos felt a sense of pride and unity and found a sense of strength in their numbers. In the Journal of Human Relations, Dr. Jack Forbes wrote: "95% of the Mexicans are part Indians, 40% are full blooded, and most of the mixed bloods have more Indian ancestry than non-Indian and are therefore a racial as well as a cultural minority." (Forbes 1994)

A quote from Pfefferkorn, a Jesuit priest, explains the reality of our indigenous heritage. In the 11 years that he was in Sonora, prior to being expelled in 1767, he stated: "There is hardly a true Spaniard in Sonora; there are very few that can trace their origin to a Spanish family of pure blood. Practically all those who wish to be considered Spaniards are people of mixed blood." The reality is all Xicanos on both sides of the border, are indigenous.

Thus, Xicano militants proudly regained their indigenous cultural roots and served as the vanguards in the defense of civil rights. At the same time many of the police, federal, and state agencies were secretly making lists of Xicano militants in order to arrest them without justification because they feared that the militancy would get out hand. (Nava)

Today, Xicanos are cognizant of their indigenous roots similar to their predecessors, "Xix-zanotls," the defenders of Cuauhtémoc. Contrary to common belief, a Mexican-American is not automatically a Xicano because a Xicano is one who

Joaquin Murrieta

fights for their culture and defends their heritage.

During their struggle against the Spaniards, Cuauhtémoc, along with his personal guards Xicanos paraphrased the term "Xicanismo." Cuauhtémoc was the first to defend his culture (which was the treasure) against the Europeans. He encouraged his people to defend their treasure, and their "knowledge." Cuauhtémoc is proclaimed "El Tata" (grandfather) of El Xicanismo because of his first struggles against the European invaders in 1521.

Spain ruled the Mexica for 300 years until 1821 when they were ousted. The Mexica had only been free for 27 years when they again were subject to European foreign rule only this to time they suffered a tragic oppression by the Manifest Destiny of the United States of America, in another attempt to totally eradicate indigenous traditions and their freedom to roam throughout the land as they had done for thousands of years.

The Mexica continued to experience atrocious injustices during the Gold Rush of 1849 in California from the newly arrived Anglos who were doing everything in their power to dominate the west. Among those suffering the consequences of the invading Anglo Saxon was Joaquin Murrieta, a miner from Trincheras, Sonora, Mexico. Joaquin suffered injustices and tragic cruelty at the hands of the racist Anglos who raped and murdered his wife. They also beat him and left him for dead. This was after they had murdered his brother, Jesus. Once he recuperated, Joaquin organized a rebellion against the United States Government. He fought fiercely to bring justice to the Mexica and help them defend their rights and regain California back to Mexico. Thus, the Early Xicano Movement began and Joaquin Murrieta was proclaimed "The Father of the Xicano Movement."

Today, as modern day Xicanos continue to struggle to preserve their culture, leaders have surfaced in the face of injustices against the Xicano communities. Humberto "Bert" Corona was proclaimed the Father of the Modern Day Xicano Movement for his life time dedication to the fight for the civil rights of Xicanos. His commitment to this struggle took him to a height unmatched by no other. (See Chapter 10.2, Bert Corona)

The true meaning of the letter "X," represents the merging of Cosmic Father and Mother Earth. The Spanish conquerors knew the importance of this symbol and banished it from the Nahuatl language and replaced it with the "ch" to further sever the connection between the indigenous and their traditions.

Today, through the cosmic measurement of time, we know the time has come for all Xicanos to return to their roots and break down the barriers that have kept us from fully understanding our origins and our culture. Today, Xicanos are the vanguards of the truth of Aztlán.

Chapter 9.2
The Xicano Poem

(Revised September 4, 2009)

By: Rosa Elvira Alvirez, 1973
Dedicated to La Escuela de la Raza Unida.
Translated by Rigoberto Garnica

The following poem expresses our over arching theme of our research based on the historical revelation of La Cuna de Aztlán. It takes us goes back to our indigenous roots and focuses on the "Birth of the New Knowledge." Xicano pride and struggles are also well manifested within this poem and the words express the Xicanos' longing for the truth of their origin.

Xicano

La palabra Xicano es un reproche
Una angustia con algo de esperanza
Semilla por la peña soterrada
Flor ahora, tal vez árbol mañana
Es un reto, quizás una bandera
Un estandarte terco de una Raza
Trasplantada a un oasis o a un desierto
Es un dolor moral hecho palabra
Un silencio en voz alta y en voz nueva
Sed de siglos le abrasa la garganta
Broto como las fuentes subterráneas
Viene de lejos, Llega del Anáhuac
Que importa un nombre! Viaja con la sangre
Azteca, Mayas, Navajos, Araucans...
Es un largo silencio que hoy nos habla
Y al mundo clama en forma de palabra
La palabra Xicano es una flecha
Y el arco es el aliento de una Raza.

Xicano

The word Xicano is a reproach
Anguish with a ray of hope
A seed thwarted by sorrow
A flower now, perhaps a tree tomorrow
It is a challenge. Like a flag it is
The unyielding banner of a race
A desert longing for a fair oasis
This word was shaped by an inner pain
A new voice, an outcry that broke the silence
Thirst of centuries burning in our throats
A bursting forth of a half buried dream
From Anahuac it came, relentlessly
What matters the meaning of a name
If the blood of many identities
Flows through our veins?
Azteca, Mayas, Navajos, Araucans...
This word has broken a long silence
And now speaks to the world at large
The word "Xicano" has become an arrow and the bow is the breath of a race.

Chapter 9.3
The Renaissance of Aztlan & the Xicano Student Movement

The quest for the location of Aztlán remained one of the main goals of the Xicano Student Movement in the 1960s and 70s. An overall acceptance, that the southwest United States was indeed the Xicano spiritual homeland was quickly established. Modern day Xicanos reaffirmed their cultural connection to their indigenous heritage that can be traced back to Aztlán and Anahuac. Xicanos felt a strong need to maintain identification with their indigenous roots, rejecting labels imposed on them by the media and the United States government such as Hispanic and Latino.

The term, "genizaro" was widely used in the old days to describe indigenous people who had lost their formal tribal identity and who had totally accepted the religion, language and customs of the Spanish conquerors. The usage of this term continues to be used in New Mexico, where the repugnant Spanish aristocrats would distinguish themselves from the rest of the indigenous population. It is also used in Mexico, but only as a derogatory term like "Es puro genizaro".

Today this term could be compared with what Xicanos call a, "Vendido, Tio Taco, Agabachado, Agringado, and one who has accepted all the ways of the Anglo."

During the early 1960s and '70s the universities and high schools were under pressure by the Xicanos to establish a Xicano Studies curriculum. As the movement extended throughout the southwest, Xicanos demanded to learn the truth about their heritage. They rejected the Hispanicized interpretations of their history as it was presented to them in their classrooms. In college, one of the most popular classes that Xicanos enrolled in was anthropology and history because

they wanted to know more about their ancestors, their culture and traditions.

The Xicano Movement was brought to new heights during the late 1950s and early 1960s due to the civil rights, anti-war, and political movements that swept the continent. Organizations such as the Mexican American Political Association, (MAPA) and the United Farm Workers (UFW) fueled these movements for change within the justice and political systems. This was the rude awakening of the Sleeping Giant; the Xicano! One of the major events that sparked the Xicano Student Movement was the Xicano Youth Liberation Conference held in Denver, Colorado. This conference took place on March, 1969 and was led by Rodolfo "Corky" Gonzales. Corky, was one of the main Xicano leaders and organizers at that time.

At the conference, the approval of the document "El Plan Espiritual de Aztlán," authored by Professor Alberto Alurista, was a major accomplishment. This plan provided the foundation for the movement. At the conference, the Nahuatl term "Aztlán," was first introduced to the over three-thousand Xicano youth in attendance. It provided the much needed motivation for the rallying cry of the Xicano Movement, which was "Viva Aztlán." The magnitude of the enthusiasm and pride energized the movement and inspired all young Xicanos to search for their indigenous roots, and reject all other labels imposed on them: "They were Xicanos and they came from Aztlán."

In the United States, "El Plan Espiritual de Aztlán" became the motto for the Xicano Student Movement. In addition, a great variety of ambitious goals evolved, which included self-determination, auto-sufficiency and independent alternative schools. As a result, all negative aspects of the Anglo dominating society were exposed at the conference and a plan of action was developed to help the students combat the injustices within the educational, political and judicial system.

The excitement of the Denver conference had not yet settled down when "El Plan de Santa Barbara" conference was held at the University of California Santa Barbara in April 1969. Those in attendance at the conference approved a manifesto for the implementation of Xicano Studies at all universities and colleges. This also served as a major boost for the Xicano Movement and the Xicano student group, (MECHA) "Movimiento Estudiantil Chicano de Aztlán." Today, unfortunately, 40 years after these historical events took place, most of the participants of those conferences have comfortably settled for mediocre jobs. They have been absorbed into the framework of the same system they were fighting against. The rallying cry of Xicano Power of the 1960s and 70s has become meaningless rhetoric to our Xicano youth of today.

The Xicano Student Movement did motivate some communities to pursue their goal of establishing independent alternative schools. Escuela de la Raza Unida, (ERU) is an excellent example of how Xicano students were motivated to organize their own Xicano Alternative School. La Escuela de la Raza Unida, in Blythe, California was organized on May 1, 1972. May 1 is May Day, celebrated as Labor Day in the world except in the United States. May 1 is also significant because it is 52 days prior to June 21, the summer solstice, which is the duality date of August 13, (52 days from June 21) the coming of the energies, thus, emphasizing the importance of May 1 to the Mexica. ERU is one of the only true independent Indigenous/Xicano school to survive for the past 40 years in "Occupied Aztlán", as paraphrased by prominent professor Dr. Rodolfo "Rudy" Acuña.

One of the main organizations that inspired the pursuit to seek the truth of Aztlan was the founding of the Escuela De La Raza Unida. The successes of ERU are fulfilling part of that Mexica prophecy of cultural rebirth. ERU was born out of conflict and throughout its thirty-nine years of existence, it has been able to expand and overcome numerous barriers brought upon by that same conflict and struggle, as a means of

growth.

The birth of the Escuela de la Raza Unida and the Xicano Alternative School Movement served as the catalyst that opened the door to a new horizon, escalating the quest and persistence in the revelation of the truth of Aztlan and of our indigenous origins on the Colorado River.

One may ask, "Why wasn't the location of Aztlán revealed before?" The response is that the time had not yet arrived to reveal the truth. However, now, with the evidence that has been found in the La Cuna de Aztlan, and in the Lower Colorado River Basin, the time has come to reveal this truth.

Time is measured. For five hundred years, the indigenous people have lived in the Era of Obscurity, similar to the dark ages that took place in Europe. The indigenous people suffered, first, due to the Spanish invasion, and then, under the United States Manifest Destiny. Still, Xicanos have surpassed these dark ages and will continue to rise as a people, in light of the hundreds of years of European oppression.

If the Xicano Movement is to truly fulfill its obligation as said in El Plan Espirito de Aztlán, they must rise above the superficial ideals. They must stay motivated to create change and substantiate their "rallying cry for justice." Xicanos must regain their consciousness of being XICANO!

Chapter 9.4
Philosophy & Reencounter With Indigenous Cosmic Tradition and Philosophy

As traditional indigenous people, the spiritual reencounter with their cosmic cultural traditional roots generates a renewal of self-identity and a reexamination of human values.

For years, anthropologists have pondered the following questions: "Where did humans come from? When did they come? Why are they here?"

All these questions coincide with a worldwide quest for consciousness manifested in different movements: The New Age, Age of Aquarius, Awakening of the Heart, the New Sun and Birth of the New Knowledge, etc.

On August 11, 1987, one of the New Age movement events that received worldwide interest and participation was the Harmonic Convergence lead by Jose Arguelles. The main ceremony began at sunrise and was held at Joshua Tree National Park, which encompasses Eagle Mountain Range.

Design by Alfredo A. Figueroa and Florencio Yescas

For years people have been deeply concerned about the forth coming of the Azteca/Mayan Calendars date of 2012. The perspective of the calendars is that "change" will occur in 2012. This will be the time of culmination of the prophecies and the end of Pisces. Pisces is the era of blind faith, and now we are entering the era of Aquarius, which is based on facts, and where "seeing is believing."

The 2012 revelation has created fear and distress in many people because they do not know what to expect. Thus, many believe that 2012 will be a devastating year. Millions of people are entombed and awaiting a new beginning, while others are skeptical and are fomenting an outright mockery denouncing the culmination of the 2012 prophecies.

Yet, in 2008, many scientists and experts participated in a worldwide academic reunion in Paris, France, in order to study the Mayan Culture more in-depth. For first time the world took into consideration indigenous ideology. At this conference, the topic was the Year 2012 and what will happen in 2012. The fictional and factual predictions of the end of the world were discussed and analyzed.

In the past several years, changes have taken place in the world that had never occurred before. One can not deny the consequences of global warming and the circumstances brought about by the great climatic changes that are currently taking place. The financial collapse of the capitalist world has created dramatic changes throughout the world, as in Portugal and Greece, and is evidenced by the 14 trillion dollar or so debt of the United States. Natural disasters such as earthquakes and tsunamis have occurred more so in the last few years than ever before. The Middle East political unrest and turmoil, the starvation of millions of people in Africa, also contribute to crises' world wide.

We cannot ignore these changes. If we want to understand the future, we must understand the past. Since time immemorial, the Mexica elders knew that time was measured by the Pleiades, the Seven Sisters Constellation, rising to its zenith every 52 years.

John Collier, in his many writings of indigenous people and as director of the National Indian Institute of the United States, wrote that all the world governments should be like the pre-American native. The traditional way of life is respect for all living things on earth and respect for the guidance of the cosmos. Learning to maintain an equilibrium and connection with the universe is the only salvation for humans.

The change of humanity in a new era was recently found to be inscripted in an important piece to the Mayan Calendar that fulfills the predictions of December 21, 2012. The Instituto Nacional de Antropologia recently found this piece/stela which was identified as "estela numero seis" and was found in the mountain, (cerro), El Tortuguero. Reportedly, it is one of three recently found archaeological pieces and contains entries on astrological predictions of 2012. It is considered to be the sixth and final stela that completes the puzzle of the Mayan calendar, substantiating the prophecy of 2012.

So, again, when people ask: What is going to happen in 2012? They must be reminded of: What happened to the indigenous population of the Continent of Anahuac 500 years ago, with the European Invasion?

Ancient Azteca Prophecy

Our Grandfather

Our Grandfather ordered us to inform our people of the future,
the Sun of our culture would rise and reach its power and realize its grand destiny. Now the time has come. The time was measured and the people of the future have thus become ourselves not a few of us but all of us, not one group nor an organization, but all of us this generation.

Nuestro Tata

Nuestros abuelos ordenaron avisar a los mexicanos del futuro, que el Sol de nuestra cultura se levantaría, alcanzaría fuerza y realizaría su grandioso destino. Ahora, el tiempo ha llegado. El tiempo estaba medido y los mexicanos del futuro somos nosotros. No unos pocos sino todos. No un grupo, ni una organización, sino todos nosotros esta generación.

Ancient Footprints of the Colorado River 99

Chapter 10

La Cuna de Aztlan Sacred Sites Protection Circle

La Cuna de Aztlán Sacred Sites Protection Circle, under the auspices of the Escuela de la Raza Unida, a non-profit organization, signed a Memorandum of Understanding (MOU) with the Bureau of Land Management (BLM) to preserve the Blythe Giant Intaglios and other sacred sites, on March 14, 2008.

The Sacred Sites Protection Circle became the guardians dedicated to physically protecting the Blythe Giant Intaglios, and several hundred sacred sites that are located along the Colorado River from Needles, California to Yuma, Arizona. Under the guidance of the Chemehuevi Nation, their mission is to protect, preserve, and share the indigenous history that was deceitfully concealed from the world for more than five centuries. More importantly, their mission is also to educate the general population of the sacredness that is represented by the Blythe Giant Intaglios and other geoglyphs that are remnants of the "Ancient Footprints" left here on the Lower Colorado River Basin Valleys thousands of years ago.

Some of the Sacred Sites Protection Circle members had previously been involved defending sacred sites on the Lower Colorado River Basin. In 1992, members, Ron Van Fleet and Alfredo A. Figueroa organized the Colorado River Anti-Ward Valley Coordinating Committee under the auspices of Fort Mojave Nation. The committee members travelled to Mexico City seeking support and to unite indigenous cultures across the continent. The committee ultimately stopped the proposed construction of the Ward Valley Nuclear Toxic dump. The dump was proposed to be built 20 miles west of Needles and it was going to contaminate the aquifers that lead to the Colorado River. They were successful in getting the five indigenous reservations of the Colorado River to join together to fight the proposed dump. After struggling for 8-years together with the help of over 200 environmental organizations in the United States and Mexico they were able to stop the construction of the proposed Ward Valley Dump.

Today, the Sacred Sites Protection Circle, envision the Blythe Giant Intaglios including the Big Maria Mountains and Little Maria Mountains, the McCoy Mountains and the Mule Mountains, to one day, become a National Park and eventually, a World Heritage Site for all to respect, appreciate, learn from the indigenous culture.

The Mexica Creation story that has mystified the world for centuries will be exposed through the deciphering of the Blythe Giant Intaglios. These sacred icons will no longer be viewed simply as ancient relics of unknown origin. They will finally be given the respect and reverence they deserve and their greatness will be recognized

Thomas Banyaca and Phil Smith at Hotevilla, on the Hopi Reservation, 1996. (Photo by Alfredo A. Figueroa)

Ron Van Fleet standing at Palo Verde Peak Point petroglyphs that indicate the end of the first sun, of the Aztec Sun Stone Calendar where Ehecatl is hitting the head of Huemac. (Photo by Alfredo A. Figueroa)

Mateo Leivas, Steve Lopez, Alfredo A. Figueroa and Angel Alvarez at the Tlatelolco Ruins, site in Mexico City where the defeat of Cuauhtemoc took place, August 13, 1521.(Photo by Alfredo A. Figueroa)

as the ancient footprints of the Colorado River, which have now begun to speak. As stated briefly in the Prophecy of Cuauhtemoc, "Our Sun has gone from our vision, but Our Sun will shine again."

The geographical images in the mountains, geoglyphs, petroglyphs, and pictographs, all represent the treasures Quetzalcoatl left and prophesized to return for on the Colorado River.

The Mexica Creation story of the ancient people of the Colorado River Valleys and the surrounding area will be the greatest revelation of the new millennium. It will be the end of the Dark Ages for all indigenous people.

La Cuna de Aztlan Sacred Sites Protection Circle is working in collaboration with local tribes and other concerned citizens and environmentalists to prevent the destruction of the giant Kokopelli, geoglyph, the Cicimitl geoglyph, the Tosco geoglyph and hundreds of sacred sites and images threatened by the proposed mega solar power plants.

The Blythe Solar Power Project/Chevron, Genesis Solar Energy and Palen Solar Power Project/Chevron are just a few of the numerous solar power projects that form part of the fast track large solar projects to be built on BLM land, with President Barack Obama stimulus monies. These stimulus monies have since disappeared but the plants are still on track to be build. The members of the Sacred Sites Protection Circle have made it clear that they are not against renewable energy, but are protesting the destruction of these specific sites and cultural resources.

The giant geoglyphs of the Kokopelli, the indigenous hunchback icon with a flute, as well Cicimitl, and Tosco lie within the right of way acreage of the proposed Blythe Solar Project. The Kokopelli site is ten miles west of Blythe and six miles west of the original 1865 Colorado River Indian Tribe Reservation boundary. The reservation's western boundary was the high

flood water mark on the west mesa of the Palo Verde Valley. BLM officials have visited the site of the Kokopelli, yet they continue to sign off on the paperwork in pursuit of the implementation of the proposed solar power plants. We are currently in search of assistance in protecting the Kokopelli and over 25 other indigenous sacred sites that are exposed to destruction by off road vehicles and now, mega-solar power plants. The Sacred Sites Protection Circle and other environmentalists have joined together and filed a lawsuit currently pending.

Chapter 10.2
In Memoriam of Humberto "Bert" Corona

Humberto "Bert" Corona was a "Xicano of all Seasons," because he was a leader, labor organizer, professor, and activist of the community.

He was born in El Paso, Texas on May 29, 1918 and was "the son of the Mexican Revolution of 1910." His father Noe Corona was one of "Los Dorados de Pancho Villa" (General Villa's Personal Escorts), and his mother Margarita Escapite Salayandia, was a teacher.

Bert's family lived in El Paso. As a young child, Bert was raised by Doña Luz Corral, Pancho Villa's widow in Chihuahua, Chihuahua, Mexico. Pancho Villa and Doña Luz Corral were very close to Bert's parents and they were in their wedding as Godparents. (Padrinos de Bodas.)

Bert had an extensive education. He attended Harwood Boys School in Alburquerque, New Mexico and Bowie High School, in El Paso, Texas. Later in 1936, he received a basketball scholarship from the University of Southern California (USC) where he studied law. He left USC in 1938, to become a labor organizer with the Congress of Industrial Organization (CIO), Mexican American Movement (MAM), the International Federation of Longshoremen and Warehousemen Union (IFLWU).

Bert was founder and member of many organizations and institutions, including El Congreso de los Pueblos de Habla Hispana, National Association of the Mexican Americans, Community Service Organization (CSO), Mexican-American Political Association (MAPA), Hermandad Mexican Nacional, Centro de Action Social Autonomo (CASA), Mexican American Legal Defense & Education Fund (MALDEF) and the National Council of La Raza (NCLR). Bert was also instrumental in the founding of the La Raza Unida Party, in California.

In 1967, under the leadership of Bert Corona, MAPA's Educational Committee was fundamental in getting Governor Pat Brown to approve the first EOP program (Educational Opportunity Program) in California which was the forerunner of today's EOP programs. It was a pilot program designed to recruit 50 low income Xicano students from los barrios and enroll them at University of California, Los Angeles (UCLA). The success of the EOP program has allowed hundreds of thousands of young Xicanos to graduate from a four-year college, thus, opening the door of a new horizon for the Xicano Student Movement.

In the late 1960s and '70s Bert was teaching Xicano Studies at three different universities during same week and was able to personally contact and encourage thousands of young Xicanos to continue their struggle for social justice.

Bert was always involved in political campaigns and has been recognized by United States Presidents and Governors. In 1958, he participated in the "Viva Kennedy", presidential campaign of John F. Kennedy. Later in 1968, he was the California State Director of the "Viva Kennedy" presidential campaign for Senator Robert 'Bobby' Kennedy.

In the beginning stages of the United Farm Workers Union (UFW), he was deeply involved with Cesar Chavez. He was also influential in

the founding of La Escuela de Raza Unida in 1972 in Blythe, California.

Bert was one of the main advocates in the fight for Amnesty for the undocumented immigrants, through the Hermandad Mexicana Nacional and CASA. This earned him the so rightfully given the name of "El Tata Del la Lucha Del Movimento de los Indocumentados," (The Grandfather of the Undocumented Movement). At the time of his death, on January 15, 2001, Bert Corona was the National Executive Director and President of the Hermandad Mexicana Nacional.

Throughout his life, this humble man dedicated himself in serving humanity. This was his passion in life. His favorite song was, "Libro Abierto" (Open Book) and his life-long theme was: "Un daño contra uno, es un daño contra todos" (An injury to one, is an injury to all). He never ran for political office because he was true to his belief: "One cannot be a politician and a community organizer at the same time; a person cannot serve two masters." This is why he was proclaimed a Xicano of all Seasons and he has been declared the Father of the Modern Day Xicano Movement, by Xicano activists.

On May 13, 1999, Bert Corona wrote the preface to the first edition of this book, "Ancient Footprints of the Colorado River."

Chapter 10.3
In Memoriam of
Professor William Hensey, Jr.

Professor William "Bill" Hensey Jr., was born on January 2, 1912 in Los Angeles, California and died February 23, 2008. He was laid to rest in the Calvary Cemetery, in East Los Angeles.

Mr. Hensey was a graduate of the University of California in Los Angeles, (UCLA) and had a Masters in Political Science from University of Southern California (USC). He was one of the most outstanding recognized debaters and received various national awards. He also served as editor and writer of various university newspapers. Mr. Hensey was also a decorated veteran of the United States Army during War World II and was discharged as a First Lieutenant.

He was a professor at Palo Verde High School from 1939 to 1947. In 1947, he was one of the founding members of Palo Verde Junior College in Blythe, California. As the main recruiter for Palo Verde College, Mr. Hensey recruited hundreds of Xicanos students from California, Arizona and New Mexico, etc., to Palo Verde Junior College. The college was fundamental in organizing the Spanish-speaking community and encouraged them to pursue a college education. Thanks to Mr. Hensey's involvement, Palo Verde had the highest number of Xicano graduates per capita in the southwest during that time.

His contributions to the progress of the Xicano Movement were overwhelming. He diligently served the Xicano students that attended Palo Verde Junior College as a counselor and mentor. He was a man with great vision and was an enthusiastic community activist. The community will forever be thankful for his efforts in promoting educational opportunities for Xicanos and others.

All the successes achieved by Palo Verde Junior College occurred prior to the existence of any California state educational aid programs, and the only program was available was the G.I. Bill for veterans. Many Xicanos attend college with the assistance of educational aid programs such as Cal works and EOPS.

In 1972, Mr. Hensey was also one of the founding professors of La Escuela de la Raza Unida. During this time the majority of the people in the Southwest rejected the efforts of Xicano families who sought to establish their own alternative schools. One of his famous quotes was, "Why can't Xicanos build their own schools if your Azteca ancestors were the builders of some of the greatest pyramids in the world and the biggest city, which was Mexico/Tenochtitlan?"

Mr. Hensey was one of the few Anglos who understood the Mexican culture and tradition. He was also one of the main advisors who encouraged this author, Alfredo Acosta Figueroa, to pursue his investigations of the Mexica culture in Mexico City, which he finally achieved in 1990.

Mr. William "Bill" Hensey will always be remembered by numerous generations of students that passed through his classroom. He will also be remembered by this author as an old friend, professor, informer and political advisor.

Carlos Llegar, Patrick Connolly and Mr. Hensey in front of ERU 1974

Mr. Hensey in his 1914 Model T in front of Caarmen Figueroa's home.

Editor's Comments

When we began to work and summarize this book, many memories of the past 55 years were relived, the joyful cherished moments and events, and the sorrowful pains of a growing consciousness of the truth of our indigenous roots and cultural experience.

Thanks to the Creator, we have flourished and succeeded in bringing forth the truth of our native culture. All humans must come together as a family; Anglo-Saxons, Blacks, Indigenous and Asians, etc. Like the ancient Nahuatl teachings of 'Tloque Nahuaque,' which is represented by the fingers on the hand, separate, different sizes and shapes, yet joined all together at the palm as the human race, symbolizing, *"that among all we do all for the benefits of all."*

The solution for human salvation is for us to focus and regain our traditional roots. We must bring back the culture, respect for elders, morals, and respect for our fellow humans, animals and environment. I leave you with Jose Burciaga's words, "Eat, drink, sleep, and live cultura!"

The outer Circle of the universe, the two snakes are Cihuacoatl, the duality, as also shown on the Aztec Sun Stone Calendar, the hand is Tloque-Nahuaque, and the eye is the symbol of Ipalnemohuani or God's' eye.
(Moundville Moore, Alabama Museum of Natural History, Book of Sun Circles and Human Hand, The Southeastern Indians by Emma Lila Fundaburk)

Tlazocamatli-Thank you

Primary Resources
Personal Interviews

Acamapixtli, José Manuel García Castillo:

Acamapixtli, is a professor of the Nahuatl language, writer and investigator of the Mexica Codex. He is a traditionalist, healer and interpreter of the Astrological Aztec Sun Stone Calendar. He is also a member of the board of directors of the Yankuikan Anahuak AC. One of his major projects is to return the headdress of Moctezuma back to Mexico from Austria.

He has traveled extensively in Mexico and the Southwestern United States, bringing forth the birth of The New Knowledge of Cuauhtémoc, and since 1992, he has been one of the authors close advisors and teacher of the Mexica traditions and language.

Thomas Banayaca:
Banayaca was a staunch Hopi Traditionalist elder who was entrusted with the ominous prophecies by the Hopi Elders Council. Banayaca traveled worldwide interpreting the prophecies and creating an awareness of the evils of war and of the destruction of Mother Earth, beginning with the atomic bomb of WWII in Nagasaki and Hiroshima.

He ardently pursued the enforcement of the Treaty of Guadalupe Hidalgo, which included all the indigenous treaties. He was in the forefront of the movement to unite all indigenous nations throughout the Western Hemisphere, beginning with the Uto-Aztecans, and the southwest indigenous nations as well as the Mexica.

Fray Toribio de Benavente:
Fray Benavente also named Motolinia by the natives, was one of the first twelve European priests who came to evangelize the conquered indigenous peoples. He was a very good priest and is credited with burying the remains of both Cuauhtémoc and Fray Juan de Tecto in the old

momozle (pyramid) of Ixcateopan in 1530.

He was also the one who insisted that the Chontales keep Cuauhtémoc's remains a secret. His writings are some of the most respected by the Rodriguez family, who retain some of his original manuscripts.

Fray Francisco Javier Clavijero:
Fray Clavijero was a Jesuit historian and geographer of the Mexica Nation and its culture. His history books "Historia Antigua de Mexico" and "Historia de Baja California" have been instrumental in our research. His findings are the most supportive in the theory that Aztlán was located above the confluence of the Colorado and Gila Rivers.

Benjamin Celaya Crespo:
A native of Caborca, Sonora, Mexico who is recognized as the most knowledgeable historian of the area, and an amateur archaeologist, who is famous for his expositions and lectures throughout Sonora.

He has found over fifteen burial mounds with three-legged "molcajetes" on top of the burial urns, confirming the pattern of burial rites of the migrating nations, as they left from the Colorado River. These findings have been instrumental in our research pertaining to La Cuna de Aztlan.

Francisco Figueroa:
Professor in Trincheras, Sonora, he is the author's cousin, who was the first to introduce the author to Laureano Calvo Berber's book "Naciones de Historia de Sonora." (Published in 1958)

This book was essential in sparking the author's interest in researching the origins of Aztlán. The book has a map that located Aztlán north of the confluence of the Gila and Colorado River. (This is approximately the area where the Palo Verde Valley is located)

He also encouraged the author to continue his research of the Joaquin Murrieta legacy in Trincheras, Sonora.

Eulalia Guzman:
Guzman was one of Mexico's most prestigious anthropologists at the Insitito National de Antropologia y Historia (INAH). She presided at the exhumation of the remains of Cuauhtémoc in 1949 in Ixcateopan, Guerrero. She was also the main spokesperson who confirmed that the remains were those of Cuauhtémoc.

Boma Johnson:
Johnson is a retired Bureau of Land Management Archaeologist and Cultural Resource Management Specialist who worked out of the Yuma, Arizona office for 25 years.

Johnson holds two Masters Degree, one in Archaeology and the other in Ethnology from Brigham Young University, in Salt Lake City, Utah. He also completed a Cultural Resource Management Program at the Arizona State University.

As the BLM Chief Archaeologist, he was in charge of overseeing historical indigenous sacred sites along the Lower Colorado River Valleys and while working in the area his research focused on locating and identifying the origin and purpose of the thousands of petroglyphs, pictographs and geoglyph. His research was also centered on the oral histories of the indigenous people.

Johnson is one of the most knowledgeable archaeologists regarding geoglyphs and has written a highly informative book describing the images that are unfortunately, deteriorating or are being destroyed.

His work became indispensable to our research for more the 20 years. He was very instrumental in supporting the struggle, opposing the construction of the Blythe Energy Plant because his study revealed that the plant was being built on top of one of the most Sacred Sites in the valley.

Since his retirement on January 1, 2000, he still continues to be active in the struggle to preserve our indigenous culture. He is now living in Ivin, Utah, and is still doing what he enjoys the most, which is giving presentations, and teaching classes at Dixie State College (DSC). He also conducts rock tours specializing in petroglyphs and Intaglios. Johnson truly enjoys sharing his knowledge regarding ancient indigenous artifacts and their meaning.

Charles A. Lamb:
Former museum director for the Colorado River Indian Tribes in Parker, Arizona, (from 1973 to 1989), Lamb is both a historian and an archeologist. He has acquired extensive knowledge of the Mojave's culture by working together with the Mojave elders, in order to preserve the language, culture, and customs.

Gilbert Leivas:
Leivas is a Chemehuevi and Colorado River Indian Tribes member. He is very knowledgeable of the four indigenous cultures that now populate the Colorado River Indian Tribes Reservation which include: Mojave, Chemehuevi, Hopi and Navajo.

Leivas' assistance from within the reservation has been fundamental to this research. He was a former president of La Cuna de Aztlán Sacred Sites Protection Circle. In 2008, the Protection Circle together with the full support of the Chemehuevi Tribe received a Memorandum of Understanding (MOU) from the Bureau of Land Management (BLM), to serve as the guardians of the Blythe Giant Intaglios and several hundred other sacred sites, located along the Colorado River from Needles, California, to Yuma, Arizona.

Steve Lopez:
Lopez was the nephew of Llewellyn Barrackman, past chairman and vice-chairman of the Fort Mojave Council.
Lopez was also on the council, and served as historian and editor of the official newsletter, Ech-Kah-Nav-Cha. He gained most of his oral traditional knowledge from his uncle, a respected Mojave elder. Lopez was also an organizer for the Spirit Mountains (Avi-Kwame) Spiritual runs.

In 1992 and 1996 he participated in the Peace and Dignity Journeys. He is also one of our main resources of the Colorado River Mojave culture and traditional beliefs.

Lopez was the spokesperson for the Five Nations of the Colorado River Native Alliance against the proposed nuclear toxic dump at Ward Valley, (Near Needles, CA) which was ultimately defeated. He also traveled to Mexico City and Ixcateopan, Guerrero to visit the tomb of Cuauhtémoc together with the author and other environmentalist.

Hunbatz Men:
Hunbatz Men is a Mayan historian, lecturer, writer, spiritualist, and founder of the Center for Mayan Studies in Merida, Yucatan.

Hunbatz Men is one of the few Mayan natives who has deciphered part of the Mayan Codex. He was also a co-organizer of the Cuauhtémoc Spiritual Pilgrimage of December 7, 1985. Hunbatz Men led the march from Ixcateopan, Guerrero Mexico to the Colorado River which ended on February 23, 1986 in Los Angeles, California.

He was sent to California by Dr. Salvador Rodriguez Juarez, to bring the news of the Birth of the New Knowledge to the people of the United States. He has been one the authors' confidantes in the Mexica/Mayan culture and has visited the Blythe Giant Intaglios and La Escuela de la Raza Unida on numerous occasions.

Hunbatz Men is also a member of the group petitioning the government of Austria for the return of the original Copilli-Quetzal (head dress) of Moctezuma to Mexico. His books include: "Los Calendarios Astronomicos Mayas y HUNAB K'U" and "Secrets of Mayan Science/Religion" which have been very important in comparing the native culture and beliefs

of Mexico and the Lower Colorado River Valleys.

Estrella Newman:
Professor and director of the Taller Escuela Julian Carrillo in Mexico City, she is a renowned artist and sculptor who worked for more than 20 years under the famous painter and muralist, David Siqueiros.

She was Dr. Salvador Rodriguez's personal confidant and in 1985 was authorized by him to plan the historical Cuauhtémoc Spiritual Pilgrimage, Mexico/Ixcateopan- Los Angeles/Aztlán.

Newman also organizes the annual Cuauhtémoc festivities on February 23 in Ixcateopan, Guerrero. She has been one of the most reliable sources of Mexica culture and the history of Cuauhtémoc. She is one of the founders of the Mexicanidad Movement to seek and regain our Mexica culture.

On April 2010, Newman came to Blythe to help stop the proposed Blythe Solar Power Project which threatened the destruction of the giant Kokopilli, Cicimitl and El Tosco geoglyphs.

Richard Robles:
Local amateur outdoor enthusiast, he has been instrumental in guiding us to some of the most sacred indigenous historical sites located around the Palo Verde/Parker Valleys. These sites are some of the most sacred that have alluded to the overall identification of the Creation Story in the Colorado River.

Jairo Rodriguez del Olmo:
Son of Dr. Salvador Rodriguez Juarez Chimalpopoca Moctezuma, he is the 13th descendant of the Cuauhtémoc Dynasty. It is his responsibility to continue propagating the Birth of the New Knowledge of La Mexicanidad.

He is now the guardian of the family codex, historian, amateur anthropologist and caretaker of the Tomb of Cuauhtémoc, and Altar of the Nation in Ixcateopan de Cuauhtémoc, Guerrero. He has been a reliable resource regarding Cuauhtémoc Mexica/Chontal lineage that ties with the Colorado River Tribes of the Hokan/Uto-Aztecan families and history.

Dr. Salvador Rodríguez Juárez Chimalpopoca Moctezuma:
He was the 12th descendant of the Dynasty of Cuauhtémoc and in charge of the "live (oral) letter" of the secret of Cuauhtémoc Tomb. Dr. Rodriguez was the universal heir of the remains of Cuauhtémoc and executor of the Sacred Commission appointed by President Miguel Aleman that preserved the knowledge of the whereabouts of Cuauhtémoc' Tomb.

Our meeting with Dr. Rodriguez in December, 1990 was one of the highlights of our lives. His writings and inspirational meeting were essential in our research in the correlation of the Colorado River Nations with the Descendants of Cuauhtémoc.

Dr. Ignacio Romerovargas Yturbide:
Director of the "Cultura de Anahuac Instituto de Investigacion" and Professor of History at the Universidad de Michoacan, Mexico, he was the President of the Academia de Leyes de Anahuac, and Asociacion de Abogados de Mexico.

Dr. Romerovargas had nine doctorates degrees and spoke 30 languages. His lifelong quest was to seek the truth of Mexica cultural, traditions and beliefs.
His most famous writings have been "The Socialist Governments of Anahuac," and "Political Organization of the Pueblos de Anahuac" and the three volumes of "Moctezuma Xocoyotzin." Dr. Romerovargas was the most knowledgeable person pertaining to indigenous law and rights. He concluded that comparing all forms of government, no government was comparable to the socialist governments of the Azteca Calpullis. According to Dr. Romerovargas, the forms of government closest to the Calpullis were those of Russia and China.

When the Chinese reorganized their government after the Red Guard Cultural Revolution of 1975, they implemented a modified version of the Calpullis of the Anahuac, based on Dr. Romerovargas' writings. As a result, of Dr. Romerovargas precise in-depth study of the Azteca life, Chairman Mao Tse-Tung bestowed on him one of China's highest awards, which was the Hero of Labor award.

Ron Van Fleet:
Tribal member of Fort Mojave, Van Fleet is the grandnephew of Sukulai-Homar (Peter Lambert) last of the great Mojave traditionalist chieftains (spokespersons). Sukulai-Homar was the son of Empote-Quatcheech and grandson of Homoseh-Quahote, the great chieftain who was forced to surrender to the U.S. army in 1859.

Van Fleet organizes the Spiritual Renewal Runs that are part of the old Mojave tradition, and was a co-organizer of the campaign against the proposed Ward Valley nuclear toxic dumpsite in the Aha- Macave (Mojave ancestral homeland). In 1992, he was one of the Peace and Dignity Journey organizers and has provided vital resources concerning the Colorado River native oral history traditions. He is currently a member of La Cuna de Aztlán Sacred Sites Protection Circle.

Florencio Yesca:
Gran Maestro of the Explendor Danza Azteca. In 1970, he was sent to the United States by Dr. Salvador Rodriguez to prepare the way for the coming of the Cuauhtémoc Spiritual Pilgrimage. This Pilgrimage was to start at Ixcateopan, Guerrero via Mexico/Tenochtitlan and end in Los Angeles/Aztlán on February 23, 1986. The objective of the Pilgrimage was to reveal the Birth of the New Knowledge which was the Birth of the New Sun.

He was the founder of the Danza Azteca Movement and set out to organize danzantes throughout the United States. Through the Danza he spread the teaching of the New Knowledge, "La Nueva Sabiduria," of Cuauhtémoc's prophecy.

He was one of the first people from Mexico who supported and reinforced the basis of our research regarding La Cuna de Aztlán in the Colorado River.

Nahuatl/Mexica Glossary

ACACITLI: A=atl-water, Ca=calli-house, Citli= Jackrabbit. Acacitli means "Jackrabbit in the tules." Acacitli was an island, which was the duality of the island of Aztlan in the Colorado River Indian Tribe Reservation. This was the original name of "El Barrio del Cuchillo" in west Blythe.

AHUITZOTL: Eighth Tlatoani of the Confederation of Anahuac. He was Cuauhtémoc's grandfather and not his father as written by historians. He is credited with having conquered the Chontales of the south around Ixcateopan, Guerrero; he died in 1502. (Carranco)

AHUIZOTO: The son of Ahuitzolt and father of Cuauhtémoc, referred by Bernal Diaz del Castillo. His image is also on the logo of the cape of Hernan Cortes and used this symbol after he defeated Cuauhtémoc on August 13, 1521. (Carranco)

ANAHUAC: Was the original Nahuatl name of today's North American Continent.

ATEZCATL: Lake.

ATLACHINOLLI: A=atl-Water, Tla= tlalli- Earth, Chinolli=Fire. Atlachinolli means "Water, Earth and Fire." This is a geoglyph that is located at the Blythe Giant Intaglio group.

ATOTONILCO: A=atl-Water, Toto=Hot, Nil= nilli-Within, Co=Place. Atotonilco means place of the thermal water, "agua caliente."

AZCATITLAN CODEX: Fold #12 has a picture of the Cradle with the new born baby which represents the geographical base of the White Thunderbird Eagle on the Big Maria Mountains facing towards Blythe, California with its wings spread out.

AZTATL: Blue Heron, symbol of Aztlán.

AZTECA: This name is interchangeable with Mexica, and is associated with today's Xicano/Mexica. Azteca were given the name because they were from Aztlán. In the last part of the 3rd Sun, Mecitli changed the name of the Azteca to Mexica in honor of the Creator when he descended from the cosmos.

AZTECATL: Azt=Aztlán, Tecatl=Person. Aztecatl means person from Aztlán singular, Azteca is plural.

AZTLAN: Azt=Aztatl-Heron, Tlan=Place. Aztlan means Land of the herons, Land of whiteness, Land of the first Sunrise. This is the origin of the Nahua nations where civilization began on the Colorado River Indian Tribe Reservation.

CABORCA: Means Turtle-Shell in the Tohono-O'odham language. Caborca is a town in Sonora, Mexico and is one of the Mexica migration stops when they left from the Colorado River.

CALLI: Calli-Earth/House. One of the Four-Astros on the Azteca Sun Stone Calendar which represents earth in the Colorado River.

CALMECA: Cal=Calli-House, Meca=mecate-Measurement. Calmeca means long house, and the Mexica institution of higher learning. (Sahgun)

CALPULLI: Barrio, suburb, social institution, similar to a native clan. The form of government that was used by the Mexica based on a highly socialistic form of equality.

CHICANO: See the word Xicano.

CHONTAL: Cuauhtémoc mother was a Chontal, who lived in Ixcateopan, Guerrero. Chontal are related to the Hokan linguistic families of the Colorado River and Seris of Sonora, Mexico.

CHONTALCUATLAN: Chontal pueblo that changed its name to preserve its identity.

CICIMITL: Cici=Magnetic North, Mitl=Arrow. Cicimitl means, the Arrow that points towards Magnetic North and he is also called "El Cucuy," in the Mexica language. Cicimitl is the Great Spirit that takes human spirits to its final resting

place at Topock Maze. The Cicimitl geoglyph is the twin of the Kokopilli geoglyph.

CITLALTEPETL: Citlal=Citlalin-Star, Tepetl=Mountain. Means "Cerro Estrella", located at Iztapalapa, suburb of Mexico City, where the 52-year New Fire Ceremony took place.

CODEX: Original manuscript painted glyphs. Painted on Amatl= Bark paper, by the Mexica "Tlacuillo" artist.

CONFEDERATION OF ANAHUAC: All the nations that belonged to the Confederation from the Shoshone on the Rocky Mountains in the north down to Nicaragua in the south.

CUAUHTEMOC: Cuauh=Cuauhtli-Eagle, Temoc=Descend. Cuauhtémoc means "Eagle that Descends." This symbolizes the Nahualli of the descending sun and the eleventh Tlatoani. The descending sun is manifested on Eagle Mountain and is seen from the Palo Verde Valley.

CUAUHTLEHUANITL: Cuauhtl=Cuauhtli-Eagle, Huanitl=Ascend. The White Thunderbird Eagles image is the Nagualli of the sun and is seen perched on the top ridge of the Big Maria Mountains overlooking the Palo Verde Valley, north of El Barrio del Cuchillo.

CUAYAHUITL: Mother of Cuauhtémoc, Chontal tribe of Ixcateopan, Guerrero daughter of Cuayautitla, known as "El Señor de Zompancoahuitl", and Atl from Coatepec. (Rodriguez)

CUAYAUTITLA: Señor de Zompancoahuitl and grandfather of Cuauhtémoc. Cuauhtémoc was born in his house, in Ixcateopan, Guerrero, where his remains were found by Fray Motolonia.

CUITLAHUAC: Tenth Tlatoani of the Mexica Nation, brother of Moctezuma Xocoyotzin who lead the first Mexica victory against Cortes on June 30, 1520, known as "La noche que lloro Cortes, en el Arbol de la Noche Triste."

CULHUACAN: Col=Colli-Grandfather, Hua-Possessor, Can-Place. Also called Huey Colhuacan, "Place of the divine Grandfathers."

EHECATL: Wind-Morning Star, twin of Xolotl-Dog-Evening Star. The nagualli of Ehecatl is the woodpecker. Venus represents Ehecatl, Xolotl and Quetzalcoatl.

HUE: Old, ancient.

HUEHUETLAPALLAN: Huehue-Ancient-Ancient, Tla=Tlalli-Earth, Pallan-Red Tinged. Huehuetlapallan means "Place of the Ancient-Ancient Red Tinged Earth," and place where the Nahua Nations left from Aztlán around 1160.

HUEHUETLATOLLI: Huehue- Ancient-Ancient, Tlatolli-Knowledge. "The Ancient-Ancient Knowledge."

HUEMAN: Gran Señor of the Toltecas who wrote the divine book and guided them on their migration south from the red regions of Huehuetlapallan on the Colorado River Valleys. (Esther Perez)

HUITZILOPOCHTLI: Huitzil=Huitzilin-Hummingbird, Opochtli-Left handed, "The Left-handed Hummingbird." The Hummingbird is the nagualli of the sun at 12:00 noon when it is at its zenith during the day and during the summer solstice it is the longest day of the year. During the solstice daylight is the same for 4-days. Solstice means "Standing Sun" and the Hummingbird is the nagualli because it can stand in mid-air.

IPALNEMOHUANI: The Creator, the giver of life and all that exists, whom we live for, symbolized by the "Divine Eye," and the northern point of the Omeyocan Diamond in the Palo Verde/Parker Valleys.

IXCATEOPAN: Also known as "The Altar of the

Nation," and the "Birth of the New Knowledge." Modified from Izcatemoteopan; A town in the state of Guerrero Mexico where Cuauhtémoc was born and his remains are located.

KOKOPILLI: Koko=hurt/crown of head, Pilli=Our Lord, "Kokopilli our Lord is hurt." Kokopilli is known as the hunchback flute player, and the original geoglyph is located in the surrounding Palo Verde Valley. Kokopilli is hurt and is leaving because humans have abused Mother Earth.

MALINALXOCHITL: Malinal=Macuili-Vine/Five, Xochitl=Flower. Mother of Copilli as shown in the Azcatitlan Codex and her image is seen in Big Maria and San Jacinto Mountains.

MALINCHE: Soldiers called Hernan Cortes "Capitan del la Marina" and the natives called him Malinche, and after Cortes married a native, they called her Malinche. La Malinche knew different native languages especially Nahuatl and Maya.

MECITLI: Me=Metztli-Moon, Citli=Jackrabbit, "Jackrabbit in the Moon." The Creator's image that descends from the cosmos at Tamaoanchan, "Granite Peak." Mecitli is the one who changed the Azteca name to Mexica when they left the Colorado River at the end of the 3rd Sun. This is why people in Mexico are called Mexica, in honor of Mecitli the Creator.

MEXICO: Me=Metztli-Moon, Xi=Xictl-Umbilical/Center, Co=Place. The name Mexico was derived from Metztli, "The Center of the Moon." It is a mountain peak that is seen from the Colorado River Indian Tribes Reservation which resembles the umbilical.

MICHOACAN: Mich=Michi-Fish, Oa=Possessor, Can=Place, "Place of fish." State in Mexico and Michigan State in the United States, both share the same Nahuatl name and meaning because the Nahua left to the 4-directions. (Ester Perez)

MICTLAN: Mic=Micqui-Death, Tlan=Place, "Place where the Spirits Repose." Mictlan is Topock Maze, located near Needles, California.

MIXCOATL: Mix=Cloud, Coatl= Serpent. "Cloud of Serpents,""The Milky Way."

MOCTEZUMA: The 9th Tlatoani of the Mexica that was killed by Cortes in 1519.

NAGUALLI: Your spiritual or animal, animus/counterpart.

NAHUA: Na=Beginning, Hua=Possessor. The original Uto-Aztecan nations that migrated from the Colorado River.

NAHUATL: The Nahua language.

NAHUI-OLLIN: Nahui=Four, Ollin=Movement, "The Four Movements."

NELTILIZTLI: To seek the roots of the truth based on Mother Nature and Cosmic Traditions.

NICARAGUA: Nica=Nican-Here, Aragua=Nahua- "Up to here came the Nahua."

OMECIHUATL: Ome=Two/Spiritual & Physical, Cihuatl=Female Energy. Omecihuatl's represents Mother Earth. She is one of the giant geoglyphs of the Blythe Giant Intaglios located on the Colorado River.

OMETECUHTLI: Ome=Two/Spiritual & Physical, Tecuhtli=Male Energy. Ometecuhtli represents the Cosmos. He is one of the giant geoglyphs of the Blythe Giant Intaglios located on the Colorado River.

OMETEOTL: Ome=Two/Male & Female Spirits, Teo=Energy. The Creator of all things; the duality of female/male, night/day and good/bad. Ometeotl's giant geoglyph image forms the point of the arrowhead which is located at the Blythe Giant Intaglios.

OMEYOCAN: Ome=Two/Spiritual, Yo=Yolotl-Heart, Can=Place, "Place of the two Hearts."

Metaphysical home of Ometéotl, the 13th Level of Knowledge. Diamond of Infinity overlapping the Palo Verde/Parker Valleys.

PAN-CHE-BEK: (Mayan) "to seek the roots of the truth." (Hunbatz Men)

PILLI: Señor-Elder; Our Lord.

POCHO: Pochi=Tacopotzi-Bobtail/Short tail Rabbit. Opata-Sonora language term. Colloquialism-Pocho is interpreted as one of Mexican heritage born in the USA or Mexican national immigrated to the USA. One who is anglicized and has adopted the English language, custom and lost most of his Mexicanidad.

POCHTECA: Merchants who sold their goods at the Tianguis-Marketplace and traveled all over Anahuac.

QUETZALCOATL: Quetzal=Quetzalli-Precious/Plumed, Coatl=Serpent/Twin, "The Plumed Serpent." Quetzalcoatl is the principle image of the Creator and is represented by Venus, the Morning Star, Ehecatl-Wind and the Evening Star/Xolotl-Dog.

TAMOANCHAN: Ta=Tata-Grandfather, Moan=Descend/Meet, Chan=Chante-house, "Tata descends to his house." Described by the natives as "The place where Sky meets Earth." Tamoanchan is mountain peak seen northwest from Blythe that looks like a pyramid.

TECUICHPOCH: Wife of Cuauhtémoc and daughter of Moctezuma Xocoyotzin.

TELPOCHCALLI: schools for young children, in Anahuac.

TENOCHTITLAN: Te=Tetl-Rock, Noch=Nopal/Cactus, Ti=Merging, Tlan-Place, "Place were the Cactus grew from the Rock." Tenochtitlan is the island where Mexico City is located.

TENOSIQUE: Place where Cuauhtémoc was killed by Hernan Cortes in 1525. Tenosique, Tabasco, Mexico was the main center of the Chontal-Maya Nation which are related to the Hokan linguistic families of the Southwest.

TEOCALLI: Teo=Teotl-Energy, Calli=House, "House of Energy" commonly called pyramids.

TEOMAMA: Teo=Teotl-Energy, Mama=Mother. The four energies, bundle carries that are shown in the Boturini Codex that took the knowledge from the Colorado River to all parts of the world.

TEOTIHUACAN: Teo=Teotl-Energy, Tihua= Coming, Can= Place, "Place of the coming of the Energies," which is represented by August 13. Teotihuacan is located 30-miles northeast of Mexico City, where the pyramids of the Sun, Moon, and Quetzalcoatl are located.

TEPEYAC: Tepe=Tepetl-Mountain, Yac=Nose, "Nose Mountain." Tepeyac was the place of veneration of Tonantzin-Mother Earth before the Spaniards built the Virgen of Guadalupe shrine on top of it.

TEZCATLIPOCA: Tez=Tezcatl-Mirror, Ca=Calli-House/Mother Earth, Tli=Tlilli-Black, Poca=smoke/ reflection, "The Black House of the Mirrored Reflection." Tezcatlipoca means your conscience.

TIANGUIS: The marketplace of the Mexica Culture. The Pleiades in the cosmos, "The Seven-Sister Constellation."

TLACUILO: Painter and writer of Codices. "The Knowledge Keepers."

TLALOC: Female energy, duality of Huitzilopochtli, associated with rain, water. The staff of Tláloc represents lightning connecting the cosmos, humans and Mother Earth. Tlaloc is fertility and reproduction and its nahualli is the frog whose symbol is the stone frog peak at Spirit Mountain and its geoglyph is the eastern corner of the Omeyocan Diamond, opposite of

Huitzilopochtli.

TLALOCAN: Place of Tláloc, the Terrestrial Paradise where the spirits repose, mansion of silence, which is located near the Colorado River at Spirit Mountain.

TLAPALLI: Where the night (sunset) merges with the day (sunrise), reflecting a reddish color, representing the spirit of Quetzalcoatl.

TLAQUIMILOTLI: Bundle Keepers of Knowledge, who took the knowledge of the Creation Story from Aztlán to all parts of the world.

TLATELOCO: Twin city of Tenochtitlan, place of the last battle and stand of the gallant Mexica warriors led by Cuauhtémoc, in defense of the Confederation of Anahuac. Cuauhtémoc was captured leaving Tlatelolco on August 13, 1521, by the European forces led by Hernan Cortes.

TLATOANI: Tlatoa-Word, Ani=Speaks, "He who speaks the Word." Spokesperson of the Tlatocan/Senate. One could be elected Tlatoani from the following five categories: a warrior, spiritual leader, poet/dancer, teacher, or merchant-pochteca. He was never a king or emperor, as it existed in Europe. (Rodriguez)

TLATOCAN: Tlato=Tlatoa-Word, Can=Place, "Place where the word is Spoken." Supreme Council of the Confederation of Anahuac which was comprised of "52-elders, 26-females and 26-males." The Tlatocan members elected their Tlatoani-male and Cihuacóatl-female to be their spokespersons. All decisions were made by the majority vote.

TLOQUE-NAHUAQUE: Supreme law, the close and together, the energy of everything, symbolized by the fingers on the hand, different sizes and shapes but all coming together in the palm of the hand based on the concept. "Among All, we do All, for the benefit of All."

TONANTZIN: To=Tonali-Sun/Energy, Na=Nana/Mother Earth, Tzin=Respect/Veneration, "Our Venerated Mother." Tonantzin's image is seen in the surrounding mountains of the Palo Verde Valley on December 21, from 3:15 to 3:45 pm and is the southern point of the Omeyocan Diamond.

TONATIUH: Tona=Sun/Energy, Tiuh=path. The first sun ray breaking dawn during the equinox at the Moon Mountains at the Colorado River Indian Tribe Reservation. Tonatiúh is the center face of the Aztec Sun Stone Calendar. The face of Tonatiúh is Ozomatli and its nagualli is the monkey, whose image is located on a mountain surrounding the Palo Verde/Parker Valleys.

TRINCHERAS: Town in northwest Sonora, Mexico, center of the Trincheras culture. The third stop on the Nahua migration south, also the birthplace of Joaquin Murrieta "El Patrio". (Figueroa)

TZOMPANTLI: Tzompa=Head, Pantli=Above/Banner, "Skulls on rows that depicted change of Eras." The Spaniards falsely stated that they were human sacrifices. When the main temple in Mexico City Zocalo was excavated it was discovered that the skulls were made out of clay and definitely not from any type of human sacrifices.

UAHUNCHE: Symbol of protection of the Mayan culture. A strategy used by the traditionalist indigenous to preserve their culture. When the Priest would preach their religion, they would "See, but not observe, hear, but not listen". This is how the Mexica/Mayan traditional culture has survived the 500 years of European rule. (Hunbatz Men)

UATZUPIN: Gachupine. Boots with thorns: "One who kicks with the point of the foot." Name given to the vicious Spaniards by the natives because of the cruel and inhumane treatment imposed on them.

UTO-AZTECAN: Largest linguistic family in the western hemisphere. They extended from Montana in the north, down through the Upper

and Lower Colorado River Basin, west to the San Clemente Islands and east to Texas, and south to Nicaragua. Millions of descendents of these families still speak Nahuatl.

XALCIHUITES: Jade, Emerald, symbol of green precious gems, together with turquoise, which forms the merging of the sky and water.

XAPULTEPEC: Chapu=Chapulin-Grasshopper, Tepec=Tepectl-Hill, "Grasshopper Hill." Famous hill in Mexico City, named in honor of Chapultepec which represents Palo Verde Peak, after they migrated from the Palo Verde Valley.

XIUHTECUHTLI: The fire energy, he who dwells in the navel of fire, energy of the center of Nahui-Ollin. This image is depicted in the Big Maria Mountains.

XICANO: One who defends his culture and seeks his indigenous roots. Also see Xhix-zanotl.

XICHIMECA: (Chichimeca) Chichi=Breast, Meca=String/Measurement, "Measurement of Breast." One of the tribes shown on the Boturini Codices leaving Aztlán that later became Chichimeca-Mexica. People that came from the Colorado River that has 4-sets of twin peaks extending from the MacChester Peaks from Needles, California, Turtle Mountain Peaks, Big Maria Mountains twin peaks and Picacho Peaks in Yuma, Arizona. (Van Fleet)

XICOMOZTOC: Xicom=Seven Organs, Oztoc=Cave/Vulva, "Seven Organs of the Woman Womb." Place of origin of the Azteca/Mexica. Xicomoztoc symbolism is well manifested at a location along the Lower Colorado River in the Palo Verde/Parker Valleys.

XIX-ZANOTL: Forerunner of the word Xicano.

Bibliography

Acamapixtli García, J.M. Gobernantes de Anáhuac, Artes y Reproducción, S.A., México, 1989

Aconcagua Ediciones. Ichcateopan, La Tumba de Cuauhtémoc, México, 1973

Acosta, Joseph de. Historia Natural y Moral de las Indias, Fondo de Cultura Economica Mexico, 1940

Acuña, Rodolfo "Rudy." Anything but Mexican: Chicanos in Contemporary Los Angeles, 2000

Acuña, Rodolfo "Rudy." Occupied America: A Chicano Struggle towards Liberation, 1972

Alemán Velasco, Miguel. La Isla de los Perros, Editorial Diana, México, 1980

Alcalá, Manuel. Hernán Cortés, Cartas de Relación. Editorial Porrúa, 1985

Almada, Francisco R. Diccionario de Historia, Geografía y Biografía Sonorenses, Instituto Sonorense de Cultura, México, 1990

Alvarado Tezozómoc, Hernando. Crónica Mexicana, Editorial Leyenda, S.A., México, 1944

Alvarado Tezozómoc, Hernando. Crónica Mexicayotl, Imprenta Universitaria, México, 1949

Anders Ferdinand, et. al. Introducción y explicación del Códice Borbónico, Fondo de Cultura Económica, México, 1991

Anderson Bertin ET. " Birds of The Lower Colorado River Valley " U of A Press 1991

Anzures, María. Coyolxuahqui Nuestra Madre Cósmica, Consejo Nacional de la Cultura Náhuatl, 1991

Barlow H., Roberto. Los Mexicas y La Triple Alianza, Obras del Instituto Nacional de Antropología e Historia (Traducción, Jesús Monjarás Ruiz), 1990

Barnes, Will C. Arizona Place Names, University of Arizona, 1960

Basurto, Carmen G. México y sus Símbolos, Editorial Avante, S.A., 1983

Berkowitz, Franz. Rayón, La Antigua Nacameri, Sonora Mágica y Desconocida; Hermosillo, Sonora, Méx., 1990

Bernal, Ignacio. Tenochtitlan en una Isla, Secretaría de Educación Pública, 1984

Bierhorst, John. Codex Chimalpopoca, The Text in Nahuatl, U.A. Press, 1992

Bierhorst, John. History and Mythology of the Aztecs, Codex Chimalpopoca, U.A. Press, 1992

Bonilla, Manuel. De Atlatlan a México, Peregrinación de los Nahoas, Mazatlán, Sinaloa; México, 1942

Broda, Johanna The Great Temple of Tenochtitlan, University of California Press

Buelna, Eustaquio. Geográficos Indígenas de Sinaloa, Peregrinación de los Aztecas, Del Agua Impresiones, 1887

Burland, C. A. Montezuma Lord of the Aztec, G.P. Putmans and Sons, 1975

Byland, Bruce E. Introduction and Commentary of The Codex Borgia, Dover Publication, 1993

Caine, Ralph L., Historic Aztlan and the Laguna de Oro, Los Angeles, 1962

Calvo Berber, Laureano, Nociones de Historia de Sonora, Manuel Porrúa, S.A., México, 1958

Capillio Cuautli, Héctor. La Nación Mexicana, Fernández Editores, S.A., 1965

Carrasco, David, Moctezuma's Mexico Visions

of the Aztec World, University Press of Colorado, 2003

Carrasco, David, Quetzalcoatl and The Irony of Empire, University Press of Colorado, 2000

Caso Alfonso Dr. "El Teocalli de la Guerra Sagrada" SEP. Mexico 1927

Castillo, Cristóbal del. Historia de la Venida de los Mexicanos y otros Pueblos e Historia de la Conquista, INAH, 1991

Chavero D., Alfredo. Los Aztecas o Mexicas, Fundación de México/Tenochtitlan, Jorge Porrúa, S.A., 1984

Chavero D., Alfredo. Historia Antigua y de la Conquista, México a Través de los Siglos, Editorial Cumbre, S.A., México, 1976

Chimalpáin, Francisco de San Antón Muñón. Relaciones originales de Chalco Amaquemecan, Traducción de S. Rendón. FCE, México, 1965

Clavijero, Francisco Javier. Historia Antigua de México, Editorial Porrúa, S.A., 1982

Codex Aubin, Manuscrito Azteca de la Bibloteca real de Berlin anales en mexicano y Geroglificos desde la salida de las tribus de Aztlán. Sr. Bernardino de Jesus Quiroz. Editorial Innovacion, s.a. Mexico

Codex Azcatitlan, Journal de las Sociedades Americanistas de París, 1949

Codex Bodley. Maarten Jansen. The Boldeian Library, 2005

Codex Borgia, Los Templos del Cielo y de la Oscuridad. Ferdinand Anders. Fondo de Cultura Economica, 1993

Codex Borbonico, El Libro del Ciuacoatl. Ferdinand Anders. Fondo de Cultura Economica, 1991

Codex Boturini, Su Caminar de los Aztecas. Lic. Lucio Carpanta Baron. Fundacion Cultural Secografica A.C. 1992

Codex Chimalpahin, Volume 1. Arthur J.O. Anderson. University of Oklahoma Press, 1997

Codex Chimalpahin, Volume 2. Arthur J.O. Anderson. University of Oklahoma Press, 1997

Codex Chimalapopoca, Anales de Cuauhtitlan y Leyenda de los Soles. Primo Feliciano Velázquez. Imprenta Universitaria Mexico, 1945

Codex en Cruz. Charles E. Dibble. Mexico 1942

Codex De Solei.

Codex El Lienzo de Tlaxcalla, Alfredo Chavero. Editorial Cosmos, 1979

Codex Fejervary-Mayer, El Libro de Tezcatlipoca, Señor del Tiempo. Ferdinand Anders. Fondo de Cultura Economica, 1994

Codex Florentine, General History of Things of New Spain, Fray Bernardino de Sahagun University of Utah Press, 1975.

Codex Laud Carlos Martinez Marin. Instituto Nacional de Antropologia e Historia Mexico 1961

Codex Magaliabecchi, An Anonymous Hispano-Mexican Manuscript preserved at the Biblioteca Nazionale Centrale, Florence, Italy. Zelia Nuttall. University of California, Berkeley, 1903

Codex Mapa de Siguenza, Museo Nacional de Antropologia, Bibliteca Central de INAH, 1982

Codex Nuttall, A Picture Manuscript from Ancient Mexico. Zelia Nuttall. Dover Publications, 1975

Codex Ramirez, Relacion del origen de los indios que habitan en la Nueva España según sus

historias. Colección de Documentos Conmemorativos del DCL Aniversario de la Fundación de Tenochtitlan Mexico, 1975

Codex Siguenza, Los Mexica parten de Culhuacan.

Codex Telleriano-Remensis. Ritual, Divination and History in a Pictorial Aztec Manuscript. Eloise Quiñones Keber. University of Texas Press, 1995

Codex Vaticano A, Religion, Costumbres e Historia de los Antiguos Mexicanos. Ferdinand Anders. Fondo de Cultura Economica, 1996

Codex Vindobonensis, Origen e Historia de los Reyes Mixtecos. Ferdinand Anders. Fondo de Cultura Economica, 1992

Codex Xolotl, Charles E. Dibble. Universidad Nacional Autonoma de Mexico, 1980

Coe, Michael D. México, Praeger Publishers, 1966

Colin, Mario. Nombres Geográficos Indígenas del Estado de México, Biblioteca Enciclopedia del Estado de México, 1966

Cook, Fred S. History of Parker and Area, Parker, AZ, 1985

Current, Richard N., et. al. American History: A Survey

Davies, Nigel. Los Antiguos Reinos de México, Fondo de Cultura Económica, 1995

Davies, Nigel. The Toltecs until de Fall of Tulla, University of Arizona Press

Day, Jane S. Aztec, Denver Museum of Natural History, Rivehart Publishers, 1992

Dellenbaugh, Fredericks S. The Romance of the Colorado River, Dover Publications, 1998

Dibble, Charles E., Códice en Cruz, México, 1942

Domínguez Hidalgo, Antonio. De Hombres y Dioses, El Colegio de Michoacán

Durán, Diego. The History of the Indians of New Spain, (Traducción al Inglés: Doris Heyden), University of Oklahoma Press, 1994

Emmerich, Andre. Art before Columbus, Simon and Schuster, 1963

Emory, William Major. United Sates and Mexican Boundary Border Commission Report 1853-1854

Fabila, Alfonso. Las Tribus Yaquis de Sonora
Fields, Virginia M., Zamudio-Taylor, Victor. The Road to Aztlan, Art from a Mythic Homeland, Los Angeles County Museum of Art, Los Angeles, Ca.

Forbes, Jack D. Only Approved Indians, University of Oklahoma Press, 1994

Forbes, Jack. Aztecas del Norte, The Chicanos of Aztlan, Fawcett Premiere Book, 1973

Forbes, Jack. Native American of California and Nevada, Nature Graph Publisher, 1969

Forbes, Jack. Warriors of the Colorado River, University of Oklahoma Press

Fradkin, Philli L. A River no More the Colorado River and the West, UA Press, 1981

Franch, José Alcina. Códices Mexicanos, Fundación MAPERE América

Fulson, Charles Scrivner. Mojave People, Naylor Comp., San Antonio, TX, 1970

Fundaburk, Emma Lila. "Sun Circles and Human Hands-The Southeastern Indians," Moundville Moore, Alabama Museum of Natural History.

Galindo Trejo, Jesús. Arqueoastronomía, Editorial Equipo Csirius, S.A., 1994

Gallo, Edwardo. Cuauhtémoc, Ultimo Emperador de México, Editorial Innovación, S.A., 1980

Galving, John. Fray Francisco Garcés. A record of Travel in Arizona and California, 1775, 1776, Howell Books

García Contreras, Guillermo. Los Códices Mayas, Secretaría de Educación Pública, 1975

García Quintana, Josefina. Cuauhtémoc en el Siglo XIX, UNAM, 1977

Garibay K., Angel María. Historia de la Literatura Náhuatl, Primera y Segunda Parte, Editorial Porrúa, 1953

Garibay K., Angel María. Llave del Náhuatl, Editorial Porrúa, 1961

Garibay K., Angel María. Teogonía e Historia de los Mexicanos, Tres Opúsculos del Siglo XVI, Editorial Porrúa, México, 1965

Gomora, A. (Xokonochtletl), Juicio a España, Testigos Aztekas, Editorial Tlamatini, 1988

González Obregón, Luis. Cuauhtémoc, Jorge Porrúa, S.A., 1984

González Rul, Francisco. Tlatelolco: Ciudad Gemela de Tenochtitlan, Secretaría de Relaciones Exteriores, 1993

Gordon, Willey R., Trincheras Culture: An Introduction to American Archaeology, 1966

Grey, Herman. Tales from the Mohaves, University of Oklahoma, 1970

Gruzinski, Serge. The Aztecs, Rise and fall of an Empire

Gutierre, Tibón, Historia del nombre y de la fundación de México, 1993

Gutiérrez Gutiérrez, Arturo. Reminiscencias de Malinalco, Instituto Mixicanense de Cultura, 1995

Gutiérrez Solana, Nelly. Códices de México, Panorama Editorial, S.A., 1990

Guzman, Eulalia. Donde estuvo el Aztlan de los Mexicas. Organo de la Sociedad de Investigaciones. Historia de Mexico, Boletin Cuatrimestral, Nov., 1966, Abril, 1967

Hassler, Peter. Human Sacrifice Among Aztecs. P. Lang Publishers, Berlin, Germany, 1992

Haenszel M., Arda. The Topock Maze: Commercial or Aboriginal, San Bernardino County Museum

Henderson, Randall. "Giant Desert Figures have been Restored." Desert Magazine, 1957

Heyden, Doris. México, Origen de un Símbolo, Mito y Simbolismo en la Fundación de México/Tenochtitlan, Colección Distrito Federal, 1988

Heyden, Doris. México, Orígenes de un Símbolo, INAH, México, 1998

Hinton, Leanne, et.al. Spirit Mountain, an Anthology of Yuman Story and Song, University of Arizona Press, 1984 History of the Colorado River Reservation, CRIT, 1947

Infante Díaz, Fernando. La Estela de los Soles o Calendario Azteca, Panorama Editorial, S.A., 1999 Instituto de Investigaciones, Historias del Estado de Baja California; II Simposio de Historia, marzo 21, 1986

Johnson, Boma. The Arizona Archaeologist, Number 20, Earth Figures of the Lower Colorado and Gila Deserts, 1970.

Kirchhoff, Paul, et. al. Historia Tolteca-

Chichimeca, Consejo Nacional para la Cultura y las Artes, México, 1992

Kroeber, A. L. Seven Mohave Myths

Kroeber, A.L. Handbook of the Indians of California, Dover Publications, 1976

Kroeber, A.L., et.al. A Mojave War Reminiscence 1854-1880, Dover Publications, 1973

Kroeber B., Clifton, et. al. Massacre on the Gila, University of Arizona, 1992

Laird, Carobeth. The Chemehuevis, Malki Museum, Banning, California, 1976

Landa, Diego de. Relación de las Cosas de Yucatán, Consejo Nacional para la Cultura y las Artes, 1994

Langston de Salazar, Manuelita. San Ignacio Río Muerto, Municipio de Guaymas, Estado de Sonora, Ciudad Obregón, Sonora, 1979

Lejarazu, Manuel A. Herman. La Creacion del Mundo según el Codice Vindobonensis, Ediciones Tecolote, 2007

López-Austin Alfredo. Tamoanchan y Tlalocan, Fondo de Cultura Económica, 1994

López Navarro, Raúl, El Número 13 en la Vida de los Aztecas, Proculmex, S.A., 1994

López Navarro, Raúl. El Peregrinar de los Aztecas, Costa-AMIC Editores, S.A., 1996

López Velarde, Ramón. El Códice de Cuauhtémoc, UNAM, 1980

Lowell Bean, John, et.al. Cahuilla Indians of California, Malki Museum Press, 1967

Macazaga Ordeno, César. Nombres Geográficos de México, Editorial Renovación, S.A., 1980

Magaloni Duarte, Ignacio. Educadores del Mundo, 1971, Costa-AMIC Editores, S.A., 1996

Manchip White, Jon. Hernán Cortés, Ediciones Grijalbo, S.A., 1974

Martínez, Pablo. Historias del Estado de Baja California, Instituto de Investigaciones, Mexicali, B.C., 1986

Martínez Pérez, Héctor. Cuauhtémoc, hijo del sur. Taxco, Guerrero, 1962

Martínez Pérez, Héctor. Cuauhtémoc, Vida y muerte de una cultura. Gobierno del Estado de Campeche, 1993

Masterworks of Mexican Art, Los Angeles County Museum of Art, 1963-1964

Matos Moctezuma, Eduardo. The Great Temple, INAH, 1992

Men, Hunbatz. Los Calendarios Astronómicos Maya y Hunab Ku, Ediciones Horizonte, 1983

Men, Hunbatz. Secrets of Mayan Science/Religion, Bear Company, Santa Fe, New Mexico, 1990

Meza Gutiérrez, Arturo. Reminiscencias de Malinalco, Instituto Mexiquense de Cultura, 1995

Miller Dean, Ronald, et.al. The Chemehuevi Indians of Southern California, Malki Museum, Banning, California, 1967

Miller, Mary, et.al. An Illustrated Dictionary of the Gods and Symbols of Ancient Mexico and the Maya, Thames and Hudson Publisher, 1997

Millon, Rene. Teotihuacan, University of Texas, 1973

Millon, Rene. The Teotihuacan Map, University of Texas, 1973

Molina, Felipe S., et.al. A concise Yoeme and English Dictionary, Tucson Unified School Dis-

trict, Bilingual Education and Hispanic Studies Department, 1993

Molina Molina, Flavio. Nombres Indígenas de Sonora y su Traducción al Español, Hermosillo, Sonora, 1972

Molina Molina, Flavio. Relación de Saguaripa 1778, Hermosillo, Sonora, 1974

Moreno Toscano, Alejandra. Hallazgos de Ichcateopan, 1949-1951, UNAM, 1980

Moreno, Marco Antonio. Historia de la Astronomía en México, S.E.P., 1986

Motolinía, Toribio. Historia de las Indias de la Nueva España, Editorial Porrúa, 1990

Munro, Pamela, et. al. A Mojave Dictionary, UCLA Linguistics Dept., 1992

Muñón, Don Francisco de San Anton. Relaciones Originales de Chalco Amaquemecan,

Fondo de Cultura Economica
Native America, The. An Illustrated History, Turner Publishing, Inc., 1983

Olivera de Bonfil, Alicia. La Tradición Oral Sobre Cuauhtémoc, UNAM, 1980

Nava, Julián. My Mexican-American Journey.

Nicholson, H.B. Topiltzin Quetzalcoatl: The Once and Future Lord of the Toltecs. University Press of Colorado, 2001

Nicholson, Irene. Mexican and Central American Mythology, The Hamlyn Publishing Group Limited, 1975

Nowotny, Karl Anton. Tlacuilolli, University of Oklahoma Press, 2005

Orozco y Berra, Manuel. Historia de la Ciudad de México, Desde su Fundación hasta 1854, Secretaría de Educación Pública, 1973

Ortiz de Zárate, Gonzalo. Petroglifos de Sinaloa, Fomento Cultural Banamex, A.C., México, 1976

Pérez R., Esther. Orgullo de Aztlán, Una Reseña. Historia Mexicana, Guadalajara, Jalisco, 1972

Portilla León, Miguel. El Mito del Nacimiento de Huitzilopochtli, Códice Florentino

Portilla León, Miguel. Aztec Thought and Culture, University of Oklahoma Press, 1982

Portilla León, Miguel. Los Antiguos Mexicanos, Fondo de Cultural Económica, 1965

Portilla León, Miguel. Quince Poetas del Mundo Náhuatl, Editorial Diana, 1994

Reyes García, Luis. Documentos Manuscritos y Pictóricos de Ichcateopan, Guerrero, UNAM, 1979

Robledo, Cecilio A., Diccionario Náhuatl

Rodríguez, Salvador. Cuauhtémoc, Ixcateopan, Guerrero, Mayo 18, 1987

Romero Quiroz, Javier. México, "En el Centro de la Luna", Gobierno del Estado de México

Romero Quiroz, Javier. Nacimiento de Huitzilopochtli: Solsticio de Invierno en Malinalco, Instituto Mexicanense de Cultura, 1990

Romerovargas Yturbide, Ignacio. Los Gobiernos Socialistas de Anáhuac, Romerovargas Editor, S.A., 1978

Romerovargas Yturbide, Ignacio. Motecuhzoma XocoyoYtzin o Moctezuma El Magnífico y La Invasión de Anáhuac, Romerovargas y Blasco Editores, S.A., III Tomos, Primera Edición 1957

Romerovargas Yturbide, Ignacio. Organización Política de los Pueblos de Anáhuac,

Romerovargas y Blasco Editores, S.A., Primera

Edición 1964

Rurner R., Paul. The Highland Chontal, Secretaría de Educación Pública, 1973

Sahagún, Bernardino de. Florentine Codex, General History of Things of New Spain, The School of the American Research, University of Utah, 1970, Charles E. Dribble

Sahagún, Bernandino de. Historia General de las Cosas de Nueva España, Editorial Porrúa, 1989

Sahagún, Bernandino de. Primeros Memoriales, University of Oklahoma Press, 1997

Saxton, Dean. Dictionary Papago/Pima-English, U.A. Press, 1983

Seguy, Rose Marie. Aztlan: Terre des Azteque; Images d'un Nouveao Monde, Bibliotheque Nationale Paris, 1976

Seiler Hans, Jakob, et.al. Cahuilla Dictionary, Malki Museum Press, Banning, CA, 1979

Setzler, Grady. Another Wilderness Conquered, Palo Verde Valley Times, Segunda Edición, 1972
Scofield, Bruce. Signs of Time: An introduction to Mesoamerican Astrology, One Reed Publications, 1994

Shaw, Anna Moore. Pima Indian Legends, U.A. Press

Sherman, James E., et.al. Ghost Towns of Arizona

Simeon, Remi. Diccionario de la Lengua Náhuatl o Mexicana, Siglo Veintiuno, S.A., 1981

Smith A., Gerald. The Mojaves, San Bernardino County Museum, 1977

Sobarzo, Horacio. Vocabulario Sonorense, Fomento y Cultura del Gobierno de Sonora, 1991

Soutelle, Jacques. Daily Life of the Aztecs, Standford University Press, 1970

Soutelle, Jacques. El Universo de los Aztecas, 1991

Spicer N., Edward. Cycles of Conquest, University of Arizona Press, 1992

Spier, Leslie. Yuman Tribes of the Gila River, Dover Publications, 1978

Sten, María. Codices of Mexico, Panorama Editorial, México, 1990

Teja Zabre, Alfonso, Breve Historia de México

Tezozomoc, Fernando A. Cronica Mexicayotl, Imprenta Universitaria Mexico, 1949

Tezozomoc, Hernando A. Cronica Mexicayotl, Editorial Leyenda, S.A. 1944

Torquemada, Fray Juan de. Monarquía indiana Volumen 1, 2, 3. Universidad Nacional Autonoma de Mexico Instituto de Investigaciones Historicas Mexico, 1975

Toscano, Salvador. Cuauhtémoc, Fondo de Cultura Económica, 1975

Vaillant G., C. Aztecs of Mexico, Pelican Book, 1966

Velázquez Primo, Feliciano. Códices Chimalpopoca, Imprenta Universitaria México, 1945

Verrill Hyatt, A., et.al. America's Ancient Civilization, J.P. Putnam Sons, 1953

Von Humboldt, Alexander. Political Essay on the Kingdom of New Spain, Alfred Knopf, 1972

Wagoner Jay, J. Arizona Territory, 1863-1912, A Political History, University of Arizona Press, 1980

Waters, Frank. The Colorado, Shallow Press, 1984

Magazine and Other Sources Consulted:

American Archaeology and Ethnology, Vol. II, No. 4, February 10, 1915

Apodaca, Paul. First Voices: Indigenous Music of Southern California, Bowers Museum Pamphlet

Avalos, Enrique de Lira. Zona Arqueológica de Piedra Verde, El Sol de Durango, agosto 30 de 1991

Barrie, Steven. Inland Catholic Newspaper, June, 1996

Bassett, Carol Ann. Mystery of the Desert Giants, American West Magazine, March/April, 1986

Boynton, Margaret. Chief Francisco Patencio: Stories and Legends of the Palm Springs Indians, Times Mirror Press, 1943

Brumgardt, John R. Historical Portrait of Riverside County, (Ed.), Riverside County Historical Commission, 1977

Castetter, Edward, et.al, Yuma Indian Agriculture

Ce-Acatl: Revista de la Cultura de Anáhuac # 6, Noviembre, 1991, México D.F.

Champe, Waters Flavia. The Matachines Dance of the Upper Rio Grande: History, Music, and Choreography, University of Nebraska Press, 1983

Cibola National Wildlife, Refuge, U.S. Department of Interior, Pamphlet

Dekens, Camile. Riverman, Desertman, Press-Enterprise

Devereux, George. Mojave Chieftainship in Action, Northern Arizona Society and Art Plateau Vol. 23, No. 3, 1951

Figueroa A., Alfredo. La Ira del Aguila, Documentary script, 1973

Figueroa A., Alfredo. ¡Salven Nuestros Sitios Antiguos Sagrados…! Southwest Network for Environmentl & Economic Justice, 2005

González Soto, Guillermo Jaime. Ingeniería Humana, La Ciencia de Los Mayas, panfleto

Guzmán, Eulalia. Donde Estuvo el Aztlán de los Mexicas. Organo de la Sociedad de Investigaciones. Historia de México, Boletín Cuatrimestral, Nov., 1966, Abril, 1967

Johnson, Boma. Earth Figures of the Lower Colorado and Gila Rivers Desert, Arizona Archaeological Society, 1985

Johnston, Francis J. & Patricia. An Indian Trail complex of the Central Colorado Desert California, Archeology Journal, April 1, 1957

Los Angeles Times, West Magazine: Alfredo's Aztlan. December 24, 2006

Los Angeles Times, In the desert, a stern glare for solar plants, April 25, 2010

Marshall C. George. Giant Effigies of the Southwest, National Geographic Magazine, September 1952

McDonald, Observatorio. Ascienden las Pléyades, noviembre 14 de 2003, página de Internet de la Universidad de Texas

Morton, Paul K. California Division of Mines: Geology and Mineral Resources of Imperial County, 1977

Ortiz, Rubén, et.al. Frontier Land (Documen-

tary), 1995

Publication in American Archaeology and Ethnology, Vol. II, No. 4, February 10, 1915

Sherer, M. Lorraine. The Clan System of the Mojave Indians, So Ca Quarterly XLVII, March, 1965

Swerdlow L., Joel. Human Culture, National Geographic Magazine, January 1998

The Californian Historical Journal, Vol. 2, No.3, 1994

The Sun Runner Magazine, The Sun Shines on Aztlan, April/May 2010

Thomas, Cyrus. Indian Languages of Mexico and Central America, Smithsonian Institution, Bureau of American Ethnology, Bulletin 44, 1911

Alfredo at the Cicimitl site. Photo by LA Times

BIOGRAPHY
Alfredo Acosta Figueroa

Alfredo Acosta Figueroa was born in Blythe, California, in 1934. He is the fourth son of a fifth-generation family of Indigenous-Xicano heritage from the Colorado River Indian Reservation, which encompasses the Palo Verde/Parker Valleys.

Alfredo's family was the only existing mining family that began mining during the famous La Paz, Arizona-Colorado River Gold Rush in 1862. He retired in 2006.

Alfredo's mother, Carmen was a long-time midwife and volunteer social worker and was well known for her resourcefulness and generosity to the community similar to what her mother Dolores Mollinedo, was, on the reservation.

His father Danuario was of Yaqui-Pima descendant from San Jose de Pima, Sonora, Mexico. He instilled in his sons a strong independent virtue as self-employed miners and he would say, "Your boss is your biggest enemy." He believed that we should share with others and that the biggest crime one could commit was to deny workers a just wage.

For the past 54 years, the Creator, "Ometéotl," has guided Alfredo in his struggles and helped him overcome life's obstacles. These obstacles have been a test of his resistance and strong determination. He accredits his mother, father and brothers for his healthy and strong upbringing as a youth and this has been the fundamental base of his family.

Alfredo and his wife, Demesia, have been blessed with nine children, twenty-seven grandchildren and twenty-three great grandchildren, all are the cornerstone of his multiple activities.

Alfredo and his brothers grew up in "El Barrio Del Cuchillo," a neighborhood in Blythe referred by the Chemehuevi natives as, "Barrio de la Liebre," "Ancient Acacitli."

During his youth, Alfredo was active in all kinds of sports and other activities together with the rest of the youths who lived in El Barrio. There were 13 teenagers; 11 Xicanos and 2 Anglos, who would always play together and excel in most of their activities. One of their favorite sayings was "this is one for the book" whenever there were triumphs against all the odds. They always had the vision

that one day they were going to write a book about, Los Figueroas and El Barrio del Cuchillo.

While Alfredo was growing up, the Anglos in Blythe wielded all the power in the public schools, city government, local and county law enforcement, Border Patrol, U.S. Customs and the judicial system. Most Anglos were associated with the growers who were the major employers in valley.

In the 1950s and 60s, there were close to 5,000 Mexican "Braceros" contracted to work as farm laborers in the Palo Verde Valley. The presence of the braceros fomented more racial discrimination and prejudice by the Anglos, making the braceros an easy target for abuse, physical brutality, harsh treatment for them and the local Spanish speaking population.

In the late 1950's, Alfredo and his brothers became actively involved in politics. During this time Blythe was known as "The Little Mississippi" because of the rampant racial discrimination by the Anglo-dominated powerbrokers against Xicanos and other minorities. The Figueroa brothers fought against civil injustices in Blythe and throughout California.

His life has taken him through many trials and tribulations that have given him a myriad of experiences and a wealth of knowledge. He has worn many hats and undertaken numerous roles including that of a "gambusino" (miner) all his life, a community leader, civil rights activist, humanitarian, labor organizer, staunch environmentalist, anti-nuclear activist, historian, political coordinator, community developer, boxing coordinator, folkloric singer and guitarist and indigenous traditionalist.

His fascinations with his geographical surroundings and cultural heritage have been the main focus of most of his interests and accomplishments.

Alfredo's work experience spans for more than sixty-years that began with Dan Figueroa and Sons which included mining gold, lead, manganese, copper and driftwood stone. Later, he became independent from his brothers and opened the Driftwood Stone Quarry, which operated until the year 2006, when he retired.

He was fortunate to have served for many years under the personal leadership of two highly respected Xicanos leaders, Humberto 'Bert' Corona and Cesar Estrada Chavez. His experiences with Corona and Chavez deepened his esteem for humanity and encouraged him to pursue his goals.

He has been deeply involved in political organizations and served as coordinator and organizer of the Mexican American Political Association (MAPA), member of the board of directors of CASA, Hermandad Mexicana Nacional, along with Bert Corona. He was vice-president of local chapter of the NAACP and youth coordinator in the Palo Verde Valley. Alfredo was also the Palo Verde Valley representative of the Riverside County board of directors of the Office of Economic Opportunity of the "War on Poverty" and served as its area coordinator as well as an advisor to the Brown Beret Organization.

In 1975, Alfredo and his family represented Xicanos at the Smithsonian Folk Life celebration in Washington DC. In 1976, he was invited again to the Bicentennial celebration.

Alfredo was the organizer of the Tri-Valley Xicano Caucus, which included the Palo Verde, Imperial, and Coachella Valleys. He was the organizer of the development of the "Viviendas Populares de Ripley y Blythe," a community-based housing organization that became the Colorado River Community Action Council.

In 1960, Alfredo's involvement in the farm worker movement began. He first joined the Agricultural Workers Organizing Committee (AFL-CIO/AWOC) lettuce strike in the Imperial Valley as a volunteer organizer to organize in the Imperial and Palo Verde Valleys. The AWOC strike ended that same year because

newly elected President John F. Kennedy ordered it stopped, he did not want an international crisis. The union fought to end the Bracero Program that had become an outright exploitation against the braceros, union and local farm workers.

In 1963, Alfredo's life changed forever when he was brutally beaten by a couple of local Anglo police officers. Alfredo was arrested and beaten inside a local restaurant, "El Sarape," located on North Main Street in Blythe. After winning his case in the Justice of the Peace Court in Blythe, his family then sued the police officers and the City of Blythe. And after 4 years on April 17, 1967 he was able to win his suit in the Superior Court in Indio, California. This victory energized the Figueroas and they became more involved in organizing Xicanos to fight for their civil rights.

His case became a "Cause Célèbre" in the Civil Rights Movement because he was one of the first Xicanos to sue City Hall and the police department and win in the State of California. His case appeared in the 1970 publication of the "Mexican Americans and the Administration of Justice in the Southwest," a report issued by the United States Civil Rights Commission (Washington, DC, March 1970). This case was the first in a series of legal entanglements battling the numerous abuses that Alfredo was subjected through his political involvement.

In 1962, Cesar Estrada Chavez started organizing the United Farm Workers Association (UFWA) which later became known as the United Farm Workers, AFL-CIO. In 1966, Alfredo once again became involve in organizing campesinos to fight for their rights. Thus, Alfredo went and joined the newly formed NFWA struggle, which had been one his lifelong commitment in organizing campesinos.

During the early years of the Coachella Grape Strike he was involved in what was publicized as the Coachella Four Clap- Down Case. Alfredo was arrested and incarcerated with three other men, Raul Loya, Thomas Patrick Kay and Jim Caswell. They were accused of disrupting a public assembly, when Alfredo lifted the United Farm Worker Flag during a 4th of July 1968 celebration at the Dateland School Field in Coachella, California and the crowd cried out in unison "Huelga, Huelga, Huelga." This case was appealed all the way to the California Supreme Court and won after one of the defendants Jim Caswell died because of lack of medical attention after spending fifty-two days of a 120-day sentence in the Riverside County jail.

The Supreme Court ruled it as a gross violation of the defendant's constitutional rights The case was very historical and set precedence in the free-speech movement.. This case ultimately resulted in the abolition of the Justice of the Peace Court system in California. (See West's California reporter 83, p. 686, in re: Thomas Patrick Kay, et al, Habeas Corpus).

The Cough Syrup case, of 1969, is another incident that involved the physical abuse and unjustified incarceration of Alfredo and his brother Gilbert by U.S. Customs officers. It started in Calexico, California at the border crossing and that ended in the 9th U.S. District Federal Court of San Diego, California.

Alfredo and Gilbert sued the Customs officers and in the case of Figueroa v. Donald Quick. The presiding federal judge, Clifford Wallace issued the historical memorandum opinion that stated that: "any violation of the Fourth Amendment could not be considered within the scope of the official duties of an officer of the government and therefore he has no immunity for such acts". Prior to this case, Customs and Border Patrol Officers of the U.S. Department of Treasury had always been immune against lawsuits. This case became a landmark which provided the rights of abused victims to sue the U.S. Department of Treasury.

Alfredo's family has also suffered the injustices by the Anglos. On April 6, 1972, Alfredo's daughter Patricia was manhandled by the prin-

ciple of Blythe Junior High School. They were having a "MECHA" (Xicano student organization) meeting and were showing a 8mm video where the United Farm Workers were protesting against the former U.S. President Richard Nixon at the Los Angeles Convention Center. The Blythe Junior High principal Earl Trout came in and became upset because two high school students were showing this movie in the meeting. He then disconnected the movie camera, grabbed Patricia and threw her out the door where she landed on her shoulders causing her injuries.

There were over 70 young Xicano students present who became enraged. This lead to a four week boycott of the high school and junior high. After seeing that the principal had not been reprimanded, the students and parents decided to start their own school at the city park. Thus, La Escuela de la Raza Unida officially began on May 1, 1972, under the famous phrase, "A la sombra de un arbol, una aula escolar, haci a los cuatro vientos," (a classroom under the shade of every tree, to the four winds).

In 1982, ERU started their own Bilingual Educational Radio station KERU (88.5 FM) which is now affiliated with Radio Bilingue from Fresno, California.

Under the leadership of Alfredo in 1976, ERU was instrumental in organizing local and international opposition against the proposed Sun Desert Nuclear power plant of the San Diego Gas and Electric Company. It was to be built 15-miles southwest at the base of sacred Mule Mountains of Blythe. SDG&E purchased 10,000 acres to obtain the water rights to supply the proposed Nuclear Power Plant displacing hundreds of local farm workers. This plant posed a major threat to the contamination of the Lower Colorado River.

The proposed Nuclear Power Plant was the first plant in the United States that was stopped by local opposition. Alfredo was able to get the support of the United Farm Workers Union at their convention in Fresno, California, as well as the support of the Department of Hydraulic Resources, of Baja California, Mexico and the native tribes of Riverside County. ERU joined the anti-nuclear groups and ultimately the State Atomic Energy Commission, under then- California's popular governor Jerry Brown, who denied the licensing for the construction of the nuclear power plant.

Continuing with the anti-nuclear campaign in 1992, Ron Van Fleet and Alfredo, under the auspices of Fort Mojave Nation, organized the Colorado River Anti-Ward Valley Coordinating Committee. This committee was organized to stop the proposed construction of the Ward Valley Nuclear Toxic dump. The dump was proposed to be built 20-miles west of Needles, California and it was going to contaminate the aquifers that lead to the Colorado River. They were successful in getting the five indigenous reservations of the Colorado River to join together to fight the proposed dump. After struggling for 8-years together with the help of over 200 environmental organizations in the United States and Mexico they were able to stop the construction of the proposed Ward Valley Nuclear Toxic Dump.

In 1982, the Figueroa brothers were instrumental in lobbying for the construction of the Chuckawalla State Prison located outside of Blythe.

Throughout, his life, he has received many recognitions and awards. He was the recipient of the prestigious "Taller Escuela Julian Carrillo" Honorary Award for his cultural investigations of Aztlan and its association with the Tomb of Cuauhtémoc. He is also a descendant/ founder and president of the "International Association of the Descendants of Joaquin Murrieta" which was founded in 1987 and from 1988-2002 he was co-organizer of the annual "Caravana Del Recuerdo" celebrations in Trincheras, Sonora (birthplace of Joaquin Murrieta).

In 1992, he was the coordinator for the Colorado River area Peace and Dignity Journeys that

begin in Alaska and Tierra del Fuego, South America. These journeys began simultaneously on May 1, 1972 and ended in Teotihuacan, Mexico on October 12, 1992 (Commemorating 500 years of European resistance) and he participated again in 1996.

Alfredo was one of the primary sponsors of the annual Cinco the Mayo Fiestas in the Palo Verde Valley. Beginning in 1960, as part of the Mexican Consul Patriotic Committee and ending in 2007, when, after 47 years, the committee disbanded.

In 2000, together with the indigenous communities of the Lower Colorado River Basin and environmentalist groups, they managed to stop and detour the north route of the proposed Pacific Gas & Electric Company PG&E natural gas company line route, which went from Blythe, south to Baja California, Mexico. The proposed route threatened to destroy some of the most sacred sites of Palo Verde Peak. Thanks to their efforts, the sacred sites were preserved.

During the North Baja Pipeline Campaign, Alfredo's daughter, Carmela, and her husband, Rigoberto Garnica, became the interveners against the construction of the Blythe Energy Plant, Phase 1. Despite the protest, it was built on top of the sacred cross-roads and it destroyed over 1,500 acres of citrus trees for usage of the water to supply the plant. Thus, displacing more than 500 citrus pickers, and creating one of the biggest unemployment in the history of the modern day Palo Verde Valley.

Today, La Cuna de Aztlan Sacred Sites Protection Circle are fighting one of the biggest struggles of their lives in their efforts to protect the sacred giant geoglyphs of Kokopilli, Cicimitl and El Tosco. As well as hundreds of other sacred sites, trails that stand to be destroyed by the construction of the approved mega solar power plants funded by government fast track stimulus monies.

In spite of the enormous obstacles that he has encountered throughout his life, Alfredo is not one that will give up.

His long-life desire is to share, educate, and organize and regain our native cosmic Mexica traditional culture which is the solution for human salvation. One of his famous sayings is, "La Lucha Indeterminable," The Never Ending Struggle. The compelling force behind Alfredo has been his strong dedication and persistence in the belief of "El Nuevo Saber," The Birth of the New Knowledge, the Neltiliztli, meaning "to seek for the roots of the truth without a shadow of a doubt."

Finally, 10 years after printing his first edition of "Ancient Footprints of the Colorado River," we were able to print this revised edition. This second edition reveals more facts of the Creation Story in the Palo Verde/Parker Valleys.

For that reason, the Palo Verde/Parker Valleys have been rightfully declared, La Cuna de Azltan (The Cradle of Aztlan) and "El Valle del Puro Triunfo," (The Valley of Triumph).

This is Alfredo A. Figueroa.

Blythe, California

www.ingramcontent.com/pod-product-compliance
Lightning Source LLC
Chambersburg PA
CBHW060315240426
43661CB00059B/2774